BRADFORD ON AVON

Comments about Keith Berry's last book, The Trowbridge Schools Revisited (1996):

"Mr Berry has written in masterly fashion ... This is not a dry-as-dust official history. He has used the memories of former pupils, teachers, and Heads to give life to the official record, with anecdotes, comments, photographs of school groups, sports teams, lists of teaching staff with dates of coming and going, to produce something eminently readable, which must be a source of delight to all former pupils who read it."
(Michael Lansdown, former editor of the Wiltshire Times)

"I have read your book on the Trowbridge Schools from cover to cover and found it quite fascinating. What machinations and personality clashes and false economies are exposed in it ... Altogether enthralling. And all of it unknown to us pupils."
(Lorna Lyall, former pupil, Scotland)

"I have just finished reading The Trowbridge Schools Revisited and I should like to say how much I enjoyed it ... It was most interesting to hear of all the trials and tribulations attendant upon the development of the two schools ... The book was so well written and flowed beautifully; even if I hadn't been a pupil I would have found it enthralling."
(Gwenda Grimstead, former pupil, Blagdon, N Somerset)

Cover illustrations clockwise from top left: refer to pages 2, 194, 66, 166, 153, 56, 174, 89

The Rt Hon Lord Fitzmaurice, Chairman of Governors 1904-1935. This small portrait (actual size) was taken by Lambert of Bath in 1911 to hang in the school library. An enlargement was commissioned in 1936 for the entrance hall to the school, and it is this larger version that can be found today at the Leigh Park Hotel, Lord Fitzmaurice's old home.

BRADFORD ON AVON'S SCHOOLS

*The story of education in
a small Wiltshire town*

Keith Berry

EX LIBRIS PRESS

Published in 1998 by
EX LIBRIS PRESS
1 The Shambles
Bradford on Avon
Wiltshire

Design and typesetting by
Ex Libris Press

Cover printed by Shires Press
Trowbridge
Wiltshire

Printed and bound by
Cromwell Press
Trowbridge
Wiltshire

ISBN 0 948578 96 3

© Keith Berry 1998

Contents

	Acknowledgements	7
	Preface	9
	Introduction	11
1	THE FREE GRAMMAR SCHOOL (1712-1903)	19
2	THE ELEMENTARY SCHOOLS (1806-1927)	27
3	THE BRITISH GIRLS' SCHOOL (1854-1925)	35
4	TRINITY CHURCH OF ENGLAND SENIOR SCHOOL, AND TRINITY SECONDARY MODERN SCHOOL: 1928-1980	57
5	*A Brave Beginning* THE COUNTY SCHOOL: 1897-1904	67
6	*A White Elephant?* THE COUNTY SCHOOL: 1904-1912	83
7	*Acceptance and Growth* The County School: 1913-1923	97
8	*Under New Management* THE COUNTY SCHOOL: 1924-1935	113
9	*Mainly About Buildings* THE FITZMAURICE GRAMMAR SCHOOL: 1936-1938	137
10	*The Second World War* THE FITZMAURICE GRAMMAR SCHOOL: 1939-1947	147

11	*A New Team* THE FITZMAURICE GRAMMAR SCHOOL: **1947-1954**	**169**
12	*A First-class School* THE FITZMAURICE GRAMMAR SCHOOL: **1954-1968**	**185**
13	*Endgame* THE FITZMAURICE GRAMMAR SCHOOL: **1968-1980**	**207**
14	Towards 2000	223
	Appendix A	229
	Appendix B	230
	Appendix C	232
	Index	233
	About the Author	239

Acknowledgements

A number of books have been of assistance to me in my writing of this history. They include: *Bradford on Avon: A History and Description* by the Rev W H Jones (revised by J Beddoe, Dotesio, 1907); *The Victoria County Histories of England*, vol VII (London 1957); *Bradford on Avon Past and Present* by Harold Fassnidge (Ex Libris Press, 1993); *Christchurch School, Bradford on Avon* by Ivor Slocombe (1978, unpublished); a student dissertation, *The History and Development of Fitzmaurice Grammar School 1890-1975* by Stephen Wicheard (1973), and *The Origins and Lineage of St Laurence School Bradford on Avon* by Philip Steele (1994). Back copies of *The Wiltshire Times* have frequently been consulted, but the principal source of written information has been the vast store of archival material held at the Wiltshire Record Office. My thanks go to the staff of that Office for their unfailing helpfulness.

Directories – Kelly's, Pigot's, Robinson's, Hunt's, Slater's, and the Post Office – covering the years 1793 to 1931 have also been useful, as has *Bradford on Avon: A Pictorial Record*, edited by Fassnidge and Maundrell (Wilts Library and Museum Service, 1983). Board of Education and Ministry of Education Reports on Schools have been referred to, and I wish to acknowledge the help given to me by the staff of the British and Foreign School Society Archive Centre at Isleworth.

The core of the information on which the book depends, however, has come from individuals – past pupils and teachers and Governors, sons and daughters of former members of staff, and people in Bradford who just have long memories and know a lot about what went on in the town years ago. All have been generous with their time and patient with me in my probing about the town's schools in the past, and what went on in them. I am very grateful indeed to them; they include: John Benjamin, Ciaran Brady, Noreen Brady, Lilian Brown, Roma Challis, Roger Clark, Colin Davison, Jennifer Fox, Jack Gingell, Graham Hayter, David Hester, Les Hills, Margaret Hore, Sidney Johnson, Betty Knowles, Eric Le Grove, Joe Lucas, Hilary Lywood, Peter Maundrell, Chris Penny, David Rees, Gerald Reid, Ken and Vera Revill, Ilse Ryder, Claude Say, Ivor Slocombe, Nicholas Sorensen, Patrick Squire, Joan Stickland, Jo Uncles, Betty Wayling, John Weeks, Enid Wicheard, and Stephen Wicheard.

There are undoubtedly inadvertent omissions in this list of contributors. I apologise to them and to all those not mentioned who, in casual conversation, have given me clues, probably unwittingly, that have led on to bigger things.

Preface

After being Head of the Tom Hood Senior High School in the East End of London, I came to Wiltshire in 1979 to take up the headship of the John of Gaunt School, Trowbridge, retiring from that post in December 1991. So for 20 years, first as a teacher and then in retirement, I have lived in Wiltshire – for most of that time in Bradford on Avon. I spent some of my newly acquired leisure during the period 1992-1996 in writing two books about the Trowbridge High Schools – *The John of Gaunt School and the Trowbridge High School: the First One Hundred Years* (1994) and *The Trowbridge Schools Revisited: an Extended History* (1996). They were well received and I certainly derived great pleasure in researching and writing them. The question of what I should do next then arose.

On my way to and from work every day I passed the imposing frontage of the Fitzmaurice Grammar School which, when I first saw it, was a living school; it then sank into disuse and dereliction, and was finally resurrected as a block of retirement homes. So I had what might be called a passing acquaintance with the place. What better subject, then, for a further history than a well respected grammar school that had fallen on hard times and been closed in pursuance of current political dictates. But it turned out not to be quite like that.

It soon became clear that not a lot of sense could be made of finding out about the development of the Fitzmaurice Grammar School unless something was learnt of the old Free Grammar School and Trinity School as well, which led to researching the history of Bradford's nineteenth century elementary schools. And in the end what was evident was what I should have understood from the beginning – that the study of one school in isolation was impossible and that what I had really embarked upon was the story of how Bradford on Avon built, developed, reorganised, and sometimes closed its schools to meet the ever-changing needs of the town and the times.

The story, too, proved to be essentially about people rather than stones and mortar – interesting and dedicated and up-to date and vigorous people – some of whom I soon began to feel that I knew very well. I made many new friends, albeit at a remove, in such as Frederick Cowlishaw, Agnes Boaden, Johnny Crompton, Dorothy Burgoine, Frank Musselwhite….

Further, I very much enjoyed the work. It has been a great pleasure to meet so many living men and women who still have vivid memories of their years in one or other of Bradford's schools, and I hope that some of my pleasure may be transmitted to the readers of this history.

Introduction

BRADFORD ON AVON'S SCHOOLS have a complicated history. To understand how they have come to be what they are today, it is probably necessary to look at the national picture of the last two hundred years, pick out educational landmarks, and relate them to what was happening locally. Over two centuries, the pieces of the jigsaw were created bit by bit; they were frequently moved about and shuffled into new combinations; some were rejected and new pieces were needed; they moved in accordance with governmental decree; and they finally settled into the pattern with which we are now familiar.

The first real school to feature in Bradford's history was a charity school of the sixteenth century. Its life was short, however, and many years were to pass before the next school, the Free School, was set up in the Saxon Church in 1712. In 1874, it moved from the Saxon Church to the building a few yards away that is today Old Church House, and here it eventually became known as the Free Grammar School for Boys. Its dilapidated state and the opening of the County Day School in Junction Road in 1897 presaged its closure, and this duly occurred in 1903. By stages, the County Day School of 1897 became the Fitzmaurice Grammar School, which endured until 1980 when, in new premises, it was merged with Trinity Secondary Modern School to form the St Laurence Comprehensive School.

The British Boys' School probably opened informally in 1806 in a building in what is now the St Margaret's Street car park, and in 1836 Trinity Church National School was established in Old Churchyard, Church Street. A second National School – Christ Church Mixed at Bearfield – opened in 1847, with a building specifically for infants added in 1879. The balance between National and British schools was restored with the opening of the British Girls' School in Old Church House in 1854.

The British Boys' School disappeared in the late nineteenth century. The British Girls' School survived (but only just) until 1925 when it was replaced by, rather than became, the Trowbridge Road Council Junior School which opened in 1928 and which is today the Fitzmaurice Primary School.

Christ Church National School is now also a primary school – Christchurch Church of England Controlled Primary School in new buildings set behind its former premises in Mount Pleasant.

What happened to the Parochial National School is rather more complicated.

It outgrew its original home in Old Churchyard and in 1896 expanded into new buildings in Newtown. Under reorganisation, it became a senior mixed school in 1928, and later a secondary modern school which moved from Newtown to Ashley Road in 1962. As has been said above, it combined with the grammar school in 1980 to form a voluntary controlled comprehensive school for all the pupils of secondary age in the town and surrounding villages – today's St Laurence School.

These openings, closures, removals, expansions, contractions, successes and failures are explicable in part by reference to those who taught in the schools and to the efficiency, or otherwise, with which they were managed. In part, however, they were also in line with national trends, and it is to these larger influences that we turn first. Thereafter, the gradual development of Bradford on Avon's schools during the 19th and 20th centuries will be glanced at, with much more detailed attention then being paid, first, to one of the elementary schools - the British Girls' School, which in some ways was the least fortunate and is now the least well remembered of the pioneering establishments – and, secondly, to the town's grammar school.

The National Picture
Until the end of the nineteenth century "education" for most children was essentially "elementary education", so it is with the development of elementary education that we begin.

In the eighteenth century, the vast majority of children did not go to school. Indeed, they were at work before the age of ten. For the well-off, there were public and grammar schools, but for the children of the working classes there was virtually nothing. What minimal provision there was consisted of three types of school: charity schools, Sunday schools, and dame schools.

The SPCK (the Society for the Propagation of Christian Knowledge) was established in 1699, and one of its aims was the founding of charity schools. These were essentially for the children of the sober and God-fearing poor and were run from the subscriptions of the philanthropic rich under the guidance of the local clergy. A group of Managers would be elected who saw to it that the school was properly run; they appointed and paid the teachers, were responsible for the upkeep or the renting of the building, and visited regularly to see that all was well. The Managers, too, would ensure that, when a child left, he was apprenticed to a tradesman of the area. Reading and religious instruction were the staple, but usually some sort of basic writing and arithmetic, and a useful craft, were added. Such schools were few in number, and in any one locality catered for very few children – say 20.

Sunday schools were first established in the early years of the eighteenth century, but were popularised by Robert Raikes who opened one such in Gloucester in 1780. They were free and they accepted any child whose parents wished him, or her, to attend. In other words, they were free, elementary, one-day-a-week schools that concentrated, as did the charity schools, on religious instruction and reading. Those who taught in them were unpaid and untrained volunteers with a wide spectrum of abilities and disabilities. The significance of this movement was less in what it achieved than in its being a genuine attempt at a basic level of instruction for the children of those who could not afford to pay for education.

There was a fee for attendance at a dame school, but it was small and the level of instruction was frequently almost non-existent. Dame schools were usually little better than baby-minding establishments for those who wanted their children off their hands for a time and who could afford a copper or two for the privilege. They have a lowly and often scarcely honourable place in the history of the education of the poor.

By the end of the eighteenth century, however, under the influence of religious and social reformers, a growing demand for a much more widely based system of education was beginning to be felt, and this took the form of the establishment of British and National schools in the early 1800s.

Two men – Joseph Lancaster and Andrew Bell – came forward with the same idea virtually simultaneously. They introduced what came to be known as the monitorial system, by which method one teacher could manage a school of several hundred children. They both started schools, found that they had far more children to teach than they could possibly manage, and sought a strategy whereby these large numbers could be taught with their very limited resources. They would choose their most promising pupils as monitors, teach them, probably in the early morning, and then have them pass on what they had learned to small groups of younger or less quick witted children later in the day. Lancaster, a Quaker, opened a school in Borough Road, Southwark, and founded the Royal Lancasterian Society in 1808 in order to propagate his ideas. Two years later the first teacher training college started, also in Borough Road. The Royal Lancasterian Society became the British and Foreign Schools Society in 1814 when Lancaster fell out with, and was rejected by, his colleagues. The Rev Dr Andrew Bell was a doctor and army chaplain in India, and it was at an orphanage in Madras that he started a school that was also based upon monitorial principles. Upon his return to England he continued his educational experiment and, in 1811, founded the National Society for Promoting the Education of the Poor in the Principles of the Established Church – the National Society.

In 1811 and 1814, therefore, we have the foundations laid for two parallel systems of elementary education – the National and the British – both based upon the monitorial system, the one Anglican and the other Nonconformist (Methodist, Quaker, Congregationalist, Baptist).

It was common for any small community to have both a National and a British School. Competition between the two was keen, and when one appeared it was usually not long before its ecclesiastical rival set up in opposition. These schools were initially financed by the congregations of local churches and by private donations, to some extent by the central societies, and sometimes by a small fee from those parents who could afford. The limitations of the monitorial system are obvious, with children in their early teens feeding younger children ill-digested information that they themselves had probably only received earlier the same day. Keeping any semblance of order was often a problem, and straying in a lesson from the strictly delineated path fraught with disaster. Nevertheless, the monitorial system, and the establishment of National and British Schools, was an enormous step forward towards a unified system of elementary education.

In Bradford on Avon, as we have seen, a British School for Boys opened in 1806, the Trinity Church National (Mixed) School in 1836, the Christ Church National (Mixed) School in 1847, and, late in the day, the British School for Girls in 1854.

If moves towards greater opportunities in education continued during the early years of the nineteenth century (English university education, for example, ceasing to be the sole preserve of Oxford and Cambridge in 1828), it was in the 30s and 40s that the greatest strides forward were taken in response to both the increasing numbers of children and to their no longer being allowed to work endless hours in factories. The first government grant (£20,000) was made in 1833 to help pay for school buildings. This was renewed annually, and oversight of its spending was given to a new committee of the Privy Council – the Committee of Council for Education (which became the Board of Education in 1899, and the Ministry of Education in 1944.) This Committee had inspectors whose job it was to ensure that the voluntary schools spent the money allocated to them effectively, and a Secretary, Sir James Kay-Shuttleworth, who saw the country's educational priority as being the creation of a properly trained teaching force. In 1846, therefore, he instituted what became known as the Pupil Teacher system.

In many ways, this innovation was the logical development of the monitorial system. Pupil teachers were twelve or thirteen year-old apprentices who, for a small wage, taught in their own schools for most of each day and received an education in the evenings or at times during the day convenient to the Master or Mistress. They were normally indentured for five years, being examined regularly during that period, and, if successful, were allowed to compete eventually for a Queen's Scholarship which gave them a place at training college and full qualification as a teacher. So, schools with a Master (or Mistress) and one or two monitors gave way to better staffed establishments with a Master, several pupil teachers and monitors, and eventually to a structure with a Head Master, one or two qualified assistants, and a clutch of pupil teachers who aspired to professional qualification. It was a system that was to endure for 50 years – in fact, until 1897.

The next milestone was the report of the Newcastle Commission of 1861 leading the following year to Robert Lowe's Revised Code – financial control through payment by results. The Commission found that there were too few schools and that most children went for a very short time, many starting as infants but having left by the age of ten. Attendance, even during that limited period, was generally extremely poor. Moreover, schools tended to concentrate on the bright and the amenable, neglecting the majority of boys and girls. The Revised Code was intended by the Education Department to alter this state of affairs and to obtain better value for the money it gave to its schools. Rather than religious instruction, the 3 Rs – reading, writing, and arithmetic – became the basis of the work. Pupils were examined annually by HMIs, and the size of the grant upon which the Managers of all schools depended, or whether any grant at all was forthcoming, rested upon the children's competence in these subjects. In each of the Standards I – VI into which schools were divided, a graduated level of competence in each of the 3 Rs was required. A further grant-attracting element was good attendance. An able child, therefore, who attended well would earn for his school an annual grant of 12/-, or about half that amount for a child under the age of 6. It follows that teaching tended thereafter to concentrate on instruction in basic literacy and numeracy to the exclusion of a wider educational and religious programme, and, despite rigorous and regular inspection, it was not unknown for attendance registers to be falsified in order to attract a larger grant. Later in the 1860s and 1870s, efforts were made to widen this unduly narrow, examinable curriculum.

It was Forster's Act of 1870, however, that introduced what could properly be called a national system of elementary education. The church schools – the National and British schools – had done a good job, but they could not cater for all the nation's children nor, any longer, for all who wanted education. They were to be allowed to continue, but in areas where this still left an under-provision of places School Boards were to be set up for the purpose of building new schools that were to be paid for from the rates. These Board Schools were to give religious education that, to be even-handed, had to be non-denominational – a requirement more pleasing to Nonconformists than to Anglicans. Education in Board Schools was to be free (that is, paid for from the rates) where parents could not afford fees. Forster's Act resulted, a few years later, in there being about 15,000 voluntary Church Schools as compared with some 4,000 Board Schools. In Bradford on Avon, despite the efforts of the Nonconformists, a School Board was not deemed to be necessary. Indeed, a motion to set up a School Board and to build a new school was defeated at a parish meeting by 53 votes to 49. And in 1893, we read that the Managers of the British School in Mason's Lane that catered for girls and infants,

> "feeling that it is necessary in the present conditions to establish a School Board in the Town, as well as its being advantageous in the interests of education to do so, and finding that there is not sufficient accommodation in the Town for the children thus to be turned from [this] school, hereby petition the Education Department to order the establishment of a School Board. As an additional argument, most of the leading inhabitants of the Town have expressed themselves in favour of the establishment of a School Board."

They failed in their petition.

The 1870 Act provided a school place for every child. Elementary education became compulsory in 1876, and free in 1891. The leaving age in 1880 was set at 10, raised to 11 in 1893, 12 in 1899, and 14 in 1918. Other turn-of-the-century developments were the abolition of payment by results in 1897, and the School Boards themselves in 1902. The Boards had been of variable quality and size, but they had gradually squeezed the voluntary schools, most of which by now were Anglican, into the position of poor relations, their teachers being less well paid, and their buildings and equipment inferior. The 1902 Act transferred the responsibilities of the two and a half thousand School Boards to County and County Borough Councils, of which there were only just over three hundred, with a consequential increase in efficiency. Board Schools, then, became Council Schools, and the size of the new bodies enabled them to develop secondary education. A further provision of the Act was to allow church schools to come under the wing of the local education authority if they so wished, with some of their finance coming from local rates, the churches' responsibilities effectively being reduced to the provision of buildings and the content of the religious element of the curriculum.

And so the elementary schools, well established by the century's end, were now producing children who wanted more than mere basic education and the focus begins to move towards secondary schooling. As yet, there were usually insufficient children in any one elementary school who wanted to stay on for more advanced work, but if a School Board collected such children from a number of schools together a viable unit resulted. In the 1890s, therefore, Higher Grade

INTRODUCTION

Schools appeared – where cash-strapped School Boards could afford such a luxury. A parallel development was that of **Technical Schools**, following the passing of the Technical Instruction Act in 1889, by the County and County Borough Councils. And these two – the Higher Grade and the Technical Schools – came together after 1902, as we have seen, when local authorities were allowed to set up Secondary Schools for pupils up to the age of sixteen or seventeen. New schools were built, too.

For the first few years – until 1907 – entry to this new secondary provision always cost money, but from 1907 a number of free places had to be offered annually, the result being the inception of what was to become the notorious 11+ examination. All places became free with the Butler Education Act of 1944; the school leaving age was raised to 15; education was organised as primary, secondary, and further; and in the secondary sector, grammar, secondary modern, and a few technical schools allowed the sheep to be divided from the goats. As is noted above, these developments had relevance for Bradford on Avon in that a long-established charity school closed just after the turn of the century, a Technical Institute was set up in the Frome Road following the passing of the Technical Instruction Act, a new secondary day school was opened by the local authority in 1897, and, following a reorganisation of the town's elementary schools in 1928, two junior schools and a senior school were formed that were to become primary schools and a secondary modern school. The latter amalgamated with the day school (by now a grammar school) in 1980 and became the St Laurence Comprehensive School which serves Bradford's teenage population today. All these developments will be looked at in more detail in later chapters.

One further strand in the story is the contribution made by private education. Historically, a child of wealthy, aspiring, or aristocratic parents would probably be educated at home by a tutor or governess, proceeding thence to public school, and then to one of the universities. In the social stratum immediately below this upper crust, education would be sought initially at decorous fee-paying institutions and then in the local grammar school, this in all likelihood having sprung from an old charitable institution for boys. And such was the case in Bradford on Avon. Small schools, seminaries and academies – some boarding, others for day pupils, and many for both – abounded in the nineteenth century, and a more substantial private school existed at Frankleigh House until comparatively recently. Today, however, private education in the town has disappeared, not least because of the proximity of Bath and the amplitude of its provision in this field.

FREE SCHOOL,
BRADFORD, WILTS
RULES AND REGULATIONS

I.

THE HOURS OF THE SCHOOL ARE ---

ON SUNDAYS,

NINE *in the Morning*, and Half-past FIVE *in the Evening*.

ON OTHER DAYS,

From NINE *in the Morning* to Half-past TWELVE *in the Morning*, and
From Two to Five in the Afternoon, in the Summer, and
From Two to Half-past FOUR *in the Afternoon*, in the Winter, except
on Saturdays, when there is no School in the Afternoon.

II.

Every Boy must be at the School five minutes before the hours named.

III.

Every Boy shall attend the Parish Church with the Master on Sundays and on other days of Divine Service and shall sit in the Gallery appropriated for the School.

IV.

Every Boy shall come clean in his person and dress.

V.

Any Boy coming late or not clean will be liable to be kept in the School after School Hours, or otherwise punished.

VI.

Any Boy absenting himself, or kept away from School or Church by his Parents will be admonished, and after the third admonition will be liable to lose the benefit of the Schhol.

VII.

No Boy who has so left can be re-admitted into the School without the consent of three of the Trustees.

VIII.

Every Boy must come furnished with a Bible and Prayer Book, and must be supplied from time to time withh all other Books, and with Slates, Pens, Ink and Pencils, as the Master, with the approval of the Trustees, shall require; or pay the Master quarterly for providing him with the same.

IX.

Any complaints which the Parents may have to make against the Master, or the Master against either the Parents or boys, must be addressed to Stephen Moulton, Esq., Honorary Secretary of the School, who will lay them before the Trustees.

X.

There are Holidays twice in the year, viz.; a Fortnight in the Summer, and a Fortnight at Christmas.

XI.

The Boys will be publicly examined every Year before the Trustees, on the Monday before the Summer Holidays, 24th of June.

The Free Grammar School
(1712-1903)

THE POORER BOYS OF BRADFORD were educated free of charge and relatively uneventfully for almost two hundred years – from early in the eighteenth century until the beginning of the twentieth. The history of this Free Grammar School is reasonably well documented, and little need be said about it here except for what happened during those few years just before and just after the turn of the century when it co-existed somewhat unhappily with the County Day School.

The earliest record of any formal teaching in the town goes back to 1524, to the chantry of Thomas Horton which embodied a small school, and we know that a quarter century later, in 1549, William Furbner, the chantry priest, was still maintaining this free school for instruction in religious doctrine and for the training of choristers. By 1559, however, it had gone. The grants to the Bradford school and a similar school in Trowbridge were transferred in that year to Salisbury, that town being more worthy of the money as " these upland towns [Bradford and Trowbridge] have small resort of gentlemen and merchants". We also know that some sort of school existed in Bradford about a hundred years later because in 1672 Christopher Wase sent a letter of enquiry to 13 schools that he had identified as existing in the county – in Calne, Corsham, Cricklade, Crudwell, Downton, Heytesbury, Lavington, Marlborough, Mere, Salisbury, Trowbridge, and Westport (Malmesbury) – and in Bradford. All record of it has now disappeared, and its existence was obviously short-lived.

And so we come to the Reverend John Rogers. He was Vicar of Bradford from 1710 to 1754, and in 1712 he started a free school for boys of the parish "for the encouragement of learning and good manners". This was in the Saxon Church, a building known at that time as the Skull House, probably because of its use as a charnel house during the middle ages. Three years later, the then lord of the manor regularised the position of the school by assigning the building to William Methuen and others for 1,000 years for conversion and use as a charity school. An interior staircase was constructed that led to an upper floor, and an extension and entrance were built on the south side. These alterations allowed the Master to live on the premises.

The school proved to be popular. It was well supported locally and

---

Left: The Rules and Regulations of the Free Grammar School, late nineteenth century.

endowments were made to it at regular intervals. Francis Smith, a maltster, for example, gave £250 in 1727, the interest on which went to the teaching of 10 poor boys, and in 1854 John Bubb's gift added 4 more children to the free list. By the middle of the nineteenth century, the little school's income was about £40 and the number of pupils had risen from 40 to 50 – that is, from 32 free and 8 fee-paying to 32 free and 18 fee-paying children by 1858. Fee-paying scholars had always been admitted to the Free School (indeed, it was their contribution to the school's finances that made its continuance possible) but they were a minority. The education of all the pupils was the same – essentially basic and elementary – but those nominated by the Trustees received it free, only having to find a small sum to cover the materials they used.

Appointed in 1819, James Grist was the Master for a considerable time in the early part of the century, to be followed by John Turner and John Thornton Butt, and it was the latter's misfortune to suffer a peculiarly modern hazard of schoolmastering; he was assaulted by an angry parent, a Mr Swift, for what he saw as Butt's cruel treatment of his children at the Free School. This was a year before the Mastership passed to Frederick William Cowlishaw in 1875.

In 1874, the Trustees of the Free School moved their scholars from the Saxon Church to Old Church House, dispossessing the girls of the British Girls' School in the process, as is described elsewhere. And from this date effectively, until its closure in 1903, the school was run by Frederick Cowlishaw. His salary was £45 a year, plus whatever he could make from private pupils, of whom there were 24 at that time, each paying 15/- a quarter in fees. Additionally, there were 36 "free" boys.

Cowlishaw's time at the Free School saw it gradually diminishing in public esteem as better accommodated rivals appeared and as it became increasingly obvious that the single room in the cross-wing at the north end of Old Church House was totally inadequate for the education of 60 boys. But he must have been a talented schoolmaster. He taught his pupils single-handedly, and year after year there are records of his young charges being successful in their examinations and of their entering the Civil Service or of gaining employment with the railways. The public entertainments they offered at Christmas and other festivals, too, were very well respected, that in 1903 being the 21st and last such event. The school held the usual prizegiving ceremonies, and round about the turn of the century it is interesting to note that some of the most prestigious awards were carried off by Master A Cowlishaw, Master F Cowlishaw, Master P Cowlishaw, and Master S J Cowlishaw!

The rules of the school in the late nineteenth century show that it met every day, Sundays included, but that Saturdays were only half days. On Sundays and other religious festivals, attendance at the parish church was compulsory with seating in the special section set aside for the boys of the school. John Benjamin was a pupil at Fitzmaurice from 1938 to 1943 (and later a Governor), and he recalls with great pleasure the stories that his grandfather told of life at the Free Grammar School. A particular favourite is his grandfather's account of how some of the boys travelled to school on horseback, stabling the animals at The Swan until school was over at 5.00 (or 4.30 in winter). At that time a race took place – first from the school to The Swan on foot, and then, mounted, up Masons Hill. One particular family of three boys rode on the same horse, and he was told of how it used to gallop away up Masons Hill with the three boys, ranged in order of seniority from its neck to its tail, urging it to greater efforts.

As early as 1891 there had been a suggestion that the Free Grammar School, which was increasingly becoming an educational oddity, should somehow or other form the basis of a County Secondary School, the setting up of which was being talked about at that time. But then, as later, the Trustees dug their heels in and rejected all idea of change. One of the difficulties was the school's title. It was not in any sense a secondary school, let alone a grammar school. It was essentially an elementary school that gave an extended education to the age of about 16 rather than the more usual 14. It was supported by fees and endowments, and it deprived the other elementary schools in the town of pupils and, as a consequence, of government grants.

A Secondary Day School was established in the town in 1897, and A E Tutton, an inspector from the Science and Art Department at Kensington, opined in 1898 that the two schools should amalgamate, or at the very least, cooperate closely rather than square up as rivals. This sort of public debate led on 7 December 1899 to a public enquiry into the Free School. Chaired by W N Bruce, an Assistant Commissioner under the Endowed Schools Acts, it had been asked for by the County Council and the Urban District Council. He found that the Free School's income was about £60 a year, derived mainly from two freehold properties in Holt, four cottages in the same building as the school in Church Street, and some interest from consols. He further found that it "provided for a class of boys who could not be sent to the rough and ready elementary school and whose parents could not afford a better class school" – the sons mainly of farmers and small tradesmen. More tellingly, he found the building inadequate; there was no playground; there were too many pupils for one teacher; and the school's finances were mismanaged. It was all pretty damning. And again there appeared a suggestion that the Free School should become a junior school preparing boys for entry to the Day School, girls also being admitted, "and this could be in the cottages restored into the school". So the north wing of Old Church House would become a sort of Prep Department for the Day School, with girls accommodated in the four cottages that formed the rest of the building.

Above: From 1712 until 1874 the upper storey of the nave of the Saxon Church served as a schoolroom for the boys of the Free Grammar School. The three-storey southerly extension, prominent in this photograph but now demolished, was the Master's house.

Below: Frederick Cowlishaw and the boys of the Free School, c1890.

Old Church House, the original home (in the far wing with the large window) of the British Girls' School and then, from 1874 to 1903, of the Free Grammar School. This photograph of 1905 shows the cottages and the derelict schoolroom, soon to become a Men's Institute, with, beyond, a private house, now demolished, which had once been the Ship Inn.

But the Trustees would have none of it.

By the end of 1899, many pupils were transferring from the Free School to the Day School anyway because parents were happier at the thought of 36 pupils being taught by 3 staff (as happened at the Day School) than of 60 being taught by one. The new school also held periodic examinations so that parents could trace the progress of their children, a system that was not in place in Church Street.

Lord Edmond Fitzmaurice was blunt in his criticism of the Free School and the way in which it was confusing the educational picture in the town. A retired schoolmaster who had run a Boys' Boarding School at Avonfield in Trowbridge Road, Sydney Septimus Lane, publicly accused Lord Edmond of trying to get rid of it, and for deliberately working for its demise so that he could sweep its pupils into his Day School. (*His* Day School because it was in many ways his creation and paid for by him.) The take-up by parents at that school, said Lane, was poor; it should never have been opened, whereas at the Free Grammar School the boys were all taught by a professional schoolmaster, without interference from incompetent Pupil Teachers, and they regularly obtained good employment.

From the other side one heard that "the bulk of the boys in the Free School got no education at all to speak of" and "its existence was a positive injury to education in Bradford on Avon as it disorganised the education in the town and caused a loss of government grants to elementary schools". Nor was there any properly elected Board of Governors.

Cowlishaw knew that, after the public enquiry, the Charity Commissioners would almost certainly close his school, and the passing of the Education Act of 1902 was the final nail in the coffin. The press debate had been unpleasant, and his pupils were seeping away, so he had had enough. After more than 25 years as Master, he offered his resignation for March 1903. In the event, he was persuaded to stay on for a few more months, but Bradford's Free Grammar School closed on 29 September 1903.

Frederick Cowlishaw "was a most genial man and held in high respect by all who knew him....He was one of the old school, a splendid disciplinarian, and though firm he proved himself to be extremely kind." Sadly, he retired without a pension, but friends and parents subscribed for the handsome presentation of an illuminated address and a purse of gold, whilst the boys gave him a clock. Cowlishaw's farewell speech left none in his audience in any doubt about the role that the Free School had played in his life.

Happily, there is life after death. Frederick William Cowlishaw continued to teach privately for the next decade at a house in Belcombe, but the old school building proved to be something of a headache for the Trustees. One of them,

John Moulton, agreed to buy it "at a proper price", restore it, and present it to the town, but he withdrew this offer in the face of difficulties that arose. It became a Men's Institute in December 1905, and in 1908 there was a suggestion that it should become a public hall; a fatal objection to this plan was that it would then be in competition with the Town Hall, thus creating an unfortunate clash of interests. The building, comprising the old Free School and four cottages (numbers 24, 25, 26, and 27 Church Street, only one of which was then occupied) was finally sold to J Merrett of Trowbridge for £275 in October 1910. This was more than the Trustees had expected to get as, by then, "the whole [was] in a most dilapidated condition and getting worse". It became a lending library in 1929 before acquiring its present dual function of Church Hall and Masonic Temple. Both Old Church House and the Saxon Church, the Free Grammar School's former premises, are today jewels in Bradford's mediaeval townscape. And the money from the charity went eventually to fund educational scholarships.

Above: The old Christ Church elementary school.

Below: The building, much restored, that housed the original Parochial National School of 1836.

The Elementary Schools
1806-1927

BRADFORD ON AVON IN THE MID-NINETEENTH CENTURY would have been recognisable to us as the forerunner of the small town that we know a hundred and fifty years later, but there were elements, then taken for granted, that would strike us today as being strange and uncomfortable – not least those seasonal epidemics that devastated the home, school, and workplace, and the immediate effects of extremes of weather on people generally. By this time, the streets had been paved and the worst effects of untreated sewage dealt with, but the gutters still carried refuse down to the river and drinking water often came from the town's small streams and wells, with the high risk of water-borne disease spreading rapidly.

As yet there was no electricity – no telephones, television, computers, fridges, freezers, or central heating – no National Health Service, antibiotics, or, happily, drug-dependency; there were no plastics, man-made fibres, ball-point pens, supermarkets, paper money, professional sport, or tyrannical youth culture. The car, let alone the aeroplane, had not yet arrived; the railway was still a novelty; the canal, horse power, and sheer physical endeavour were the principal means of transport. With horses in their various functions dominating its narrow streets and surrounded by farms, Bradford, with the parish church and the Swan Inn as its focus, was still essentially an agricultural community, despite its factories and workshops. So the urban context in which the young children of the British and National Schools lived and worked would in some ways have been very familiar to us; in other ways it was a different, a rawer, and a more basic environment.

The first of Bradford's elementary schools to be established was the British Boys' School, and its history is similar in some ways to that of its sister school, but of course it was both founded and closed many years earlier. It probably began in a fashion in about 1806 in an old Quaker meeting house that dated from 1718. This was in what is now the entrance to St Margaret's Street car park, with a narrow passage-way left between the north-east corner of the building and Westbury House. Religious meetings had ceased to be held there by 1800 and, after a tentative beginning, some more formal agreement about its use as a school seems to have been reached in 1817. The rent was £1 per annum, and there was a requirement that the Managers should keep the building in good repair. However, the British and Foreign School Society Reports of 1831 and 1832 indicate its official founding on 21 June 1830 (the 1831 Report) and in January 1829 (the 1832 Report), perhaps the former, from its precision, being the more accurate.

The fees in 1831 were two pence per week, and late that year the committee were able to speak with confidence of the progress that had been made.

> "....five months only have elapsed since the commencement of the school on the 21st day of June, at which time there were 180 boys entered on the books. From the above period, the number of boys in attendance has varied from 200 to 140, fluctuating principally during the harvest, and in getting in of the potato crop, to which latter cause the thin attendance of the boys at the present time can be satisfactorily attributed. The committee have every reason to expect, in the course of two or three weeks, the numbers will progressively increase, as was the case at the close of the wheat harvest.
>
> It is with great pleasure the committee allude to the progress made by the different boys in their learning. At the commencement of the school, there were but twenty boys out of the number that could write; they are now happy to state that the whole of the classes are able to write the words given out by the monitors from the dictating cards, many of the boys writing a good bold hand. As an encouragement, the committee have presented each of the boys in the eighth class with a copy book....
>
> The committee are happy to observe that there have been many visitors to the school who have expressed themselves much pleased with the working of the system and the improvement of the boys: to which opinion they most cordially subscribe, and also that the school will be attended with the most beneficial results to the town and neighbourhood."

There was more praise for what was obviously a very popular school the following year, and on the occasion of this, the 1832, Report there were 187 boys present, together with a few girls who could be accommodated because the room was not quite full. It measured 36' x 30' and contained 12 desks of 17 seats each.

> "The progress of the pupils appeared to be pretty good; several read fluently, and had obtained considerable scriptural knowledge, who were unable to name the letters on their admission. The master stated that an examination of the school before the parents had been very beneficial in increasing the number and in strengthening his hands, by engaging the cooperation of the parents. Although the order of this school did not appear preeminent, yet it is probable that many

on visiting it might be ready to subscribe to the following entry which we found written by a gentleman in the visitors' book: 'I have with real heartfelt pleasure visited this school, and rejoice in its excellent order and the deep attention of the children.'"

This entry is from an abridged journal of a visit to British schools in Oxfordshire, Buckinghamshire, and Wiltshire in the British and Foreign School Society Report of 1832. The writers go on to describe their continuing inspection of schools in Trowbridge, Westbury, and Warminster. At Trowbridge, where fees were also two pence a week, there was a school "conducted in a very spirited and efficient manner, under great disadvantages". But Westbury, "in every aspect under which we saw it, presented a deplorable view. Passing through it, we found a number of men loitering about unable to find employment, and the school here formed a sad contrast with the beautiful and interesting establishments we had just visited [in Bradford and Trowbridge]." Warminster was also unsatisfactory in that the visitors were not allowed to question the children about what they had read in the scriptures – "a very material evil".

Back to Bradford. The visitors acknowledged the need for a girls' school in the town, but saw little prospect of one being provided in the near future. "It is with great difficulty that the Committee are enabled to raise subscriptions to give the master any salary above the pence. The place is very poor, and the people dejected in consequence of the removal of the principal cloth factories." Some 20 years or so were to pass before anything could be done for the girls.

Six years later – in 1838 – only 80 boys were in attendance when the school was visited (the harvest or potato picking perhaps again being responsible), but "it is generally prized by the inhabitants and is under efficient management". Unfortunately, from the 1840s onwards it came under increasing pressure from its more efficient and affluent National neighbours and began the steady decline that led to its eventual closure.

John Marchant was an early Master of the British Boys' School, but for many years in the 1840s, 1850s, and 1860s it was in the hands of John Stapleton. Henry Chard and John Lewis were later Masters, and it was during the latter's tenure that, after 74 years, the school ceased to be.

A report of the Education Department, dated 14 July 1880, says:

> "The ventilation [of the building] is most imperfect; the windows on one side have to be frequently kept closed to exclude the smoke of the neighbouring factory, and on the other side the building is exposed to the effluvia of a rank and confined stable. Altogether, the position is most gloomy and depressing, and unsuited to the purpose, there being no playground but the factory yard, and the building

being overshadowed by higher walls on all sides. It would appear therefore that the building is becoming unsuitable for school purposes, and the question of the continuance of the annual grant will have to be considered seriously by their Lordships."

It closed, in fact, in September of that year.

The two British Schools in Bradford on Avon were very much the poor relations as far as both the quality of accommodation and of the instruction they offered were concerned. They did not have the financial resources of their National counterparts. But the old Quaker meeting house survived the closure of the Boys' School and for some years at the end of the century it served as laboratory accommodation for the newly established Technical Institute.

The story of the British Girls' School, which, sadly, is not one of unqualified success, is told in more detail below.

The third of Bradford's elementary schools, and the first of the two National Schools to be founded in the town, was Trinity Church (or the Parochial) National School which opened in 1836, probably under Charles Byfield, with Sarah Fry looking after the younger children. This establishment (and the building is still there, of course) was in Old Church Yard, just beyond Orpin's House at the point at which Church Street narrows to the passageway by The Chantry, and it was for both boys and girls. It contained two classrooms, the boys being on the ground floor, with the girls upstairs. Set up by local Anglicans in conjunction with the National Society, it quickly gained respect, and was referred to in 1844 as "an institution very efficiently managed". William King and Lucy England were in charge for most of the 1840s, and Charlton Clarke Stills and George Kemp followed as Masters in the 1850s. By this time some 50-60 boys and 80-90 girls were regularly in attendance at what was described as "a good school under kind and liberal management".

Masters and Mistresses came and went fairly regularly, though Thomas and Sarah Hawkins in the 60s and 70s, and Joseph and Blanche Genders in the last decade of the century achieved a degree of permanence. They taught through the medium of Monitors and Pupil Teachers, and their logs record the usual little triumphs, tragedies, and frustrations of school life.

"1885 – 'The infants' school is in good order and is very satisfactorily taught,' say HMI."

"1887 - Have had occasion to report E Morris, 3rd year Pupil Teacher. She has not done her lessons satisfactorily since I came. I examined her class yesterday, the result being very unsatisfactory, especially in reading."

"7 November 1899 – Received word today that Winifred Ovens, the little child suffering from diphtheria has died....Dorothy Ovens is suffering from the same complaint as her sister."

"17 November 1899 – Received word this morning that Dorothy Ovens is dead."

A teacher's house was built in 1869, but it was not until 1896, after inspectorial condemnation of both the Parochial School and the British Girls' School, that real expansion was made possible by the opening of new premises just behind the old building and with access from Newtown. This was the school that until recently occupied the site on which The Ropewalk retirement homes now stand, and it afforded places for 216 boys and girls and 141 infants.

Gideon Norton White (who also taught part-time at the County School) was Head from 1900 until his death in 1917; his wife, Mrs Ada White, initially looked after the girls and infants but latterly the infants only, and was in office from 1900 to 1923; and Miss D White for a few years up to 1923 was in charge of the girls' school. It was very much a family affair. Albert Harris succeeded as Head of the Boys' School in 1917, with Mrs Robinson and Mrs Alice Davis as Heads of the Girls' and Infants' Departments respectively when Miss D and Mrs A White retired.

Christ Church, a second National School, opened in 1848. There is a neat and concise history of this school – *Christchurch School* – written by Ivor Slocombe in 1978, and greater detail than is given here can be found in that study.

The church itself was built in 1840, with a school always planned as a further facility on the same site. So when land at Mount Pleasant was given by Sir John Hobhouse, the school could be built. It was paid for by Capt Septimus H Palairet and, together with a school house, opened in 1848. Thirty years later, a separate infants' department was built immediately next to the earlier school, the benefactress for this extension being Miss Isabella Poynder of Leigh Court, and the new building was opened on 24 July 1879 with all due pomp and ceremony. Today, the house and two school buildings form a unified though somewhat dilapidated whole.

Christ Church was the largest of Bradford's elementary schools, being able to accommodate over 400 pupils from 1879, and the fact that attendance was always good differentiates it significantly from its British School neighbours. During the 150 years of its life many hundreds of teachers worked there. (One of some distinction in a different profession was Arnold Ridley of *Dad's Army* fame who, as a young man, taught at Christ Church very briefly indeed in 1915, resigning without having given the requisite notice.) But even the names of some of the early Masters and Mistresses are now lost to us. Mrs Sarah Barrett was in charge in 1848, Henry and Mary Humphries in 1851, John Inker in 1855, John and Jane Perry in 1859, and, for 42 years from 1860, the seemingly indestructible Caleb and Mercy Bryant ran the school. Husband and wife teams, with the man in charge of the older children and his wife of the infants, as happened also at the Parochial School, were a common pattern in those days. The successors to the Bryants, Herman and Elizabeth Wilkinson, also served for a considerable time – for 26 years, from 1902 to 1928.

From 1924 onwards the idea of change and expansion was in the air. These old Victorian elementary schools were outdated and were unfitted to meet the needs of the twentieth century in the number of children they could accommodate, the age-range for which they catered, their curricula, and general organisation. In Bradford, too, there was an increasing need for some sort of school south of the river with the town's expansion in that direction. Reorganisation, however, was not at all to the liking of the Managers of either the Parochial or Christ Church School; the British Girls' School in Masons Lane was about to be wound up anyway, so their views on the matter were of small account. There was certainly little support for reform on the lines proposed by the Director of Education in November 1924 which was for two junior schools that would take children from their infant years up to the age of 9, with a transfer thereafter to a senior (or Central) school.

This thorough-going re-shuffle was to the great and publicly flaunted disapproval of both the Parochial and Christ Church Managers. From Newtown the message was sent: "The Managers of the Parish Church Schools beg to state that, while approving the general principle of Central Schools, they do not consider that the time is right for the drastic change suggested for Bradford." A Public Enquiry was held into the matter on 6 January 1925 and the Board of Education gave its seal of approval to Mr Pullinger's plan, "on the condition that the directions will not be enforced until a school for the infants and junior children has been provided at Bradford on Avon on the south side of the river". This school was built. It opened on time and took its place in the reorganised scheme of things, and it was known variously as the new Junior School (Council), the Council School, and the Trowbridge Road School. Today, of course, it is the Fitzmaurice Primary School.

It was made clear to the managers of both elementary schools that their chances of effectively opposing reorganisation were nil; the only influence they could wield would be in securing senior positions and favourable conditions for their preferred candidates, and throughout 1926 and 1927 bargaining went on for the appointment of suitable men and women from the 5 possible candidates (Messrs Harris and Wilkinson, and Mrs Robinson, Mrs Davis, and Mrs Wilkinson) to the 3 headships that would be available. This was the problem addressed by all the interested parties at a meeting in Old Church House on 27 January 1927, though, as a mark of their disapproval, none of the Christ Church

Managers deigned to be present.

Herman Wilkinson, from Christ Church, went as Head to the new Senior School; his wife, Mrs Elizabeth Wilkinson, remained at Christ Church as Head; and Mrs Davis, from the Parochial Infants' Department, was appointed Head of the new Junior Council School that was about to be built between the Frome and Trowbridge Roads, south of the river. Mrs Robinson made things easier for everyone by accepting a post in Bristol, but Albert Harris's position was acutely uncomfortable. It had been made clear at an early stage that he would not be acceptable for the headship of the Senior School as he was insufficiently qualified, and in the event he joined the staff of that school in a subordinate position but with a protected salary. All the other existing teachers were deployed to positions in the newly reorganised schools, which moves brought satisfaction to some (doubtless) and feelings of vexation to others.

In this new order of things, which began on 1 January 1928, Christ Church and the new Council School took infants in classes I, II, and III, and juniors in standards I and II – 259 places in the former and 100 in the new school. At Mount Pleasant, the juniors and older infants were taught in the former mixed school building, whilst the building of 1879 took 3 further classes of infants. And the Senior School, which now officially became the Bradford on Avon Trinity (Senior) School, Number 31, provided 320 places for boys and girls in standards III-VII. The other educational establishment in the town at this time was the County Secondary School in Junction Road, which catered for boys and girls who were older, abler, wealthier, and possibly more ambitious.

> THE BRADFORD-ON-AVON ANNUAL. 1887
>
> ### Public Schools.
>
> Parish Church National Schools—For Boys and Girls—Church Street.
> *Master*—Mr. H. Holt.   *Mistress*—Miss A. Bailey.
> Christ Church National Schools—For Boys and Girls—Mount Pleasant.
> *Master*—Mr. C. W. B. Bryant.   *Mistress*—Mrs. Bryant.
> British School—For Girls—Mason's Lane.
> *Mistress*—Miss A. Boaden.
> Free Grammar School—For Boys—Church St. Founded in the year 1712.
> *Master*—Mr. F. W. Cowlishaw.
> Grammar School—Young Gentlemen's Boarding School—Avonfield Terrace.
> *Principal*—W. H. J. Beechey, Esq.
> Young Ladies' Seminary—The Misses Merrick, Trowbridge Road.
>   ,,   ,,   ,,   Mrs. and Miss Venton, St. Margaret's Place.
>   ,,   ,,   ,,   The Misses Harman, Albert Terrace.

Above: A list of the educational opportunities available to the children of Bradford on Avon in 1887. The British Boys' School had closed a few years earlier.

Below: The new premises built in 1874 for the British Girls' School.

The British Girls' School
1854-1925

THE HISTORY OF THE BRITISH GIRLS' SCHOOL in Bradford on Avon is a short and, in the main, an unhappy one. It came late upon the scene and led a hand-to-mouth existence in that the quality of the teaching it offered was often questionable, with clear and repeated inspectorial dissatisfaction, its accommodation was for most of the time well below what was acceptable, parental support tended to be fickle, and it was chronically short of money.

We know that a certain James Patch left a will dated 4 June 1846 in which he asked for two cottages in Middle Rank, numbers 4 and 5, to be developed as a school for the joint benefit of the Baptists and Congregationalists in the town. These cottages, of course, were next door to the Zion Chapel and the Grove Meeting House, and they may have been the forerunner of a larger and more formal school. In any event, according to the List of British Schools of 1897, a British Girls' School opened in 1854 and finally, after many a close shave, closed in 1925.

Initially the school was accommodated in what we now know as Trinity Church Hall, or Old Church House, at the junction of Church Street and Druce's Hill. Harold Fassnidge is mistaken when he writes in *Bradford on Avon: Past and Present* that "the [British School for Girls] had been started in Church Street - the 1871 census return shows that it was held in what had been until 1842 the Hobhouse Bank, now called Church House". This is a different building altogether and is next door to what is now Lloyd's Bank. Old Church House, dating from the sixteenth century when it was built by Thomas Horton, is further along Church Street and is now in part Trinity Church Hall and in part a Freemasons' Lodge. Others, following Fassnidge, have repeated the error in more recent publications. The schoolroom in Old Church House was the large room at the eastern end of this building and it measured 31.5' x 16.5' x 18'; upstairs was a smaller classroom, the dimensions of which were 19' x 14.5' x 10'.

Virtually nothing is known about the founding of the school, its first teachers, or the triumphs and disasters of the first few years of its life. But there is evidence of its having been well regarded locally, credit for which must go to the committee of Nonconformist ladies who were its Managers and to its pioneer Mistresses. After this sound start, there was a change of leadership in July of 1863. At that time an inspector reported that it was "so satisfactorily taught a school that I certainly regret the Mistress's intention to leave". Unfortunately, leave she did, and responsibility passed to Fanny Maizey, a Certificated Mistress, who was to remain in charge for the next six years. She was assisted initially by a Pupil Teacher, Miss Long, and two Monitors, Maria Keen and Keziah Norris who received 6d each per week for their work. Miss Long was soon to complete her apprenticeship and go to Stockwell to try for a scholarship (in which venture she was successful), so Maria and Keziah were promoted to Pupil Teacher status.

By the summer of 1866 these two very young girls had completed the first year of their apprenticeship successfully, despite occasional failures in their annual examination and the discovery that Maria Keen was too young properly to have been appointed anyway. A further problem was the doctor's view that Maria was "delicate" and needed a break from her job, a decision that necessitated the appointment of more Monitors. However, Miss Maizey, with her two young helpers, Miss Keen and Miss Norris, ran what seems to have been a reasonably tight ship, and for a time there was a sense of continuity and competence that was to be singularly lacking in the not-too-distant future.

At this time – the mid 1860s – those parents who wanted a basic education for their daughters in addition to the British School had the choice of sending them to the Christ Church National School, opened some twenty years earlier, the Trinity Church National School that had been in existence for thirty years opposite the Chantry, or, if they had the means, to some private establishment. Amongst these there were several that flourished for a considerable time: Susan and Sarah Harvey's seminary for young ladies in Church Street, Ellen Fatt's little school in St Margaret's Street, and Ellen and Sophia Merrick's ladies' school that was open for many years in Wellclose House, Barton Orchard, for example. So the British Girls' School had competition and Fanny Maizey was anxious about both the numbers who enrolled and those who actually attended, there often being a considerable discrepancy between the two.

Attendance figures (and difficulties of accommodation) were complicated by the presence in the school of infants. Infants were not boys or girls; they were infants. And the temptation, because of the philosophy of payment by results, was to cram as many children as possible, both girls and infants, into what was a very restricted space. In the mid 1860s, 70 girls was an average attendance, and the log records "a crowded schoolroom" and "a full school" with between 80 and 90 present. The infants, on the other hand, confined to the smaller room upstairs, were about half this number, and in 1866 the inspectors recommended that their numbers should be restricted to 33. Accustomed as we are to open-plan architecture and the airy classrooms of schools today, Old Church House, with its perennial problems of ventilation, heating and general cleaning, would have struck us as being spartan, not to say fetid, accommodation for small children.

Throughout the life of the school, the infants were a problem one way or another. They were children under the age of 6, but, and particularly when older sisters were in the school, the little boy infants tended to stay on beyond the age of 6, and in the records of the time the British Girls' School is sometimes referred to as the "mixed" school. Indeed, the inspectors recommended in 1867 that no boy should be retained on the books beyond the age of 7, the implication being that there were some in the school who were older. There was no room for them, quite apart from the fact that the facilities of the school were inappropriate for little boys. And another problem that the infants posed was that, in their room upstairs, they were too often left solely to the care of the Pupil Teachers, Maria Keen and Keziah Norris. So incensed were the inspectors about this that in 1864 they decreed that one tenth should be deducted from the grant given to the school. "The infants should be properly superintended by the Mistress." Fanny Maizey semi-solved the problem by bringing the older infants downstairs into the main schoolroom and teaching them herself, but this compromise did not find favour either. The under-6s, it was decreed, must be taught as a single class.

It seems, however, not to have been an unhappy school under Fanny Maizey, official criticism being largely offset by the enthusiasm and approbation of the local committee of Nonconformist ladies whose responsibility it was. So the young Bradford girls of the 1860s whose parents chose to send them to this little school in the old building at the bottom of Druce's Hill learned their letters and their numbers, began to read and write, and, as they reached the age of 9 or 10, had their horizons widened by the lessons handed down to them by Maria, with her object lessons on "Tea" and "The Cow", for example, and Keziah (whose speciality appears to have been "Coffee"), and the Mistress. After that, going to work at home, in the town's shops and factories, or on farms was their lot.

In 1869 Fanny Maizey accepted the offer of a post in London and was given a testimonial in recognition of her services to the school. Eighteen months of confusion ensued.

Mrs Smith was Mistress from June to December 1869, being followed by Emma Livermore for five months, Jane Swinfield for two, and Lydia Read for six. Misses Livermore and Swinfield appear to have been stop-gap appointments, but more had been expected of Mrs Smith. From her first day, she was a severe critic both of the behaviour of the children and of the abilities of her staff, her daily record oozing dissatisfaction. "Some boys for mischief have covered the school door with mud before school time. Sent to the police to have them spoken to." And some of the pupils behaved appallingly. Miss Edmonds, in particular, was a thorn in Mrs Smith's flesh, disobedient, subversive, and always fighting –

"she has been forbidden to do it, but she persists." And as for the wretched Keziah Norris: "I find that her manner in giving lessons is very poor, her grammar shockingly bad, and the interest of the gallery not kept up at all. I shall look for great improvement." (The gallery was a typical feature of schoolrooms at the time, consisting of tiered rows of benches at one end of the room, thus forming a separate teaching area or enlarging the schoolroom into a sort of lecture theatre.) Keziah did improve. Her lesson on "Growth" was not good, but she was better on "Iron" – perhaps having benefited from the Mistress's demonstration lesson on "The Circulation of the Blood".

Mrs Smith's zeal took her on several evening visits late in 1869 to the homes of her pupils to enquire about their absence from school. Most were suffering from scarletina, which infection Mrs Smith herself contracted as a result of her assiduity. She resigned in December, and the inspectors ungenerously, but unambiguously, reported: "The intermediate Mistress who left at Christmas seems to have let down the school very much." So, after Mrs Smith, Miss Livermore and Miss Swinfield, came Lydia Jane Read.

Like Mrs Smith, Miss Read was unimpressed by what she found. Good order and discipline had suffered "through great change of teachers and loss of senior Pupil Teachers", but, again like Mrs Smith, she was to be merely a passing influence. After a few weeks, she felt that matters were improving. Nevertheless, complaints about her organisation of classes were soon heard and she left in December 1869. "Not having been trained for a British School, I find the Committee lack confidence in my plans." She was bitter about not having been given a chance. "The progress of the school has duly rewarded my toil. This has not been fully tested by the Committee." And she felt that the real reason for the Committee's lack of support for her lay elsewhere. "My not residing in the town seems to be the chief [complaint] of some of the ladies." So she, in turn, gave way in January 1871 to Agnes Boaden who was to remain as Mistress of the Bradford on Avon British Girls' School for 20 years and 7 months.

By the beginning of 1871, Maria Keen and Keziah Norris had gone – Maria to College having done well as a Pupil Teacher, Keziah into academic obscurity, having failed. So Agnes Boaden, Probationary Certificated Mistress being paid £35 per year, was assisted by Caroline Tiley and Gertrude Howell, Pupil Teachers, and Mary Likeman as Monitor. It was not long before Miss Boaden lost her probationary status, but Miss Howell soon had to leave as a financial economy. These were difficult years in some ways because the rooms being used in Old Church House were really not adequate for the number of children being crammed into them, and there was the serious problem of one qualified teacher having two classrooms on two different floors to supervise. The inspectors from the Department said in 1871: "The infants....are taught only twice a week by the

Mistress herself and otherwise are left to a young Pupil Teacher in a separate room....My Lords infer that the infants are usually taught upstairs. My Lords consider this objectionable." Nor were rules being observed as to what was being taught to the different classes. "A deduction of two tenths is made from your grant for faults of discipline and for faults of instruction. A larger deduction will have to be made next year unless...." These were menacing words. My Lords were clearly displeased, but in the financial strait-jacket within which a Nonconformist voluntary school operated a viable solution was not easy to find.

One thing that could be done was to remove the infants. Most of them went to "a room over the Baptist Chapel in St Margaret Street", a room that is still there, looking out on the junction of St Margaret's Street with Station Approach and masking the passer-by's view of the chapel itself. Old Church House, in consequence, was for a time much quieter. But – and this happened more than once in the school's history – no sooner had they gone than provision was made for them to start drifting back, and by December 1871 we hear that the Committee was again willing to admit girls between the ages of 5 and 6, provided they had an older sister in the school.

Caroline Tiley and Mary Likeman (for by the beginning of 1872 there were again two Pupil Teachers) were another anxiety. They were constantly having to be reproved for silliness or not keeping good order or not attending to their lessons or being late or being away....There seemed to be no limit to their ingenuity in finding ways to exasperate the Mistress. Indeed, one gets the impression that they often required more disciplining than did the younger children. From the daily log one reads of the other small difficulties and dramas that punctuated the school's routine. "I unwell, so my sister looked after the school," wrote Agnes Boaden. "Attendance of only 15 today as the roads are impassable after snow." And we learn of the death of one of the pupils, Emily Tucker, who was drowned in the Avon, this little tragedy compelling the attendance of others of the girls before the Coroner as witnesses to what had happened.

The number of girls attending at this time was usually about 70 or 80, but bad weather, as with the snow early in 1873, could reduce attendance considerably. Epidemics in Bradford could also affect the numbers attending; measles, scarletina, or simply "fever" effectively stopped work and not infrequently led to the British Girls' School's being closed, along with all others in the town. A phenomenon strange to us today was the closure of the school for a variety of celebrations, both local and national. Had there not been an official holiday, events such as the Foresters' Fete, the Flower Show, the Wilts Friendly Society Festival, the Harvest Festival, and the arrival of the annual fair would all have closed the school anyway, so important were these local attractions before the advent of mass home entertainment.

Inflation, then as now, was a problem. The 6d per week earned by Monitors in 1863 had risen to 1/- eight years later. And there was agitation in Bradford in the early 1870's, as elsewhere, for the setting up of a School Board – a move that was fought off then as it was to be again some years later.

The real bombshell, however, was the appearance of a notice affixed to the door of Trinity Church, the same information being repeated in the local press, to give warning effectively of the termination of the Girls' School's tenancy of their home in Old Church House by 1 March 1874. The Trustees of the Saxon Church, having just acquired the whole property, wished to exchange it for the Old Church House, moving the Free School into that building from the Church and ejecting the girls in the process. Their intention of doing this was the momentous news contained in the notice on Trinity Church door.

Headed "Charity Commission", and dated 10 May 1873, the notice read:

> "In the matter of the Charity called the Free School, in the parish of Bradford on Avon in the County of Wiltshire. Notice. The Trustees of the Charity propose with the Authority of the Charity Commissioners for England and Wales to effect an exchange of the messuages and tenements belonging to the said Charity described in the first schedule hereto, for the messuages and tenements belonging to the Rev W H Jones of Bradford aforesaid, which are described in the second schedule hereto, the said W H Jones paying all the expenses attending the transaction...."

The first schedule referred to the "property belonging to the Trustees of the above named Charity, the Free School premises now belonging to the said Trustees situate in or near the Churchyard of Bradford aforesaid" – the Saxon Church - and the second schedule related to the "property belonging to W H Jones, four messuages and tenements, school buildings and premises situate in Church Street, Bradford on Avon" – Old Church House.

An Emergency Committee meeting of the Managers was convened. They met with the Managers of the British Boys' School, the gentlemen, albeit with a strong element of self-preservation in their actions, showing commendable solidarity with the ladies. A deputation waited upon the Vicar, but their advances were repulsed.

So the exchange of the messuages and tenements took place. The boys of the Free School went to Old Church House, and the British Girls were rendered homeless, out in the cold. This was a severe blow, its severity increased by its total unexpectedness. Everett's Room at first seemed a possibility as alternative accommodation, but it proved not to be available, and prospects were bleak until a Mr Joseph Sparks came to the rescue with the suggestion of his building entirely new premises for the girls in Mason's Lane. His offer was accepted. He was thanked, as were the gentlemen of the Boys' School Committee for their support and advice, and the future for the little school organised by the town's Nonconformist ladies again seemed assured.

What Mr Sparks did was build a new schoolroom on the site of a derelict cloth factory which had been burnt down in 1869 in what was generally thought to have been some sort of insurance scam. (William Wilkins, a Trowbridge clothier, had occupied the property for some four or five years for the making of waste into yarn, employing about 40 workmen. The blaze of July 1869 had been so intense that "the very stones were calcined, and a pump some short distance from the burning pile melted like butter in the sun".) This building of Mr Sparks still stands in Mason's Lane, its grim and unprepossessing bulk giving little impression from the road of its grace and lightness within, and the magnificent views of Bradford that it offers from the garden. Today it is numbers 9, 10, and 10a Mason's Lane, the House of Inner Tranquillity, a Buddhist Monastery and meditation centre, in the Western Tharavadin tradition.

Before they were able to enter their new home, however, Agnes Boaden and her girls were to suffer a year of upset. The Mason's Lane building would not be ready by the time they had to quit Old Church House, and so, as a temporary measure, the Trustees of the Wesleyan Chapel in Coppice Hill offered them the use of their schoolroom for six months – from 17 April to 24 October 1874. And the silver lining to the cloud of their being removed from Church Street was the extra room that they found in the Wesleyan schoolroom. It was much pleasanter and roomier, so much so that infants could once again be admitted to the school. A measles epidemic provided even more room, attendance in the June of 1874 being down to just over 30. The completion of the Mason's Lane building still dragged on, so three more weeks were granted in their temporary accommodation, to be followed by an enforced holiday from 13 to 23 November to gain more time. But finally - at 09.16 [sic] on Monday 23 November 1874 – the new schoolroom in Mason's Lane was opened by the Rev H Howard, the Wesleyan minister. There was a good attendance at the ceremony, several ladies of the Committee being present, but few pupils because of the danger, as their parents saw it, of the new walls still being damp.

The main schoolroom in the new building was 49' long, 23.5' wide, and just over 14' high, with a small reduction in space for a lobby and a store. An adjacent classroom (for the infants – who else?) was over 41' long, rather less than 10' wide and almost 11' high. The dimensions of this latter room, and in particular its narrowness and darkness, were to cause problems in the future. Both rooms are still clearly recognisable in the Buddhist Centre today. The larger area, now a room for worship, lies parallel to Mason's Lane, access to it being through 10a. The narrow room, once part of the factory building, is at right angles to it and is reached via the road that runs through the central arch of the building. Between the two is a garden, once the school yard, but the school's small toilet block which in recent years was found in a corner of the garden has now completely disappeared.

This, then, was the British Girls' School of November 1874, staffed by Agnes Boaden, Mistress, and Harriet Jones and Mary Likeman, Pupil Teachers. Caroline Tiley had just left for Stockwell College in order to sit for a Queen's Scholarship.

The sixteen years or so of Agnes Boaden's rule at Mason's Lane, from 1874 to 1891, sound to have been relatively happy, but one is always conscious of the fact that parents had the option of sending their children to Trinity or to Christ Church, both of which were in a much sounder financial position, and with more commodious buildings, than the Girls' School. Even so, it was with a touch of pride that the Mistress recorded in 1886 that gas had been laid on to the school and that its name had been painted on the outside. (The words "British School" were still misleadingly visible above the doorway of the building until comparatively recently, but they are now painted over.) And her pride was even clearer a couple of years later when she wrote:

> "The Christmas Tree was prepared by the Ladies. The children and visitors assembled at 5 o'clock when the Tree presented a very brilliant appearance, being lighted with nearly 100 coloured wax candles. The children who had attended school most regularly choosing first from the Tree, and then those who had gained the highest number of marks during the year. Each child received a gift, mince pie or bun, and an orange, and the infants sweets. Songs and recitations were rendered at intervals by the scholars, and the whole affair was a great success. The Managers and friends expressed themselves highly pleased with the arrangements, and congratulated me on the matter."

And on the occasion of the School Treat in high summer 1880, the comment was made that "Miss Boaden may be congratulated on having a very efficient and well conducted school", and that she (assisted by the Pupil Teachers, Misses Knight and Long) "is most indefatigable in her efforts to amuse the children and render it a real treat for them".

Unfortunately, these sorts of entry are not common in the Mistress's log; disaster, dissatisfaction, and disciplinary problems are more usual. "Mary Bowyer died today of a brain fever"; "I reprove H Jones [a Pupil Teacher] for knocking children on the head with a blacklead pencil"; "spoke to H Jones about keeping the store tidy and received a very impertinent reply"; Mary Arbuckle [an Assistant] sacked "on account of her neglect of duty and untruthfulness"; and there is mention of canings – strokes on the hand with a stick – for misbehaviour.

During these years, the school continued to be staffed by a succession of Pupil Teachers, some of whom came from outside whilst others graduated to the position from that of Monitor. Most stayed about 5 years, going on if successful to college, but others failed to stay the full course. Today they are just names: Mary Likeman, Harriet Jones, Minnie Broad, Jane Knight, Emily Long, Frances Jones, Emily Harding, Maud Fowle, Ada Knight....We know that some gained promotion, Harriet Jones, for example, to Seend Cleeve Unsectarian School, and Jane Knight to Oldland Common British School, Bristol. These young girls had constantly to be rebuked for their rudeness and inefficiency, but they were children themselves, often only slightly older than those whom they were supposed to teach and keep in order. Two of them were complained of by parents for slapping their charges, thumping them, and pulling them across the schoolroom, and Minnie Broad seems constantly to have been late, rude, and inattentive to her duties. "Came into school unexpectedly this morning," complains Miss Boaden, "and found the room in an uproar, children running about and calling out etc, & all three PTs in the room allowing such disorder, while they were talking loudly & increasing the noise."

But despite the trouble they caused in their younger days, some, like Frances Jones, were welcomed back as teachers in their own right. It was in 1883 that Agnes Boaden got her first full Assistant, the status of this post being between that of (Head) Mistress and Pupil Teacher. This was Rose Cook, but Rose and her successors proved to be a fragile breed. Miss Cook was fairly quickly told to resign (which she did); her successor was Mary Arbuckle, whose fate has been mentioned above; Annie Hawker stayed only 4 days "proving to be of a nervous disposition, and not fit"; and then there was Matilda Storrier before the school welcomed back Frances Jones, who enjoyed a longer stewardship.

The number of pupils attending in Mason's Lane was larger than it had ever been in Church Street. In 1875, there were 164 on roll, the highest number ever, and attendances of 120 or 130 were common. In October 1880 there were 150 pupils present, the significance of which number lay in the events of the previous month. In September 1880 the British Boys' School had closed, their premises in the Old Quaker Meeting House in what is now the St Margaret's Street car park having been condemned, and it is clear that from that date a number of boys either stayed on at the Girls' School from the infants' class or enrolled there when they were older. So in 1882 there is mention of 191 pupils being in attendance.

Attendance, of course, was erratic. The leaving age was 10, but children often drifted away before then; epidemics of childish illnesses were common; and the vagaries of the weather led to large-scale absence. Agnes Boaden frequently records outbreaks of whooping cough, measles, scarlet fever, diphtheria, and chicken pox which devastated attendance. And, again, one reads, perhaps with surprise, of repeated and regular natural phenomena which prevented the children from getting to school – "the hurricane" of October 1877, frequent floods (but particularly that of 1882), heavy rain, snow and blizzards (not occasionally but, it seems, several times annually), and excessive cold or heat. The infants in their long, dark and narrow classroom suffered particularly and from time to time they had to be brought into the larger room because they either could not see properly or were feeling the cold. These conditions could bring the school to an early close or sometimes prevent its opening at all.

Before it all started to go wrong in the 1890s, inspectorial reports throughout the 70s and 80s tended to be favourable. The girls' work was centred on reading, composition, grammar, dictation, spelling and recitation; arithmetic; and some history, geography, needlework, music and singing. Much was learned by rote. Specific targets had to be met, and there was little room for imagination or initiative.

It is with some surprise, therefore, that we read: "I allowed the girls to write as an exercise in composition an account of the horrible murder committed last Friday night" – an indiscretion that would today bring down censure upon such a misguided teacher. Lessons then were generally more mundane and less open to flights of the imagination. But in 1890, after the visit of the inspectorial team, the school for the first time in many years received a clear vote of no confidence. "The girls are orderly but their instructions not satisfactory....The first and second standards, comprising more than one third of the upper school, are taught by two of the older children....The staff should be at once increased." And after mention of "the backward state of the school", there is the threat of a reduced grant for the following year.

At this point - March 1891 - Agnes Boaden submitted her resignation. She was to be married, but the recent criticism of the inspectors may have hastened her departure. A presentation was made; she was persuaded to stay on a few extra months because of the difficulty the Managers were having in finding a replacement; and she left on 24 July, to become Mrs Agnes Waygood.

Applications to Westminster College and to the British and Foreign Schools Society for a new Mistress had initially produced no result, but eventually, and in time for an August start, a Miss Georgina Little was appointed. She was Mistress of the school for 5 years, from August 1891 to June 1896, unfortunately producing in that time much aggravation, trouble, and disharmony, and setting the school on an inexorably downward path.

Poor Miss Little did not get off to a good start. Her school could not open on time because of an outbreak of scarletina which closed all the schools in Bradford for two weeks in September 1891, but when she did get going she "found the girls in fair order and the teachers able to manage their classes". Soon, however, having examined the whole school, she found the arithmetic "a total failure" and proclaimed that the previous five months had been utterly wasted. The new broom was obviously going to sweep clean, and a start was made by the appointment of new staff in line with the inspectors' recommendations. Emily Harding, a former Pupil Teacher at the British School, returned from the Portsmouth Board School to be appointed Assistant at a salary of £30 per year. This was a disaster. Georgina Little had not foreseen the consequences of such an appointment. Internal bitterness and wrangling ensued, and Frances Jones resigned. She had been promised the coveted job of Assistant and now had been passed over. The spat was patched up, however, by the stratagem of Miss Jones also being appointed Assistant, at the same rate of pay as Miss Harding, and Ada Knight took over the unpopular job of infants' teacher. But the seeds of mistrust and suspicion had been sown.

The germination of these seeds was rapid. First Ada Knight found a new post, leaving the unglamorous teaching of the infants to be shared by the two unwilling Assistants, and her resignation was followed by that of Frances Jones who gave as her reason Miss Little's interference with her teaching. In a letter to the Managers, in addition to her specific complaint, she also questioned in general terms the way in which the school was being run. The consequence was an official enquiry into Georgina Little's capabilities, but she was cleared of blame, the anger of the Assistants, it was found, being due to "friction occasioned by a strict supervision of their work to which they were not used". Perhaps it was so, but in the light of the Mistress's future troubles it seems likely that she had something to answer for. The end of the matter was that a plea was made by the Managers to Emily Harding, the one remaining Assistant, to be loyal to the school and to Miss Little.

By this time – 1892 – there were 180 children on roll in Mason's Lane, 110 older pupils (including a few boys) and 70 infants. And amidst all the staff unhappiness positive innovations took place. A Penny Savings Bank was started in collaboration with the Post Office; ambitious extra classes, for which the girls would have to pay, in cookery, drawing and French were planned; and a Mrs Beddoes began to provide cooked dinners during the winter months for girls who travelled from a distance or whose parents were out working in the factories.

But, overall, as 1893 dawned the situation was bleak, and again it was the infants' department that was at the centre of the storm. HMI were extremely unhappy about the conditions in which these small children were being taught.

There were too many of them; their classroom was narrow and dark; "better accommodation must be provided". The Managers discussed the matter but resources to effect improvements were not available, and HMI refused in any way to soften their stance. The infants room had to be closed immediately, and it was made clear that no temporary accommodation would be tolerated in its place. This decision placed in jeopardy the future of the whole establishment and the following announcement was made: "The Managers do close the said school [the infants' schoolroom], and not having means to build another, or of long continuing the Girls' School....hereby petition the Education Department to order the establishment of a School Board." Sparks was given 12 months notice of the school's intention to quit the Mason's Lane premises and a precise date – 31 December 1893 – was given for the closure of the Girls' School.

So definite did things seem that Ellen Hopkins, who by this time had succeeded Emily Harding as Assistant Teacher, left after a very short time "as she was assured that the British School would be closed in a few weeks". And Georgina Little made more waves by her failure to abide by the decision to close the infants' room. Infants were still being enrolled and she was called to account for her refusal to implement the Managers' decision. She explained that she had misunderstood the situation, and on being instructed in plain terms to dismiss the remaining infants and close the room forthwith, she tendered her resignation in a fit of pique, only to withdraw it immediately at the earnest entreaty of the Managers. The British School for Girls was not a happy school in early 1893.

Later in the year, there was a change of mood. A new spirit of optimism, born of the belief that sufficient funds could be raised to save the school if all pulled together, replaced the gloom of the winter and spring, and a number of positive moves were made. First, Bradford's Nonconformist congregations were asked to dig into their pockets. Then a plea was made to Mr Sparks to reduce his rent. Fund-raising activities were envisaged, and a stratagem was devised – £7 to £8 to be spent on a large curtain to act as a partition in the schoolroom – whereby the infants would be able to continue in attendance. And continue they did, in the same room as the older girls but now cut off from them by the curtain – not a solution, one felt, guaranteed to satisfy the authorities in London.

It was at about this time that Miss Little is first mentioned as being "Head Teacher, Certified Mistress 1st Class", rather than simply "Mistress", and in 1894 she had two Assistants, Gertrude Dyer who had just arrived in Bradford from Winchester at a salary of £37.10.0, and Clara Bull who had been appointed two years earlier from the Wesleyan Boys' School in Frome. Bessie Ford was the Stipendiary Monitor. A great fund-raising Concert and Entertainment was held, with singing, recitations, and scarf and fan drill. At least 100 visitors were unable to get in, so popular did the event prove. A new charwoman was engaged, toilets were repaired, and one has the feeling that everything that could be done was being tried in an attempt to secure the school's future. Unfortunately, HMI were not impressed.

They reported the girls as being in fairly good order, with progress being made, "but they show very little intelligence and do not understand much of what they read". "Grammar is not known sufficiently well to receive a grant." They noted with surprise that cookery was being taught. No-one had told them, so no grant could be made. The infants had made progress, but the business of their being taught in the same room as the older children, the classes separated only by a curtain, was quite unacceptable. There was an urgent need for sunblinds at the windows; the toilets were too near the school; the floor was rotten; a playground was needed.

Almost everything about the British Girls' School was sub-standard and it was hard for the inspectors not to be totally discouraging. "My Lords are clearly of opinion that the existing premises cannot be regarded as providing suitable accommodation for both girls and infants....The Managers should in future restrict the school to girls", but, with hesitation, a grant for the infants was on this occasion allowed. "I have lastly to request," writes the correspondent from London, "that the Managers will confer with the Managers of the Parish Church School at an early date upon the question of the future organisation and improvement of both buildings. In their present state, neither of them can be accepted as satisfying the conditions of grants in future." The Managers of the Parish Church School were able to act effectively and new premises were soon forthcoming; the British Girls' School was not so fortunate.

For Bradford on Avon's Nonconformist girls, therefore, 1894 and 1895 were years that switchbacked between hope and despair, between positive statements about the future from the Managers and condemnation from the Education Department in London, and between moves designed to restrict the number of children on roll and plans to expand. Changes in teaching staff became more frequent. The services of Miss Bull were dispensed with. Others – Fanny Coombs, Kate Arthur, Annie Sharp, Kate Burgess, Annie Turner, and Misses Stinchcombe, Gittings and Brayley – came and, for the most part, soon went. Miss Dyer fell from the playground wall, breaking her leg (Why was Miss Dyer on the playground wall in the first place?) but she too soon left anyway to get married. And the twin problems of inadequate accommodation generally and how to cope with the infants for whom there was really no room continued to plague Miss Little and her Managers.

Miss Little was herself a problem. She had constantly to be warned that she must not ignore the limits set on numbers by the Department. Early in 1895 she was formally requested to get "more order and discipline throughout the school", and a month or two later she bitterly asks: "Will you kindly let me know if you intend to provide accommodation for the infants. If so, and in any case, will you oblige by informing me if my services will be required after the annual examinations." She was permanently at odds with her superiors because of her abrasiveness and her sins both of commission and omission.

It was during 1894 that attempts were made to extend the school's premises. Real effort had gone into improving and bringing up to standard, as far as was possible, the existing building in Mason's Lane, sunblinds being provided, the toilets (again) being repaired, and part of the former infants' classroom being pressed into service as a sort of covered playground. Mr Sparks tried to buy neighbouring land so that the school could be enlarged, but this was unavailing. Also fruitless was the Managers' attempt to obtain the use of the Zion Baptist Church's schoolroom as temporary accommodation for their classes. (This was the building in Middle Rank, on the left as one goes up Conigre Hill, known today as Zion Baptist Chapel and in 1894 as the Grove Meeting House. It was then the Sunday school for the earlier Zion Chapel which was demolished in the 1960s. Its site today remains as an undeveloped space to the right of Conigre Hill and is used for car parking.) The Charity Commissioners blocked the move. But during the course of the following year it was finally agreed that a temporary structure could be built. "My Lords have, on several occasions, granted formal recognition to an iron building, such as Mrs Humphrey's," it was said, and so it was agreed that "a movable building, something like the technical school's" should be erected behind the Girls' School.

Planning for this new building went hand in hand with a close examination of the school's financial position, the imposing of economies, and more discussion about fund-raising. One teacher (Miss Brayley) would have to go. Salaries were closely examined, Mrs Sharp's being set at £50 and Miss Coombs' at £35; and Miss Little was to get £35 plus one third of all the grants made to the school, except that for cookery. It was not expected that she would like this new arrangement, but it would start on 1 January unless she raised objections, in which case she would be given formal notice of its imposition from 25 March 1896.

We do not know whether Miss Little objected or not. Early in 1896 the inspectors submitted their report for the previous year. It was dire. "The scholars read fairly but they are very backward in the other elementary subjects and show no knowledge of either grammar or elementary science....Were it not for the difficulties under which the teachers have to work, the school would be reported to be inefficient....The infants have no chance of making proper progress." In the light of these damning comments, it was put to Georgina

Little that it might be best were she to resign. This she did, with three months notice. Her "conscientiousness" and "faithfulness" – minimal achievements – were recorded, and she left on 24 June 1896, bringing a very unhappy chapter in the little school's history to a close.

She never saw the "iron building", the new home of the infants, no trace of which now remains. It went up in August at a cost of £163, for its benefits to be enjoyed by the new Head Mistress, Jessie McCulloch. Its life, however, was a mere 9 years.

Miss McCulloch was soon to become Mrs Ford, and she and her successor, Mrs Walker, restored a semblance of calm and good order to the British Girls' School. With Mary Clegg's appointment in 1900 a degree of permanence even seemed to have been achieved as she stayed until 1913, working with a succession of competent and dedicated colleagues. Quite a number were former Pupil Teachers who returned to the school after they had qualified – Minnie Alexander, Ada Scott, and Emily Jones, for example – and others like Misses Beath and Trapwell stayed for substantial periods, bringing a professionalism to their work that was of a different quality from the efforts, say, of Keziah Norris and Maria Keen forty years earlier.

But, as had always been the case, the Bradford on Avon British Girls' Schools faced competition. There were still Christ Church and Trinity, and there was still the alternative of private education. In the 1890s and 1900s Sydney Lane ran a boys' boarding school at Avonfield, Trowbridge Road, Ella Venton operated from 6 St Margaret's Place, and Miss Watkins, followed by Miss Blake, offered a ladies' college at Avon House in Kingston Road. After the closure of the Free School in Old Church House in 1903, Mr Cowlishaw moved to private education at an establishment in Belcombe, and Miss Cockrom's School for Young Ladies and Gentlemen, still remembered with affection by some of Bradford's citizens today, first opened its doors in St Margaret's Street in 1895. It closed in 1932. And there were others. Customers, therefore, had to be positively sought.

These were the years of conflict in South Africa, and school holidays marked events of military and political importance as well as local festivities; there were still closures for such events as the arrival in town of Sanger's circus, Haymaking Day, the Temperance Excursion, and the Hospital Parade, but to them can be added the celebrations for Coronation Day (a whole week in honour of Edward VII) and the Relief of Mafeking as well as recognition of General Elections. In December 1899, all the schools in the town closed so that a proper send-off could be given to the local reservists who were going to the front in the Transvaal War. The children marched to the railway station and lined the Approach, whilst a band and an official committee accompanied the men.

More curiously, there was another full-scale closure in the same year to mark

Mabel Cockrom and her pupils c1910. For most of these children, both names and father's occupations are known.

Back row, left to right, W Cousins, P Rose (landlord of Swan), Dorothy Jennings (rate collector), Kathleen Archard (brewery), Mary Norris (chemist), Cecil Benjamin (coal delivery and farmer), Nellie Borrett (Spencer Moultons), Norah Payne (jeweller), Wilfred Bowyer (farmer).

Half row, centre right, not known, Leslie Long (builder), Muriel Rose (Swan), Dot Maclean (poor law officer), Dolly Uncles (foundry), Ernest Chard (farmer).

Centre row, seated, Ivy Mizen (rate collector, farmer), Muriel Maclean (poor law officer), Ida Rose (Swan), Mason, Miss Cockrom, George Edwards (station master), Nell Percival (brewery), Phyllis Vennel (Spencer Moultons), Billy Mayell (builder).

Front row, Victor Borrett (Spencer Moultons), Nellie Uncles (foundry), Wheeler (men's outfitter), Bobby Cleveland (butcher), Dolly Mizen (rate collector, farmer), Cecil Weaver (ironmonger), Hilda Chard (farmer), Nellie Mizen (rate collector, farmer).

THE BRITISH GIRLS' SCHOOL

Pupils from the British Girls' School taking part in the Town Carnival of 1912.

the coming-of-age and wedding of Miss Mallinson of Wood Leigh. Patriotism and local pride were stronger then than they are now. And certainly pride is manifest, both in the importance of the occasion and in personal appearance, in the bearing of "the pupils of the Undenominational School for Girls on Mason's Hill" in an interesting old photograph that has survived. It is of participants in the Town Carnival of 1912. Conscious of their importance, the girls are immaculate in their white dresses, a credit to their parents and their school, and in the photograph they are pulling Mollie Hopkins in her chariot. (The Hopkins family lived at the start of Trowbridge Road, Mollie's father being a mechanic and engineer. It was Mr Hopkins who had made the chariot, and Mollie, who came to be a well known character in the town, followed in his footsteps by being very mechanically minded and driving an ambulance car during the Second World War.)

At the start of this period leading up to the First World War, and under a new Head Mistress, the inspectors reported that the outlook for the girls was good. They add, however, "The school has been in a low state for many years". They say that there was much to be done but that "the infants are in nice order and are likely to make good progress in their new school". The well respected Fanny Coombs left in 1897; Jennie Ransom from Spalding replaced her, but proved to be a poor disciplinarian and lasted only a few months; she herself was replaced by Miss Gunstone from Bethnal Green who immediately made a good impression; and the Monitor, Kate Burgess (who stayed until 1904 when she left to become a nurse), had her wages increased from 1/6d to 2/- per week. We know no more of her than this, but she was clearly better thought of than was another young girl, Rose Harris, because the parents of Rose arrived in school [one afternoon in 1897] "in a very rude manner and removed their two girls, because Rose is not suitable to be taken as a teacher".

The number of pupils on roll, the average attendance, the actual numbers that it was judged the accommodation would take, unjustified absence, the activities of an Attendance Officer, and the first prosecutions of parents who failed to ensure that their children were in school were all concerns of the first order for the Head Mistress and her Managers in these years. This was because they were all crucial to the school's financial well-being. Indeed, when Mary Clegg resigned in 1913, she was able to take satisfaction in there having been 82 girls in attendance on her last day as compared with 25 on her first. Just before, just after, and at the turn of the century an attendance in the high 60s or 70s was usual, with perhaps 10 more than that being average just before the outbreak of the First World War. Additionally, of course, some 40 or 50 infants were also present daily until 1905.

What this meant in terms of actual cash can be seen from the figures of any given year. In 1897, for example, the average attendance was just over 61 girls and 55 infants. Each girl was worth 21/9d and each infant 15/- at this time, so revenue from this source was £108.9.0. To this was added a fee grant of £62. Additionally, there was an aid grant from the Bristol and District British Association intended to allow for the increasing of salaries to teachers and for providing more teachers and equipment. The school's total income, therefore, was about £217. From this it can be seen that regularity of attendance was important in achieving a high average attendance figure, so Mrs Walker's lament that "about 30% attend with fair regularity, but the remainder scarcely make half time" was heartfelt. Friday absence in particular was traditional – and damaging.

In 1898 a new Attendance Officer was appointed, and girls under the age of 13 who had left school unauthorisedly were reported to him. The requirement was that by this age they must either have achieved a certain academic standard or, alternatively, have gained a somewhat lowlier award, the Required Attendance Certificate (the so-called Dunce's Certificate), if they were to be allowed to leave. This latter simply meant that they had put in the time! Mrs Walker took action, and in 1899 was able to report that she had secured a second prosecution for non-attendance, this resulting in a fine of 3/6d for the parents.

The annual reports of HMI at the turn of the century were always good, containing neither criticism nor threat. The school's statistics, however, indicated an interesting trend that sprang from there being no Nonconformist boys' school in the town by this time. In 1900, there were 85 girls on roll; in 1901, the average attendance was 69.5 girls and 3.3 boys; in 1902, 69.5 girls and 10.2 boys; in 1903,

64.1 girls and 19.4 boys....At this point HMI gently indicated that if boys were to continue to attend, proper toilets should be provided, advice that eventually seeped down to County Council level because in 1906 they issued a clear instruction that boys must henceforth be excluded. This instruction was implemented and a few of the girls also left to go with their brothers to Christ Church. Coincidental with the removal of the boys went the demise of the infants. Always a problem, they were finally ejected in 1905 when their schoolroom, the "iron building" that had only been erected in 1896, was physically removed, leaving room for a walled playground, the eastern portion covered. From this date to the closure of the school some 20 years later, it could, for almost the only time in its history, properly be called the British *Girls'* School.

After a successful headship, Mary Clegg left in 1913 with a silver teapot, a pair of sugar tongs, and a degree of bitterness. The gifts were deserved; the bitterness arose from difficulties not of her making. Mabel Beath had been absent from her teaching duties for seven or eight months because of illness, and as a consequence HMI had been unable to carry out an effective inspection of the teaching. But, unusually, they were constrained to criticise aspects of organisation – of the arrangement of classes, for instance, and of the admission of under-age children. Miss Beath's prolonged absence, too, was exhausting for Miss Clegg and her remaining colleagues, so, when a needlework inspector was, as she saw it, totally unreasonable in the way in which she carried out her duties, Miss Clegg perhaps felt that it was time for her to go. That was in May, and the summer of 1913 marked the beginning of the end for what was now officially the Bradford on Avon British School: Number 30.

An announcement was made late in 1913 that a meeting was to be held at the Baths to consider the closure of the British Girls' School and the provision of a new council school for Bradford on Avon. This meeting took place in March the following year, and the decision was taken not to recognise the school after the end of August 1915, replacing it with a new council school for 150 children. The War, of course, temporarily froze all plans for reorganisation, but from the end of 1913 or the beginning of 1914 a blight descended on the school. It had, effectively, only a limited future, and, in addition to the rigours of wartime, it increasingly felt all the implications of this death sentence.

A flavour of those wartime and post-war years is given by the closing of the school to mark the visit of the King and Queen to Trowbridge in 1917, to allow Peace Celebrations to be enjoyed in 1919, to honour the wedding of Princess Mary in 1922, and to witness the unveiling of the War Memorial in the same year. Holidays were also instituted for more mundane reasons – to coincide with the annual closure of the rubber works, and the holding of Trowbridge Fete and the Bradford Pageant – and half day school closures were ordered by the County Offices during and just after the War so that pupils could go blackberrying in order to collect the fruit and eke out food supplies. Time had to be found, too (though no holidays were declared), for what today sounds the curious business of collecting horse-chestnuts at the request of the Board of Education. Apparently they were a vital constituent in the manufacture of gunpowder, and after collection by the pupils, arrangements were made for their bulk storage and onwards transmission to processing plants.

Gwendoline Maddison followed Mary Clegg as Head Mistress. When she left two years later in 1915, Ada Burchell was appointed. She stayed until 1921, and after her came a Miss Parkinson. Thereafter, a succession of temporary Head Teachers oversaw the running down of the establishment.

By this time it had become obvious that the Mason's Lane buildings were no longer viable as a twentieth century elementary school. "The conditions under which this school has to be conducted add greatly to the normal difficulty of the work," opined the inspectors in 1923. "The classes are taught in an undivided room and the yard which serves as a playground is of such restricted area that only one class can use it for physical exercises which necessarily can only be of a limited character. (By the kind permission of a friend of the school the girls have the use of a park for organised games.) Moreover, the third class is largely made up of infants who, as has been previously reported, cannot have a suitable course of instruction in the circumstances." The "friend of the school" was Lord Fitzmaurice of Leigh whose home from 1890 to 1935 was Leigh House, now the Leigh Park Hotel. A great benefactor to education at all levels in Bradford on Avon, for many years he allowed the girls of the British School to walk up the hill and use his grounds for their games and recreation.

In 1923 HMI wrote: "The present Head [Miss Parkinson], who is assisted by two uncertificated teachers, began work here on 9 May 1921. Since that date, five assistants have had charge of the third class and have left....The good order, the manners of the girls, and the neatness with which their written work is set out are commendable features." But an Education Committee report of November 1924 says: "The Undenominational School is to be closed at Christmas. Strong representations have been made in favour of providing a council school on the site bought by the Council for that purpose on the south of the river. Though there are sufficient places in the church schools for all the displaced children, sooner or later a new school for younger children will be needed south of the river."

Mrs Alfreda Simmonds spent the whole of her school life at the British Girls' School, from 1918 to 1924. She remembers Mollie Hopkins very well. She also remembers going blackberrying and walking with her friends, two by two, up the hill to play in the grounds of Lord Fitzmaurice's home.

"The best part of our week was when we went to the Baths. Swimming was always a part of our work and if any girl was naughty she was not allowed to go. Mr Heavyside was in charge at the Baths, and when he died his wife was in charge. She was a right one! And after swimming, back to school. We went in at the door lowest down on the hill and turned left into the large schoolroom that was divided into sections with partitions. There was another room that was ever so narrow and very dark, but that was a storeroom or cloakroom. A solicitor had his office upstairs.

Miss Parkinson took us. She was lovely. She lived at Westbury and was childless, so, as a treat, she used to invite some of the girls back to her house for tea. But I was never invited."

The British Girls' School had never been well placed in a material sense. Official criticisms of the conditions under which it was run were voiced very soon after its inception, and with the passing of time they increased rather than diminished. Nevertheless, generations of young Bradford girls had received their education in Old Church House and in Mason's Lane, and successive Mistresses did their enlightened, or unenlightened, best for their young charges. But by the turn of the century, the days of the British Schools were over and the impetus for educational advance was with the new council schools. Secondary schooling, too, was developing, and girls from Mason's Lane now regularly left, either with scholarships or as fee-paying pupils, to go to the secondary school in Junction Road.

The Mason's Lane premises closed as a school at Christmas 1924, and thereafter the building served successively as a British Legion Club and as various private residences; but the Girls' School staggered on throughout January, February and March 1925 in the Congregational schoolroom in St Margaret's Hill under the headship of Mrs Arnold. During this period, staff changes were frequent and an air of impermanence hung over all aspects of the running and management of School Number 30. It finally closed on 8 April, with the children transferring to the Parochial Girls' School after the Easter holidays, pending the building of the council school.

Above: Trinity National School in Newtown. This replaced, or extended, the old building in Church Street in 1896. The site is now that of the Ropewalk retirement homes.

Below: Vacated in 1962, Trinity's Newtown buildings were demolished in 1984.

Trinity Church of England Senior School, and Trinity Secondary Modern School
1928-1980

TRINITY SENIOR SCHOOL OPENED with its new name and function in January 1928. Its premises, however, were as they had been – the old building of 1836 at the end of Church Street, together with the newer and larger addition of 1896 at the back, with access from Newtown. These were scarcely appropriate to the needs of a senior school and were to prove to be increasingly squalid and unsatisfactory quarters until a move to modern premises was effected in 1962. Herman Wilkinson was Head Master, but it was essentially a church school and the Vicar of Holy Trinity Church was always its Chairman of Managers, from which position he exercised undoubted authority. From 1915 to 1921 this was the Rev Richardson and from 1921 to 1937 Canon Clarke.

Names that are remembered from these prewar years are those of Mr Harris, Mr Musselwhite, Mr Baker, Mr Kernutt, Miss Jackson – and Mrs Cowlishaw. Mrs Ruth Cowlishaw had worked at the school for about 30 years when, in 1934, she transferred to the Trowbridge Road Junior School (where she worked for another 13) and was presented with the very latest type of fountain pen for her lifetime's work. Albert Harris, after being Head of the elementary school, continued for a number of years as an ordinary teacher, albeit on a protected salary, at the senior school. His position was unusual and uncomfortable, his feelings (one imagines) ambivalent. A rather younger member of staff in the 1930s was Frank Musselwhite, a man for whom the young George Carey, in later years Archbishop of Canterbury, came to feel great affection and respect when he, his mother, brother and sisters arrived as evacuees in 1939. Musselwhite had started his teaching career at Christ Church in 1921, moving to Trinity in 1928, and he went on to become one of the mainstays of the school. In 1937 he unsuccessfully applied for the headship, retiring in April 1961 after giving 40 years of service to education in Bradford.

Vera Jackson was appointed in 1930, and she, too, went on to give long and distinguished service to the school. She served for 32 years, 24 of them as Deputy Head. A H Baker became a Manager in the 1930s, and for a number of years up to 1961 was Vice Chairman of Governors. Combining this responsibility with multifarious duties elsewhere, he was ubiquitous in his enthusiasm for service to the town in general and to education in particular. He had joined the staff of the County Secondary School in 1905, rose to be the Chairman of that school's Governing Body, and died in 1964. And Leslie Kernutt flirted briefly with teaching in a senior school before transferring to the more rarefied atmosphere of selective education in Junction Road.

Trinity School was a tough school in those prewar years. There was private education or the County School for the aspiring and the genteel; if you were neither, and did not have cash to spare, you went to Trinity. And it was in a tough area, Tory, Newtown, Middle Rank and Wine Street not having the respectability that they have today. Even so, it was in many ways a happy school. Frank Musselwhite was able to look back on the period of Herman Wilkinson's headship, 1928-1937, and say this:

> "The school was started as a Senior School. It was formed of six or seven unwilling factions in the town and villages around. The staff consisted of men and women of various loyalties. The parents were often hostile or, if not hostile, apathetic. Few believed a Senior School would be successful. By 1933, the school had achieved unity and become a school of character. It was interested in music, art, drama. It was divided into Houses and organised inter-school games. It had small ceremonies and speech days. It made visits to exhibitions and had other local outings. It had started a Cycle Club. There was a feeling of friendship throughout the school. They all knew they were working under good direction. The school was known from Swindon to Bath. The Head Master, a man of great integrity, who had worked the school as a benevolent democracy, left a considerable heritage to his successor when he resigned in 1937."

By the time of Herman Wilkinson's retirement, Trinity had achieved a growing reputation and it was known for a range of extra-curricular activities that was unusual at that time beyond the grammar schools. That reorganisation was considered a success was evinced by a report from the Diocesan Inspector of Schools of 1933:

> "In the work of this large and important Senior School we find convincing evidence of the advantages afforded....by such proper grading of pupils as is made possible by schools' reorganisation. Here full use is being made of the opportunities which reorganisation has presented...."

Sports were held on Victory Field and cups (given by such as William Pullinger, Director of Education, various Managers, the Old Main Swimming

Club) were presented to the winning Houses – at this time, St Aldhelm, St Laurence, St Olave, and St Margaret. A sports field for Trinity's sole use was being sought, so far without success, but the most obtrusive blot on an otherwise promising picture was the beginning of a feeling that the buildings were not adequate for the school's growing needs.

It was already clear that there was no chance of the school's obtaining a playing field close to its premises in Newtown, and as the 1930s drew to a close extra classrooms, a laboratory, an assembly hall, a staff room....all became increasingly desirable or necessary. One idea that was floated was to purchase the Malt House at Abbey House, converting it to use as a gymnasium and woodwork centre. The cost proved to be prohibitive. Another idea was to build a multi-purpose wooden hall on the existing site that could be used variously as an assembly hall, gymnasium, handicraft centre, lecture theatre, dining hall, and general recreational area. The Director of Education was not unsympathetic but he suggested more ambitious plans, one of which was the conversion of the Newtown site to a junior and infants school, a new senior school to be built elsewhere. And so the seed was sown that came to germination a quarter century later, but, in the meantime, the Second World War put an end to such ambitious and potentially expensive ideas for rebuilding, as it did to so much else.

The new Head, appointed from September 1937, was G Conway Jones, described later by Frank Musselwhite as "a clever scholar". No school was able to be innovative and adventurous during those years of national emergency; the best that could be hoped for was that the line was held so that, when peace returned, forward movement could be resumed. And certainly the problems posed at Trinity by the massive influx of refugees and their teachers, on top of all the other wartime shortages, disruptions, and emergencies, can not be underestimated. Even so, Mr Jones appears to have been ill fitted to cope with them. Things went downhill. There was unease about the "tone" of the school from both parents and Managers, but despite the strength of their feelings, the Board of Managers forbore (in 1943, for example) to put their views in writing to the Head, though sorely tempted to do so.

The following year, Conway Jones had cause to write to his Managers about the quality of his new intake. He had received "an influx of undesirable children"; fifteen of them he found to be "mentally defective" and "a very real moral and physical danger to the other children". These pupils were clearly causing him grave concern, and Mr Musselwhite was put in charge of the group. Nor did his staff escape censure. Four months later he wrote again, complaining about six named teachers who were either not carrying out their duties, or were incapable of carrying them out. Mr J, for example, had been away all term, had no intention of returning, had removed all his possessions from his digs and from school, was living in Surrey, was desperately arthritic and unable to dress or undress without his wife's assistance, and "would be given a certificate of inability to work by any doctor". But he was still timetabled for classes. There were also ladies who were planning to get married with the intention of leaving the school (which was bad), or of staying (which was worse). Mr Jones's problems were not imaginary, but he seemed overcome by his inability to handle them.

Jones resigned during the course of a full inspection of the school in the summer of 1947. "He no longer felt able to cope with the situation and he would feel happier if he were allowed to relinquish the duties and responsibilities of Head Master." The Managers, unsurprisingly, allowed him so to do.

Ellis Darby, who had spent two years as Head of Science at the Fitzmaurice Grammar School, was appointed Head of Trinity as from January 1948 to begin what was to be an almost 20-year tenure. Johnny Otter, also from Fitzmaurice, and Frank Musselwhite were among the unsuccessful candidates. And for this wartime and post-war period, the Rev Philip Barry was Chairman of Managers (1937-1944), followed by the Rev Claude Green (1944-1956).

Darby had a job to do. He had to pick the school up and, as one teacher put it, "recapture the soul of the school and restore its self-respect". It was a job that he set about with vigour, and local opinion was that the first results of his more vigorous leadership were soon apparent. A prefectorial system was created; school Houses were reinstated (Horton, Kingston, Methuen, and Yerbury rather than the earlier saints); homework had to be done; the wearing of school uniform was encouraged; the behaviour of the boys (with no mention of the girls!) was deemed to be better; and, in 1959, a sort of Speech Day and Prizegiving was instituted, the first being in St Margaret's Hall in November. This was an event of some significance for the school with over 350 pupils, staff, parents, and other guests attending, Alderman Stevens, Chairman of the Wiltshire Education Committee, presenting the prizes. In line with the earliest of these initiatives, the full inspection of 1950 resulted in an excellent report

The school's situation changed; it became the Trinity Secondary Modern School, with Controlled status from July 1949, and in 1950 the Managers became Governors. Noreen Brady became School Secretary for three years in 1955 before moving to begin a very lengthy stint in that position at the grammar school. Frank Panzetta (another link with the grammar school) began his active connection with Trinity as a Governor in the late 1950s, and the local MP, Sir Robert Grimston, paid a visit to Newtown in 1958 as part of the school's campaign to secure more suitable premises. And it was this search for new premises that dominated Trinity's history in the 1950s.

When Darby was appointed to the school in 1948, as he himself said,

The whole of the Trinity School site as it was prior to 1962.

"the war had just finished and conditions were bleak. There were disgusting toilets and primitive washing conditions. One classroom in the old building was called the Black Hole of Calcutta, and school meals were taken there. A large ARP water tank took up most of the boys' playground, and there was no assembly hall, no craft room, library or labs. There were just bare classrooms."

The premises, after all, dated from 1836 and 1896.

After the school had gained Controlled status in 1949, efforts were made to bring the buildings up to a tolerable standard, but as it was soon evident that a total replacement was sooner or later inevitable, there was little point in spending money on the old premises. Ellis Darby's assessment of the situation indicates the poverty of the material provision, but increasing numbers (approaching 400 by the late 1950s) meant that not only were the buildings poor and ill-suited to the needs of a twentieth century secondary school, but they were also far too small. And so we have the main school building in Newtown, containing six classrooms and little else, and the two classrooms of the old building fronting on to Church Street that were on different floors and heated by open coal fires. Sladesbrook Hall, 900 yards and 14 minutes walking distance away, was also used, as were the Lambert Memorial Room (700 yards and 12 minutes), the Methodist Schoolroom (600 yards and 10 minutes), the Handicraft Centre close to the Trowbridge Road Junior School (1200 yards and 15 minutes), with the school garden and playing field a similar distance and time away in the other direction. The Handicraft Centre was opened in 1949, the boys having no woodwork before that date though the girls had been taught cookery on the ground floor of the old building. And after 1957 when Christ Church Junior School was rehoused, Trinity made use of a couple of classrooms on that abandoned site too. The school was incredibly dispersed – an old, bedraggled thing of bits and pieces.

More cheerfully, hand in hand with this despair about the existing premises went the search for a site on which to build a new school. Northleigh House? Berryfields? Bath Road? Eventually, a plot of land between Churches and Ashley Road was chosen as the site for a completely new school building. The contract was given to Messrs T Holdoway and Sons of Westbury and eventually the new premises cost £122,000. Whilst still at the old building, however, the Governors had time boldly to declare that the suggestion about a merging of Trinity and Fitzmaurice to form a comprehensive school was not to be entertained, and talk of a bilateral school found no favour in any quarter either.

The old Trinity School closed on 31 May, the new school coming into use immediately, with the official opening held on 12 July 1962. And this was an occasion of some moment. There was a great gathering of officers and members of the Local Authority, together with an impressive collection of clergy, local notabilities, teachers, parents, and pupils – some 500 in all. The Dedication was performed by the Archdeacon of Wiltshire, the Guests of Honour being Lieutenant-General Sir Wilfrid and Lady Linsell, the whole proceedings orchestrated by Ellis Darby and the Chairman of Governors, the Rev A F Osborne. The new premises were a striking contrast to the old, everything that had been lacking previously now being provided, with the whole building attractively

A representation of the Trinity, part of a commemorative brass to the Horton family in the north aisle of Holy Trinity Church. Much simplified, this design was taken as the badge of Trinity School.

presented in Bath stone and the more irregular Atworth stone.

Some effort was made at this time to link the opening of the new Trinity School with celebrations to mark the 250th anniversary of the beginnings of formal education in Bradford on Avon. Unfortunately, they went off at half-cock. The later-than-expected opening of the new buildings missed the February anniversary celebrations by several months. In any event, 1712, though an important date in Bradford's educational history, does not accurately record the founding of the first known school in the town. And claims that John Rogers' school of 1712 was the forebear of Trinity are somewhat forced anyway; if the precursor of anything, it was of the Old Free Grammar School that was quite distinct from the Parochial (or Trinity) National School of 1836.

The next 5 years were exciting. Darby continued as Head, with the Rev Osborne (1956-1964) and the Rev David Strangeways (1964 -1973) as Chairmen of Governors. (In this latter post, there was a brief interregum in 1965 and 1966 when Mrs C H Goschen took the Chair, and, interestingly, David Strangeways' leaving in 1973 was to enable him to take up the post of Chaplain to the British Embassy in Stockholm.) Trinity was now a school of which one could be proud; it no longer had to go cap-in-hand to find some empty building in which it could lodge the odd class, and even Speech Days could be in-house, in the splendid new hall. One long desired innovation took place as a result of the move and that was the establishing of a 5th Form aiming at external examinations. In 1962 it numbered only 14; from this small base it failed to grow, 8, 13, and 10 being the figures for the next three years, but in 1966 it began to achieve respectability with 21 pupils. Ellis Darby was disappointed at the lack of instant enthusiasm for his long desired 5th Form, but aspiration to examination success was unfamiliar and, despite his exhortations, parents were slow to grasp the new opportunities available to their children.

During the mid and late 60s, secondary reorganisation began to be discussed in earnest, and soon it was not so much a question of *whether* comprehensive education would be adopted as *when* it would be introduced. The Rev Strangeways and Miss McDonald were Trinity's representatives on the Reorganisation Working Party, and things were done in preparation for the brave new world that was about to dawn. The comprehensive school would be called St Aldhelm's; a speaker was invited to Speech Day who had first-hand experience of this new sort of education; and when Ellis Darby retired in December 1967, his successor, Vernon Atkins, was only appointed to a temporary post as everything was about to be thrown into the comprehensive melting pot.

But it did not happen. There is a terse record in the Governors' Minutes that "lack of public funds has caused the indefinite postponement of the plans for comprehensive reorganisation in Bradford on Avon". This was disturbing, as was the appointment of a new Head Master to the Fitzmaurice Grammar School. Atkins's position, therefore, was made permanent in 1969, and things went on as before. Speech Days, now well established, continued, usually with some local dignitary or one of the Governors presenting the prizes. Miss McDonald JP, MA, Vice Chairman of the Governing Body did the honours in 1971, the last occasion on which this prizegiving was held.

By 1970, eight years after the new school was opened, a further building programme took place, and this produced a new sports hall, art room, domestic science room, woodwork and metalwork shops, drawing office, and an extra laboratory. But Atkins resigned in 1971 in order to go as Adviser for Secondary Education to Dewsbury, and so in 1972 the final episode in the history of Trinity School opened.

In April, Colin Davison, previously Deputy Head of Blake Secondary School in Bridgwater, began his headship of what was by this time a large, well respected and well run secondary modern school. The buildings of 1962 had been designed for 300, but additions since then had allowed the school to expand to 500 and to over 600 by the late 1970s. The new Head did not like formal Speech Days, believing that the money they cost could be better spent elsewhere, and so they were discontinued. However, clubs of all sorts flourished; trips, both within this country and abroad were an integral part of the school's activities; a diversity of extra-curricular activities was encouraged; the results of external examinations were eagerly awaited and evaluated; and, despite the threat of eventual reorganisation, Trinity was very much a going concern with parents, staff, and pupils proud of its reputation and achievements. It even had the unusual advantage of having the remains of a Roman Villa found within its grounds, which discovery provoked more than local archaeological interest. There was a flirtation with a Sixth Form, but if this never really took off, a retiree from the staff was able to say that he was leaving a stable and happy school, with staff relationships the best he had ever known.

As his Chairman of Governors Mr Davison had the Rev D C Ritchie, and it was they who prepared for the coming of comprehensive education when it became clear that, even with a change of government, a new order was to begin in September 1980. The comprehensive school was to be on the Trinity site. The old Fitzmaurice buildings in Junction Road that had long outlived their useful life were to be abandoned, and the new St Laurence (not St Aldhelm's) School would take pupils of all abilities on the Ashley Road/Churches site. Additional buildings would be provided so that all the boys and girls of secondary age from Bradford on Avon and the neighbouring villages could be accommodated on the single campus. By then Colin Davison had gone as Head to the comprehensive school at Durrington near Salisbury, and his deputy, A J Tayler, was appointed Acting Head for the two remaining terms. Trinity had existed as a secondary school for 52 years. Like any school it had had both its high and low points, and if the low had been superlatively low, at its best, and particularly in its later years, it is still remembered as having been a very happy and successful school.

TECHNICAL INSTITUTE AND SECONDARY SCHOOL.

Built, largely by the liberality of Lord Edmond Fitzmaurice, in 1896, to the design of T. B. Silcock, of Bath. It has proved very suitable for its purpose, and is generally considered besides to be an ornament to the town.

A Brave Beginning
The County School:
1897-1904

Thou hast most traitorously corrupted the youth of the realm in erecting a grammar school....thou hast built a paper mill.

Shakespeare, *King Henry VI, part II*

THE CATALYSTS FOR THE STARTING of secondary education in Bradford on Avon were the Technical Instruction Acts of 1889 and 1891. As a result of the first of these, the County Council set up a Wiltshire Technical Education Committee which spawned Local Committees in towns throughout the County. As early as 1890 discussions about technical education took place in Bradford, and the following year a Local Committee was appointed, charged specifically with the implementation of the requirements of these two Acts. Its Chairman was Erlysman Pinckney, and one of its members was Edmond Fitzmaurice.

This movement had been stimulated by a growing awareness of the widening gulf between Britain and Germany, our closest industrial rival, in the matter of resources devoted to technical education. The problem was where the money for innovation was to come from. It was raised, in fact, by the Chancellor's putting an extra 6d income tax in his budget on the cost of spirits. Ostensibly this was to curb the incidence of drunkenness and the growth in the number of public houses that the country's prosperity had encouraged, and it was intended that this "whisky money" would be used to compensate those in the licensing trade adversely affected by the tax. In the event, however, this plan was defeated and the money went instead to the development of technical education. It was on this whisky money, therefore, that technical schools were built.

On three separate occasions in the period 1889-1891 the Technical Education Committee had tried to enlist the sympathies of the Trustees of the Free Grammar School in embarking together on some sort of venture for the starting of evening technical classes, but "they declined to alter their plans or help them in any way", so for any progress to be made Mr Pinckney and his committee had to go it alone. A decade later, this shortsighted intransigence on the part of the Trustees was to be remembered when the Free School found itself in terminal decline. In the event, the Committee moved quickly, and towards the end of 1891 took a very positive step.

A Technical Institute – "a commodious iron school-house" – was established in Frome Road (though exactly where in Frome Road I have been unable to discover) under the aegis of the County Council, with William Edward Watkins in charge. "The iron building which has been provided is a neat and useful structure, of very convenient size, and when completed will, no doubt, offer all the accommodation that can be desired for such classes as may be formed," reported the *Wiltshire Times*.

Measuring 60' x 20', it opened in December 1891 with about 50 students. They paid 1d for each lesson, with 2 classes on Monday and 2 on Thursday evenings, and with a morning class as well. A couple of years later it expanded somewhat by using as laboratories the old Quaker Meeting House in what is now St Margaret's Street car park, a building vacated some time before by the British Boys' School. So evening classes devoted to a wide range of technical subjects became established and were developed in Frome Road over the next five or six years, albeit in what was really only makeshift accommodation.

Walter Aust was the first to enrol at the new Institute – or so he claimed in two letters written 54 years later. He had been a pupil at the Free School for over 6 years (and his report of March 1890 shows that he was an excellent scholar) when he saw an announcement in the local press about the Technical Institute. Intending students were invited to apply through a Mr Patrick of Woolley Street, so he and his younger brother, A C Aust, went to see Mr Patrick and were told that they were the first to apply. He remembered, too, that some years later he was present on the occasion of the opening of the Day School.

Throughout 1893 and 1894 discussion went on about the acquiring of a more permanent home for the Technical Institute, a number of possible sites being investigated. All, for one reason or another, proved to be unsuitable. One, for example, was too close to the river to allow for the sort of foundations that would be needed for a fairly substantial building. But eventually a site in Junction Road was bought from James Taylor, a builder and contractor who lived nearby. This plot of arable land measured 188' x 160' and cost £280. A new, purpose-built home for the Institute was closer to becoming a reality. Edmond Fitzmaurice had already promised 500 guineas for such a project; this he now increased to 1,000 guineas on condition that the town itself matched the original sum. The County Council contributed £935, the UDC £500, the Department of Science and Arts £478, the Clothworkers' Company £250, and two other private individuals, Erlysman Pinckney and G P Fuller, £100 each. So with these and other gifts the £3,288 needed was found, and the new building eventually opened free of debt.

The difficult nature of the plot bought by Fitzmaurice was soon noticed. It was uneven, and there were considerable slopes which many years later were to prove to be an insuperable obstacle to the building of extensions and to the provision of play areas.

Thomas Ball Silcock whose practice was in Bath but who came of a Bradford family was the architect chosen to design the new Institute; the builders were Chancellors of Twerton. Work began in October 1895, went on throughout 1896, and the completed building was handed over to the Bradford on Avon Town Council on 25 January 1897, with the formal opening a month later. The *Wiltshire Chronicle* was fulsome in its admiration of the building:

> "Commandingly situated, handsome in design, substantially built, and equipped in the most up-to-date fashion, the new institute is indeed a thing of beauty and an ornament to the town and neighbourhood. Nothing has been left undone to make it as perfect and complete as possible....The style chosen is a picturesque type of English Renaissance, freely treated, and while keeping in view the purpose of the building, a successful endeavour has been made to secure a massive yet artistic structure, free from superfluous ornamentation, and entirely in keeping with the characteristics of the stone buildings of the district. The walling is of Bradford stone, with Winsley stone dressing, and the roof is covered with green slating. The windows are of wrought iron and filled with lead glazing."

There is then a detailed account of the lay-out of the new Institute:

> "The main entrance, which is in the centre of the principal front, heads into a well lighted hall, with the women's department on the left, and the secretary's office and two physics classrooms on the right. At the rear of the hall, outside the main building, are the men's lavatories and cloakroom, with the back entrance adjoining. From the centre of the hall a wide open staircase leads to the first floor, whilst stairs beneath lead to the basement containing the heating chamber, store room, and coal cellar. On the first floor, in the centre of the building is the chemical lecture theatre, with the laboratory, balance room, and store room adjoining, and in the other wing of the building is a large specially lighted classroom which is to be used for art classes. Special attention has been paid to ventilation, heating, and drainage arrangements, and the cookery room and the lecture theatre are to be fitted with raised galleries for the convenience of the students."

So the two principal rooms to the right of the small entrance hall on the ground floor were the physics lab (at the front) and the science classroom, both 20' x 20'. In effect, they became two smallish classrooms. The Domestic Science room was to the left. The chemistry theatre, which was raked or tiered, was above the main door and measured 29' x 15'. The chemistry lab was to the left on the first floor (again measuring 20' x 20') and it had two half rooms - the balance room and store room – behind it. Upstairs to the right was the building construction and elementary art room, this, at 40' x 20', being double the size of the labs and classroom. (Left and right are as seen from Junction Road. The staircase to the first floor described a 180 degree turn, thus, for anyone ascending, reversing left and right as seen from the road.)

This was the new Technical Institute, soon also to become the County Day School, later the Fitzmaurice Grammar School, and today, after the lifting of a threat of demolition, a complex of retirement apartments called Fitzmaurice Place. It was a huge improvement on the "commodious iron building" in Frome Road, not to mention the squalor of the still extant Free Grammar School in Church Street.

One further sentence from the *Wiltshire Chronicle* deserves mention: "If considered desirable, the building might easily be made to answer the requirements of a secondary school...."

As has been said, the building was officially handed over on 25 January 1897. The following day, Erlysman Pinckney and Edmond George Petty-Fitzmaurice signed a deed formally creating a Trust by which the new Institute and the land on which it was built was gifted to the Urban District Council. This Conveyance vested the legal estate in the UDC and stated that the Institute should be under the control and management of the Local Technical Education Committee. It was to be used "as a school for the instruction of children and adults in the pure and natural sciences applicable to industry and manufactures". This old agreement was the basis of the later Fitzmaurice Trust.

Charles G Watkins, a scientist, brother of William Edward who had been in charge in Frome Road, was appointed Principal of the Institute; T I Hallett taught art; and there were visiting teachers for a variety of technical subjects. It quickly gained a good reputation, and we read as early as August 1897 that "the new Technical School at Bradford on Avon is an admirable little institution", the science teaching being picked out as particularly worthy of praise. In that same month (in which, incidentally, the first motor car was seen on the roads of Bradford), there were more suggestions about the use of the building as a day secondary school, and these were quickly to bear fruit. A new term began at the Institute in September. Almost simultaneously advertisements appeared in the press about a County Day School for both boys and girls which it was intended should open in the same building on 11 October 1897. The fees were to be £4.10.0 a year. The school would give a thorough secondary, technical, and commercial training in all the normal school subjects, with the addition of other specialist subjects of a technical nature. The Head Master would be Charles Watkins, already Principal of the Institute, assisted by John Crompton. And so the County Day School became a reality less than a year after the new Technical Institute opened its doors to evening classes.

In some ways, the new secondary school had everything going for it; in others, the first few years were not easy. It had purpose-built accommodation, and everything was brand new. Not only that; where deficiencies were found, additions were quickly made, and if publicly provided money were not easy to come by, the little school was not short of wealthy friends. However, mixed education was still a novelty and an experiment, and a marked reluctance by Bradford parents to send their daughters to the school became increasingly clear. Indifference was one thing; positive hostility was another. And hostility both on grounds of cost and because the secondary education of the children of working folk was felt to be unnecessary did exist. A further problem was the town's geographical position. On one side was Bath, with its abundance of good schools, and on the other was Trowbridge, a larger community that at that time had two secondary schools, one established and one developing. At the latter the fees were very much lower than they were in Bradford. So a constant worry in these early years was the low number of pupils who enrolled at the school, and, particularly, the dearth of girls. It began with 3 pupils – 2 girls and a boy – but this number had risen to 12 by the end of the first term. A year later there were 31, and at this figure, or just over, enrolment stuck for three years. There were 36 pupils in 1899, 34 in 1900, and 36 again in 1901. So the new school was not universally popular, and it clearly was going to have to work hard to establish itself in public affection and regard.

Its failure to grow was a worry, and the small number of pupils made staffing difficult. Initially there were just Mr Watkins and Mr Crompton, and John Crompton was later to tell how in those first few months he taught every subject the school offered except for housewifery and woodwork. They were joined in 1899 by a Miss Johnson, but she left that same year and was replaced by Miss Lowden from Hollyhead. And then in 1900 Watkins himself left to take up the post of Secretary to the Technical Education Committee, later becoming Director of Education, in Buckinghamshire. His place as Head Master was taken by his assistant, John Crompton, a very significant change as he was to remain in that post for the next 26 years. In science Watkins was replaced by Mr I Williams. The full-time staff of the Day School in 1900, then, was Messrs Crompton and Williams, and Miss Lowden, but other part-time teachers and instructors borrowed from the evening classes at the Institute were available – Hallett for art, White for woodwork, Miss Allen for music (whose pupils were declared to be very few), and Monsieur Nourry (appointed to teach "middle-class French"). And in 1901 Sergeant McLean arrived as drill instructor.

John Crompton was 33 when he came to Bradford from the Central Board

School in Harwich, and after serving as assistant to Watkins for two and a half years he became Head in March 1900. He was a mathematics exhibitioner from Jesus College, Oxford, though at Bradford he taught English for many years. He gained his MA in 1903, and, as has been said above, he remained as Head until 1926.

Another who joined the school in 1900, albeit in a part-time capacity, was Gideon Norton White. As a part-time teacher, he taught a few classes of woodwork at the secondary school, dying in office in 1917, but his full-time job was that of Head of the Trinity National School. And Thomas Isaac Hallett should also be mentioned. Educated in Bath, he taught art at many institutions in West Wiltshire – at the Technical Institute and the Day School in Bradford, at the Wesleyan High School and the County Day School in Trowbridge, at the Trowbridge School of Art, at Monkton Combe School, at Calne County School.... Until his appointment at Bradford he had lived at Widbrook Villa, but in 1900 he moved to the Manor House in Bradford on Avon. He taught art at the Day School until 1922. (Interestingly, Watkins, White, and Hallett taught at the County Day Schools both in Bradford and in Trowbridge, Charles Watkins being, with Jimmy Henson, one of the two founding members of the teaching staff of the Trowbridge school. At the end of the nineteenth century, one taught where one could, not tying oneself necessarily to a single institution.)

Returning to the problem of low pupil numbers, room for manoeuvre was clearly limited and ambitions for a full secondary curriculum had to give way to the reality of that situation. Nevertheless, it all sounded good on paper. The school advertised itself as offering all the "normal" subjects, plus practical mechanics, practical chemistry, land surveying, practical electricity, book keeping, commercial French, practical cookery for the girls, practical woodwork, typewriting, and shorthand – and swimming in summer was also available. (Swimming always featured in the school's programme. The Public Baths in Bridge Street had opened at almost the same time as the Institute, and the fact that pupils received instruction there from the start received early inspectorial approval. The instructor from 1911 to just before his death in 1919 was the Bath's Superintendent, Joseph Heavyside.) In practice, this curriculum meant an education in the basic secondary subjects with a few exotic technical additions as and when they were available and required.

John Crompton undertook an early exercise in selection by refusing admission to two prospective entrants whom he found to be backward, and by his imposing the passing of an exam as a future condition of entry. Henceforth, though at first it could not afford to be too choosy, the County School was essentially a selective school. In the heady days of 1898, too, he declared the school full, with no more admissions possible. Even so, for those able to surmount the exam hurdle, the age of 10 was deemed to be the youngest at which a child could enter the school. A year later, 9 was thought to be the right age. And at the end of 1898, the school's attraction for rural pupils was shown by there being only 15 on roll from the town as compared with 16 from Freshford, Limpley Stoke, Winsley, Monkton Farleigh, Broughton Gifford, South Wraxall, and Atworth.

A number of other things happened in the first five years of the new secondary school's life. Improvements had been made. Very early on, for example, tennis lawns were laid and James Long and Edmond Fitzmaurice had seen to the planting of shrubs and firs. And again at the latter's expense, the building of a new gymnasium had begun in the spring of 1900. This was formally opened in February 1901, with, as evening entertainment, a lime-light exhibition of scenes of old Bradford to mark the occasion. Built as a substantial one-storey addition to the left hand wing beyond the cookery room, the gymnasium increasingly tended to become the focus of the school's social life and the venue for its larger meetings as well as serving the school's needs for physical education. It was a significant addition to the original building, and it was considered very advanced for its day. A prospectus of a somewhat later date says that "the gymnasium is exceptionally large and well equipped, giving an opportunity for physical education such as is possessed by few schools of this kind".

Fitzmaurice, too, was responsible in these early years for anonymously making up the deficit that appeared annually in the accounts. He also set up a small school library in the room used by the Head Master between the cookery room and the new gymnasium. As was always the case, this gift was given quietly, a letter from him to the Clerk dated August 1903 being typical: "You will remember that there are to be no newspaper paragraphs about my gift to the school. The entry will be as last year's in the accounts – 'Voluntary subscription'."

Outdoor sport was a bit more problematical. Football had got under way for the boys, with matches played against Trowbridge's Wesleyan High School, and Bath and Warminster Grammar Schools. Indeed, John Crompton proved to be a passionate advocate of the game. "The vaccination of football enthusiasm is a well timed preventative against the diseases of idleness and vice," he averred. Well, a hundred years later, some of us are not so sure! Cricket, however, was abandoned for 1901 because of the difficulty of obtaining a suitable field. This was still the time when what today would be looked upon as a basic amenity had to be borrowed or begged from charitable neighbours.

In these early days, the school advertised itself in the local press as providing "secondary education under public control", reminding us that private education was still the norm for older children at the turn of the century. Gratifyingly for Mr Crompton, Mr Williams, and Miss Lowden, the County Inspector, Mr Knight,

Above: C G Watkins, Head Master 1897-1900.

Opposite above: A note from Lord Fitzmaurice to Mr Rosen accompanying the photograph of Watkins.

Opposite below: The gymnasium, venue for many school activities, was tacked on to the main building in 1901.

LEIGH,
BRADFORD-ON-AVON,
WILTS.

Feb 4. 29

Dear Mr Nown

I send you a photo of Mr Charles Watkins which I have got out of an old album in my possession, as an addition to our Picture Gallery.

I am
Yrs sincerely
Litzmann

(First H.M. of his [name])

75

reported optimistically on the start that had been made made by the little school, French, English, maths and science all being favourably reviewed, and, rather obviously, the accommodation and equipment were thought to be satisfactory. More surprisingly, perhaps, by as early as 1901 former pupils were already regularly gathering to join the end-of-year celebrations and to cement friendships formed whilst they had been at the school. One such former pupil, resident in San Francisco, seemed to be particularly keen to maintain contact. It was not until 1910, however, that an Old Pupils' Society was formally inaugurated with 76 founding members.

The school was inspected by the Board of Education on 1 and 2 July 1901 and extracts from the inspectors' report give a flavour of how things were at the County School four years after its opening.

> "Bradford, though within a walk of Trowbridge, appears to have a population (4,514 urban and 5,071 rural) quite entitling it to a secondary school of its own. The Urban District, moreover, is understood to be specially characterised by weaving and rubber factories and the Rural by stone quarries. The situation of the school is described by the inspectors as central, close to the station and otherwise suitable.
>
> The buildings, erected in 1896, and approved by the then Department of Science and Art, have the advantage of including a fine gymnasium, the gift of Lord Edmond Fitzmaurice. Here, as elsewhere in the County, a Technical Institute and Secondary Day School are combined.
>
> It is noted that the room on the ground floor intended for a physical laboratory is at present used for a classroom and, for that purpose, fitted with dual desks, blackboard etc.... It is understood that a suggestion for meeting the requirements of the Board without depriving the school of one of the few classrooms it now possesses was discussed at the inspection. This would involve the amalgamation of two small rooms opening out of the manual instruction room....
>
> The school stands in the midst of a fair sized plot of ground which is however on too great a slope to be of much use as a playground. The use of the town swimming bath by boys and girls from this school is noted with satisfaction....
>
> The present salaries of the Assistant Master [Mr Williams] and Assistant Mistress [Miss Lowden] (£120 and £90 respectively) were commented on by the inspectors who were assured by the Committee that they would gladly pay more if they had the money....There is no scheme of pensions for retiring teachers of this school....
>
> The report speaks favourably of the teaching, and the general inference from the inspections hitherto conducted by the Board is that, at present at least, much industry and a degree of efficiency varying from moderate to admirable may be

secured in schools of this type for comparatively small remuneration....

The school is reported to be divided into upper, middle, and lower forms, each of which includes two sections, one being more advanced than the other....The timetable seems to be particularly well balanced and not to require any material alteration....

A few of the children remain till 16 years of age. The average age, however, seems to be under 13 and only 5 are over 14. The Board are of opinion that efforts should be made to prolong the stay and increase the average age of pupils."

The teaching in scripture, English, mathematics, science, and art was commended; in French, geography and history, however, progress was hindered by the curricula and organisation of the town's elementary schools. And " it is not clear why girls only are taught singing". Mention is made of the competition offered to the County School by a "private school for girls" and by the Free School.

"A subject of perhaps more pressing importance is the relation of the County School to the elementary schools by which it is so largely fed....The somewhat disorganizing influence of the elementary schools upon the secondary will, it is hoped, be ultimately neutralized if the natural tendency of the latter to react upon the former is fostered and regulated."

In 1902 a significant change took place. The Misses Blake, Julia and Lilian, had for some years been running the school mentioned above – a small private boarding school for girls at, first, the Parish Church Vicarage, and then at Avon House in Kingston Road. In 1897 this had been rather grandly renamed the High School for Girls, with Miss Julia Blake as its Head Mistress. Now, in 1902, after what apparently were very hurried negotiations, it was amalgamated with the Day School, bringing its pupils and the two Misses Blake to that establishment. The number of children on roll consequently rose from 39 to 54, with a further rise to 59 in 1903. Of these 54 pupils of 1902, 22 were girls – an improvement on the 9 to which number they had fallen, though the hope that had been expressed of there being a considerable rise in the number of girls as a result of the amalgamation was hardly met.

There were a number of consequences of this move. One was a change from mixed education to what was known as the Dual System, "with a girls' side entirely separate from that of the boys. Many parents have expressed a desire for some such arrangement...." So there were, in effect, two schools under one roof, and Miss Julia Blake was designated Head Mistress of the girls' section. Another consequence was that, with her arrival, the number of full-time staff rose from 3 to 5 for what was still fewer than 60 pupils, and perhaps this imbalance was a factor in Miss Lowden's decision to leave shortly afterwards to care for her elderly mother. Boarders, too, were sought. "The [Girls'] School is open to boarders who reside with the Head Mistress at the Vicarage" and "a few boarders can be received [at the Boys' School] who reside with the Head Master."

In this pre-history of the Fitzmaurice Grammar School, the focus is on the County Day School, but it should be remembered that for many years it shared the building in Junction Road with the Technical Institute, which at the beginning of the century ran part-time and evening courses for hundreds of students (242 in 1901, for example) in many subject areas; and from 1902, briefly, it was also a Pupil Teacher Centre. This closed in 1904 as it was found more economical for such students to receive their instruction in Trowbridge. The dual role that both the building and the administration of the two institutions was expected to fulfil had in-built difficulties. The Managers had two areas of responsibility, and two sets of accounts had to be kept, with the problem of apportioning salary bills to one or the other where the same teachers worked in both the evening institute and the day school. But it was the Local Technical Education Committee that managed and controlled both institutions; the Wiltshire TEC – the umbrella organisation – played no part in the management of either.

Amalgamation with the private school for girls, increased numbers, and the Dual System came in 1902, by which time Bradford's Day School could be said to have been typical in its characteristics of many in Wiltshire. Early in 1903 there were 10 similar secondary schools in the County, educating 472 boys and less than half that number – 202 – girls. (This gave an average of 47 boys and 20 girls – 67 pupils – each, so Bradford's numbers were perhaps not unusual.) Every town, with two exceptions, had such a school; and it was against this developing background that William Pullinger was appointed Wiltshire's Director of Education.

In 1902, the Day School achieved 7 successes in the Oxford Local Examinations and 1 County Scholarship, that particular student gaining the top place nationally in natural sciences. A year later there were 9 passes, and again 1 County Scholarship. And to keep pace with its academic achievements, improvements and additions were needed. It was pointed out that Bradford had been almost the first town to introduce technical education, and the school had started in a building meant for technical, not secondary, instruction. Laboratory accommodation was, therefore, already inadequate, extra apparatus, furniture and equipment were needed, and the boys' playground required resurfacing. On the credit side, benefactors still appeared, and Erlysman Pinckney donated a strip of land (conveyed to the Foundation on 20 May 1908) that he owned at the back of the school so that the playground, which had been diminished by the building of the gymnasium, could be extended. This second transfer of land to the Foundation, like other gifts of the time, was a considerable gesture and a public demonstration of faith in the importance of a system of education that was to be available to all.

The new woodwork room of 1905.

These matters were mentioned in 1903 by John Crompton in his report at the annual prizegiving when Sir John Gorst MP was the guest of honour. The year had been notable in that the number of pupils had almost – but not quite – reached 60 for the first time, a figure that thereafter remained elusively out of reach for a considerable period. (In 1904, numbers fell to 48, and from then until 1912 the roll remained stubbornly in the 50s.) But 1904 was a year of greater significance. Cricket, for the boys, finally got under way and the school could now boast 2 football teams; more importantly, there was a flurry of staff changes, the Dual System bit the dust, with a reversion to Mixed Teaching, and the Local Technical Education Committee asked the UDC to apply to the Board of Education for a "Scheme" under the Endowed Schools Act – that is, a management structure for the school similar to the one that was in operation at Chippenham and Calne. At the same time, it wished the existing management as set out in the Trust Deed of 26 January 1897 to be maintained. The UDC complied, and the Scheme was sealed on 25 April 1905.

First, the staff changes. Lilian Blake remained at Bradford for only a short time. Late in 1902 she was awarded the Teaching Diploma of the University of London, the highest qualification open to professional teachers, and it may have been this success that hastened her departure. After Miss Lowden left in 1903, Misses Snelling and Pfieffer made brief appearances, Miss Pfieffer, although her appointment was permanent, staying literally for no more than a few weeks. No re-appointment was made when she left, another staffing reduction thereby being effected to further ease the school's chronic financial difficulties. Williams, who had joined the school in 1900, also resigned at this time, his replacement being C J Colquhoun.

The Board of Education inspectors again visited the County School in the summer of 1904. Early that summer term there had been 57 pupils on roll – 37 boys (of whom 2 were boarders, one from Lancashire and one from Surrey) and 20 girls. Twelve were under 11 and only three had attained the age of 16. And although the inspectors tried to be kind about the Dual System under which the sexes were segregated, there is a sort of bafflement in their comments about the impracticality of such an arrangement with the limited resources available.

> "The girls' department is now carried on as a separate school so far as teaching and organisation are concerned. The exact relations between the Head Mistress and the Head Master appear to be undetermined. In answer to a question on this point, the inspectors learnt that the Head Master has authority over the Head Mistress. Practically in the working of the school this authority does not seem to be exercised, the organisation of the girls' curriculum, the choice of their books, and of course the whole of their discipline being entirely in the hands of the Mistress. The Head Master generally attends the meetings of the Governors, the Mistress less frequently. The two appear to work together quite well, but the present arrangement is not one which can continue indefinitely."

Many of the points the inspectors made relate to the intractable difficulties posed by this two-schools-under-one-roof policy, and one wonders whether its introduction was a condition of Miss Blake's agreeing to throw in her lot with the County School in the first place.

As is always the way with inspectors, the building's shortcomings were pointed out, and some of these were fairly severe. The only staff accommodation, for example, was the Head Master's room, a mere cupboard measuring 9' x 9', which also housed the library; this was beyond the cookery room. Criticism of several aspects of the toilet provision were also trenchant, one comment being that "the arrangement by which the boys in the Preparatory Class, many of whom are 10 years of age or over, use the girls' cloakroom and lavatories is not suitable". And it is noted that the playgrounds, small and either of grass or gravel, are supplemented by the use of the Town's football field across the road in Pound Close.

The various subjects taught to the boys and the girls were examined as though the children were in different schools, and, generally, serious weaknesses and deficiencies were observed, the teaching of French being of particular concern. The most serious and detailed denunciation, however, presented as "a little constructive criticism", was reserved for science. "The sequence of experiments is in many cases wholly unintelligible and apparently haphazard." "An experiment that leads to nothing and suggests no further work has no value except as practice in mere manipulation, and even in this the older girls showed but little skill." "A very great deal remains to be done to give this science work its full value...." And so on.

The inspectors came to their conclusion:

> "When the school was started, both boys and girls were admitted and were taught together. The number of girls, however, diminished, and it was feared that girls would cease to come to the school. An attempt was then made to start a separate girls' school in another part of the town, but failed from the difficulty of getting suitable buildings. An arrangement was ultimately made by which the Mistress of a private school joined this school, bringing all her pupils with her. At the same time, all coeducation ceased....It is needless to point out that this arrangement is a very expensive one....The time will come when it will be necessary to determine whether girls are again to be taught with the boys, or to be removed from the school altogether."

A start had been made, albeit a somewhat shaky start in several respects.

Girls' hockey XI 1912.

A White Elephant?
The County School:
1904-1912

JOHN CROMPTON COULD NOT HAVE BEEN totally delighted by the HMI report of 1904, but in one respect at least its recommendations were adopted. After a two-year flirtation with the Dual System, despite the brave words at its introduction, the County Day School reverted in September 1904 to conventional mixed teaching. It was a matter of economics and common sense, one mixed school being cheaper and easier to organise than two single-sex schools involving the same personnel. But he took up the cudgels on behalf of Mr Colquhoun, the science teacher, who was only 20, untrained, and, though willing, clearly lacking in experience, and he took exception, with some justification, to remarks by the inspectors about "frequent changes in the staff". In the previous year there had been one or two changes, but the teaching body was, and was to continue to be, remarkably stable.

As well as undertaking a re-mixing of the sexes, there was back-tracking in other areas, too, as the 1904-05 school year progressed. The lower age at which pupils were to be permitted to enter the school shifted upwards again to 10, the so-called kindergarten being disbanded. The reason for this was, again, the fewness of the total number of pupils, with the inevitable lack of opportunity for organisational manoeuvre that this implied. Pupils of different ages had to be lumped together rather than taught as separate classes, with an inevitable lack of teaching efficiency. An HMI report of July 1905 identified the problem:

> "Educationally....the position is not thoroughly sound. The numbers in attendance are not high enough to allow a proper classification, and it is practically impossible with the present staff to organise a properly graded course extending over four years and ensuring due progress in each year. The proportion of scholars in the forms above the second year of the course is quite inadequate, and the future of the school cannot but afford some cause for anxiety."

That last statement of the inspectors was as unambiguous as it was alarming.

Lord Edmond lived in the great house (later the hospital and later still the Leigh Park Hotel) on the crossroads at Leigh, and it was in 1904, a mere seven years after Bradford's first motor vehicle was spotted, that he had cause to complain: "the road up here requires strict watching owing to the destruction by locomotives". So he had his problems. By this time, however, he was Chairman of the Technical Education Committee, having succeeded Erlysman Pinckney in May 1904 (though Pinckney remained a member until 1912); and it was Lord Fitzmaurice who tried to buy back the old Technical School – "the commodious iron building" – in Frome Road with the intention of re-erecting it at the back of the new school for use as a woodwork and cookery room. In this he failed. Undeterred, he went ahead with the provision at his own expense (£242) of new premises for woodwork, together with fittings, the necessary tools, and an extension of the heating system to the room. This was the second substantial addition to the original premises, and it consisted of a separate, single-storey block at the back of the right-hand wing of the 1897 building. (To later generations it was known as the art room.) The old woodwork room became a classroom, and in 1907 the cookery room. Lord Edmond paid for the extension of the heating system to that room, too.

Other alterations that had been put in hand as a result of inspectorial criticism were the provision of separate entrances for boys and girls at the back of the school, and an extension of the cloakrooms. There were now three lavatory basins on each side of the building for boys and girls respectively, and additions had been made to the office accommodation. Purely in terms of buildings and facilities, therefore, the Head Master and the Committee had done everything to keep abreast of what was needed. In other respects, however, there was reason for concern.

In addition to the criticism about the organisation of classes mentioned above, the inspection of 1905 revealed other shortcomings.

> "The scope of the work in mathematics is hardly adequate....While the equipment for the teaching of science appears complete, it cannot be said that the provision for the simpler needs of literary instruction is at all adequate. Not only is there no good reference library, but the actual text books used are meagre and unsuitable."

These were matters that could be put right, and science had been let off the hook. But the fewness of the pupils proved for some time to be a major stumbling block to the County School's efficient organisation, and one understands its patron's rueful reflections on the difficulties being experienced by "Lord Edmond's White Elephant", as he heard it being called.

The introduction of a Scheme of Management is mentioned above. This was the establishing of the school's own Board of Governors which took over the duties previously undertaken by the Local Technical Education Committee. The

Foundation and its Endowment thereafter were to be administered by this Governing Body, all lands belonging to the Foundation to be vested in the official Trustee of Charity Lands. Consisting of both representative and co-optative Governors, the balance of this Body changed from time to time, but in 1905 it had 3 representatives from the County Council (later increased to 5), 2 from the Rural District Council, 9 from the Urban District Council (increased from the originally intended 3, but later reduced to 6), and 4 co-opted members – 18 Governors in all. Of these, a certain number had to be women. The Governing Body of the County School sat for the first time in July 1905 and Lord Edmond Fitzmaurice was elected its Chairman, with Erlysman Pinckney Vice Chairman.

A slight variation soon occurred in that the Draft Scheme of 1908 amended the Scheme of 1905, resulting in the Consolidated Schemes of 25 April 1905 and 29 April 1909, sealed by order of the Board of Education on 8 March 1911.

The Governors' first duty was to appoint a teacher to succeed Colquhoun who left in the summer term; their choice was the 23 year old Arthur Henry Baker from Upper Tooting High School. In 1905 they could not have suspected that he would stay as science master, with a gap for military service in the First World War, for the next 40 years or that thereafter he would become Chairman of Governors. Baker later told how, after one term, he had quite decided to leave the following summer, Bradford being so different from London. What tipped the scales was his joining the local Rowing and Cricket Clubs where the friendliness and sociability with which he was greeted completely won him over.

What the school charged in fees was already a matter for debate. Pitched too low, the cost of salaries and routine maintenance could not be met; set too high, they would deter parents from sending their children to the school. Initially the fees had been £4.10.0 a year. In 1904 they had gone to £6 in the unrealised hope that all the county's secondary schools would accept that level, and the new Governing Body now had to reconsider the matter, one view certainly being that they should be reduced again. They decided, however, to keep them at £6, but to include in that price a number of charges that hitherto had been separate and additional – 15/- for books, 7/- for a cap and gym shoes, and a games subscription of 8/-, leaving £4.10 as the cost of tuition. Even so, the effort to balance fees and grants from the Board of Education and the County Council on the one hand with the cost of staff salaries, the upkeep of the building, and essential books and equipment on the other was considerable and a constant source of concern. But for Lord Fitzmaurice's munificence, it is unlikely that Bradford on Avon's County School could have survived these first few years of the twentieth century.

Another decision made by the Governing Body in 1906 was to hold the school's annual sports day and prizegiving henceforth at the end of the summer term in July, and so it was for the next six years. The outdoor events took place just across the Frome Road in the Pound Close field in the afternoon, and the Head Master had the foresight always to choose a day that was fine and sunny. A local band enlivened the proceedings, William Summers, baker and confectioner in the Shambles, provided refreshments in the Technical Institute, and the prizegiving took place in the evening in the school's gymnasium. None of this involved John Crompton in much travelling, of course. He had followed Charles Watkins in living at Clifford House, 4 Junction Road, immediately next to the school, and we hear from time to time of renovations to his house that had to be undertaken, or of repairs to his garden wall, or of a resurfacing of the path that led from his property to the school. But in 1907 Lord Fitzmaurice bought the house and its garden, put it in order, and on 23 November 1907 gave it as a further gift to the Foundation, the rent paid by the Headmaster to be reckoned as income for the school.

Headmaster's house apart, already mentioned have been Edmond Fitzmaurice's initial donation for the building of the school, his part in laying out the grounds and providing a tennis lawn, his giving a gymnasium, a small library, and a woodwork room, and countless gifts of books and equipment. In the years between 1907 and 1912 he also paid for the conversion of the physics room downstairs on the right into both a study for the male teaching staff and a more substantial library, for the upgrading of the chemistry laboratory upstairs to the very best standards then available, and, in large part, for an extension to the boys' cloakroom and a rebuilding of their toilets at the back of the main school. A further gift was a photogravure of Sir Michael Forster which was hung in the science room. And, perhaps as a reciprocal gesture and as a permanent recognition of his generosity to the school, in 1911 Lord Edmond's own portrait was hung in the Library. (An enlargement of this portrait was commissioned in 1936 and was hung above the plaque commemorating the school's founder. Today it can be found in the vestibule of the Fitzmaurice Suite at the Leigh Park Hotel.)

The teaching staff, admittedly few in number, had been remarkably stable for the first years of the school's life, but it was added to in 1906 when "a thorough course of Housewifery" for the girls was introduced. A visiting rather than a permanent teacher, Katharine Willson, came from the Wiltshire School of Domestic Economy in September 1906, staying for just over three years. She was followed by Misses Street (1910), Sutton (1910-1911), and Pocock (1911-1918). Another appointment, following the recommendation of HMI for an additional permanent teacher, was that of George Breen. He joined the school in 1907, being responsible for the drill instruction of the boys and also for teaching some history, English, and French. The following year, the physical education of the girls was thought to be in need of attention, so the aid of a Miss Allen was enlisted for one hour a week, she being replaced by Miss Abrahamson in 1909. And in this roll-call of staff, W S Rawlings and Mrs K Farr should not be omitted. The latter had been the school's Caretaker since its opening, whilst Mr Rawlings acted as Secretary to, first, the Committee and, later, the Board of Governors from its creation until 1910. In that year he emigrated to Canada, being replaced by a local solicitor, Alex Wilkins. Throughout, Crompton, Baker, and Miss Blake (full time and permanent), and Hallett and White (visiting), continued as the core of the teaching staff.

It was in 1908 that John Crompton was given by the Governors the crisply official title of "Head Master of the Day School and Director of the Technical Evening Classes and other Teaching of the Institute". Miss Blake was named "Vice-Principal of the Day School". In the years prior to 1912, teachers had to argue and fight for what salary they could get. Julia Blake, for example, made repeated attempts to get her salary raised – successfully, to £130 per annum in 1904 and £140 in 1907 – but her position was complicated. On the credit side, there were the peculiar circumstances of her appointment to the school (she was Headmistress of her own school, which amalgamated with the County School, to its benefit, in 1902) and this was recognised by the Governors; on the debit side, she was unqualified as a teacher, and she was a woman. When formalised salary scales were introduced in 1912, therefore, she was deemed to be exempt from their restrictions, and continued at a salary somewhat greater than it would otherwise have been. This set salary scale, for which there had long been agitation, was determined as follows:

Headmaster	£270, plus £10 every 2 years to £300;
1st Assistant Master	£120, plus £5 every year to £150;
1st Assistant Mistress	£100, plus £5 every year to £130;
2nd Master	£100, plus £5 every year to £130;
2nd Mistress	£80, plus £5 every year to £100.

But we have leapt ahead in time. John Crompton and his Governors still had much to do before this rather neat salary structure came into being. He expelled boys (but not girls) from time to time for "offences" unspecified. He transposed the boys' and the girls' playgrounds – the boys from the eastern end of the school to the west, and the girls from the west to the east – because in their leisure time the boys were making too much noise and annoying the neighbours. In his capacity as Director of the Technical Evening Classes, he encouraged the growth of such studies as plumbing and stone-carving, and

Above: The 1912 prospectus.

Below: The new woodwork room of 1905 (taken c 1908).

88

*Above: The school library, 1908.
Below: The gymnasiuam.*

more esoteric subjects like poultry keeping and bee culture; but as the first decade of the twentieth century wore on, attendance at these courses tended to drop away. They finally faded out at about the time of the First World War. And he battled to get grants for those few pupils at the County School who lived in Somerset. Despite his protests, Somerset refused to fund them, Wiltshire finally bowing the knee after lengthy argument and footing the bill themselves.

In this first decade of its life, the County School was still fighting an uphill battle for recognition in that popular feeling locally, if not hostile, was certainly equivocal about the desirability of having such an institution in the town. There was a clearly articulated view that to give free education of a grammar school sort to the children of artisans was asking for trouble. It would lead to social upheaval. Again, there had been a direct charge on the local rates for the provision of the building, and many townsfolk felt that they personally had had to pay for something of which they did not approve. It was also felt that the teachers at the County School had all been brought in from outside and they were not, therefore, up to much; certainly they were not of the calibre of such a well respected figure as Mr Cowlishaw who had taught at the Free School for so many years. And so recognition was hard to win. As has been said, but for the unswerving support of Lord Edmond Fitzmaurice both in money and in counsel the school may well have had to close.

Gradually, of course, opposition waned. The many good things that the County School was doing were acknowledged, and, as they became better known and part of the community, the quality of the teaching staff was recognised. More than 30 years later, A H Baker remembered the tremendous fillip given to the school's reputation locally by the examination results of 1913. The details of those results that he recounted on his retirement were actually incorrect. Nevertheless, J A Cooper achieved 1st class honours in the Senior Oxford Examination, with a distinction in physics, which bracketed him 9th in the whole country, and girl called Gladys Hewett achieved a similar result in the Junior Examination, which bracketed her in 1st place nationally. These unusual honours for a small country school caused something of a sensation in the town, and thereafter the *raison d'être* of the secondary school ceased to be questioned.

Bradford on Avon's County School by 1907 was recognisably selective. That is to say, entry was by examination whether fees were paid or a child qualified for a free place, these by statute having to be 25% by number of the children admitted to the school the previous year. It aimed as a minimum at a basic 4 year course, with the taking of public examinations in year 5 desirable. Its buildings and facilities were excellent, the former being purpose-built and the latter augmented when necessary by the unstinting generosity of its creator and continuing benefactor. Inspectorial recommendations were accepted and acted upon. And yet it had failed to thrive, its pupil numbers immovably stuck in the low or mid 50s.

Latin had been dropped from the curriculum in 1907 because of organisational difficulties and pressure from other subjects, but expansion was occurring elsewhere. Mention has already been made of the remodelling of the chemistry laboratory. This actually took place in the Christmas holidays 1907, an extended holiday being granted to allow for the work's being carried out, and it followed a study of what had been done at Colston Girls' School in Bristol. A further positive move was the continual examination of the school's facilities to see whether they could be used to advantage in fallow periods by the town's elementary schools, and so it was that the gymnasium and the woodwork and domestic economy rooms all came to be used, when it was convenient and by agreement, by younger pupils.

It is unsurprising, therefore, that the inspectors of 1908 gave the school a clean bill of health. It was still comparatively new, of course, and there had not yet been time for the number of pupils grossly to overburden the accommodation available, as was later to be the case. The inspectors had recommendations to make about financial matters and the qualifications of the teaching staff, about the need for a qualified instructor to be obtained for gymnastics for the girls, and about the decorative state of the classrooms and the general unsuitability of the boys' cloakroom and toilet accommodation, all of which were swiftly implemented as far as was possible. The accommodation and equipment generally, however, were deemed to be excellent. But there were two matters at this time that caused ripples. The first concerned Mr Cowlishaw – he of the long defunct Free School in Church Street. For a number of years he had been the proprietor of a private school at Belcombe, and that, in its turn, now closed – under what circumstances is not clear. It was suggested "by certain gentlemen" that the pupils thus set adrift should be enrolled at the County School, half their fees (£3 a year) to be paid by the aforementioned gentlemen. No suggestion was made as to how the other half should be paid, so the idea was felt to be flawed and unsatisfactory and was rejected the Governors.

The second matter of concern was precipitated by the Board of Education's unhappiness about the suitability of the premises occupied by the County Day School in Trowbridge, a dispute into which Bradford on Avon's Governors were now reluctantly drawn. New premises had urgently to be sought for the Trowbridge children, and Bradford had spare capacity. Grudgingly, therefore, its Governors were forced into negotiation. Possible schemes that, it was claimed, would be of benefit to both towns were drawn up, the transfer from Trowbridge to Bradford of either their boys *en masse* or girls *en masse* being the essence of what was being suggested. The Bradford Governors declared that, though prepared to talk, they were totally opposed to the acceptance of any single sex arrangement for their school, which was the implication of these suggestions. Fortunately, events allowed the Trowbridge difficulty to be resolved in a different way, and Bradford was able to move forward untroubled by its neighbour's problem.

Before the HMI inspection of 1912, a number of things happened. A flag pole was bought and erected to the left of the steps going up to the front entrance, and there was a three-day closure to celebrate the coronation of George V in July 1911, on which occasion the school flag was flown for the first time; a large vase, carved by the stone-carving class, was presented to the UDC as an ornament for the prospective Westbury House Gardens (Is this the urn, rather battered today, that still graces the gardens?); the lot of those who brought packed lunches to school was improved by the purchase of equipment for their convenience; John Crompton was praised for his devotion to duty in spending three weeks of his summer holidays on a course at the Cirencester Agricultural College; and Miss Blake steered her pupils to success in the Wiltshire Music Festival, held in Trowbridge.

It was in 1912 that the combined sports day and prizegiving, that for some years had taken place in summer, was split, the sports being held in October and the prizegiving in December. An outbreak of measles in July was the reason. Both occasions were always lavishly reported in the press, the former being an opportunity for the recording of local junior records in obscure events, the latter for a report on the year's activities from the Head Master and an enunciation of universal truths likely to benefit his young audience from the guest of honour. So, Admiral Sir Richard Poore, for example, let it be known that "there are two great duties in life – duty to the empire and duty to one's family". And to encourage participation in sport, we hear that "the unselfish cooperation with others for a common object, the endurance of hard knocks and ill luck, unstinting submission to the decision of captain or umpire, all contribute to the strengthening of character." The expression of such sentiments would be impossible today, but they reflect the spirit of the time and a great deal of genuine optimism. Examination successes were praised. Out of 10 pupils entering the Oxford Local Examinations in 1908, 4 passed at senior and 4 at junior grade, with all 4 entrants for teaching scholarships (or Bursarships) being successful. Such results were typical of the time. News of the teaching staff, too, was given, with John Parry being thanked for the excellence of his contribution when he covered for half a term in 1912 during George Breen's absence through illness.

At the prizegiving in this particular year new ground was broken. Additional to the presentations and speeches was live entertainment, with an Elizabethan Masque prefacing the more formal part of the evening. This was an elaborately costumed musical presentation into which much hard work had gone, Ernest Blake conducting, and his sisters, Misses Julia and Helen Blake, providing the adult contribution. An ambitious undertaking, it unfortunately failed in that the costumes could not properly be seen because of the cramped conditions in which it was put on.

The most important event of 1912, however, was the full inspection of the County School, and it is with the findings of the inspection that we conclude this account of the first fifteen years of the school's life.

By now – and still with only 52 pupils on roll – it was organised in five forms. These were the Lower Third, the Upper Third, the Fourth, Fifth, and Sixth, but as the Fifth and Sixth were always combined there were only effectively four teaching groups. The ages of the pupils ranged from 9 to 16. IIIb consisted of the youngest boys and girls up to the age of about 12, IIIa was principally 13 year-olds, form IV tended to be children aged 13 and 14, and forms V and VI combined consisted of only 7 pupils aged 15 and 16. So, as well as being few in total, the pupils at the top of the school were very sparse indeed. Of the 52, only 30 came from Bradford itself, the neighbouring villages supplying the other 22. A small handful came from a professional or white-collar background; the majority, however, were the sons and daughters of artisans, tradesmen and farmers. Boarding accommodation was theoretically available, but the last boarder (a boy) had left some four years earlier.

It is no surprise to find the inspectors thoroughly complimentary about the school's premises and equipment, about the general standard of its teaching in most subjects, and about its tone and ethos, and it is equally unsurprising to find dismay expressed about its failure to grow and develop.

> "The school possesses an excellent gymnasium and laboratory and a well equipped art room. The classroom accommodation is also very satisfactory....The manual workshop is an excellent room....The school possesses a good library...."

The few criticisms that there were of the facilities were minor (but not many years were to pass before encomia on these lines were to turn to lamentations on the sub-standard accommodation that the school had to suffer in every aspect of its work). And the teaching staff were commended, even if there was perhaps a hint of some sort of divide between them and the Head Master.

> "The Head Master is most fortunate in the assistants he possesses, and would probably find it advantageous to himself and the school to take them more regularly into his counsel. The Second Mistress [Miss Blake] continues to do much good work for the school, and her personal influence maintains the high reputation

for good tone and discipline which the school enjoys in the town and the neighbourhood. The two Assistant Masters [Messrs Baker and Breen] are also valuable members of the staff, and are proving themselves capable and zealous teachers."

It is a little surprising, therefore, that what the inspectors saw and heard in class was not more highly commended. English was all right – but no more. "....the notebooks were not very carefully corrected....the literary standard of the pupils is not high....the standard of enunciation and intelligent expression is not very high...." In history, Mr Breen did too much of the work himself, the pupils were weak in their knowledge of facts, and the syllabus was open to criticism; on the other hand, he was thought to be well qualified, had a real enthusiasm for his subject, and the pupils in his classes derived great pleasure from listening to him. And so it was with all the other areas of the curriculum – unstinting praise quickly qualified by quite serious criticism. The teaching of science proved on this occasion to be satisfactory, but "the standard of mathematical work is low". Other subjects just about passed muster, except for Breen's work with the boys in physical exercise. "He is very well qualified for the work, having received a thorough training in Swedish exercises himself....The exercises were performed with precision and smartness, and the Master is much to be congratulated on the excellence of the work."

What the inspectors found really disturbing was the lack of growth of the school, pupil numbers in 1912 being no more than they had been eight years earlier, and this was a theme to which they returned throughout their report. Local apathy seemed to be partly to blame, but there was also the implication that John Crompton had not worked sufficiently hard at making known what it was that the County School had to offer. The inspectors clearly feared that it might not survive.

> "The school....will find it increasingly difficult to maintain the position that is desired for it....It is to be regretted that [it] should fail to attract the numbers that it deserves to have. It should be the constant aim of the Head Master to make the most of the opportunities he possesses, and he must spare no effort to consider ways in which to promote the general interest of the neighbourhood in the fortunes of the school."

In 1912, the Foundation was a somewhat delicate creation and there was a chance that it might still prove to have been a mistake, a White Elephant. Despite its many advantages, unless it could be encouraged to more vigorous growth its future was, at best, uncertain.

*A H Baker, teacher 1905-1945 and Chairman of Governors, 1951-1961.
This portrait used to hang in the entrance hall of the school.*

The full-time teaching staff of the school in these inaugural years was:

Head Master:	C G Watkins (1897-1900), J Crompton (1900-);
Vice Principal:	Miss J Blake (1902-)
Assistants:	J Crompton (1897-1900), I Williams (1900-1903), C J Colquhoun (1904-1905), A H Baker (1905-); Miss Johnson (1899), Miss L Lowden (1900-1903), Miss Snelling (1903), Miss Pfeiffer (1903); Miss L Blake (1902-1903); G T Breen (1907-).

Erlysman Pinckney retired from the Governing Body in 1912, moved to Warminster, and died in 1920.

Left: Mr Crompton in the front garden of Clifford House.

Below: The Gallipoli hut, erected in 1920, that was still there long after the Grammar School closed in 1980. (See also page 146)

Acceptance and Growth
The County School:
1913-1923

By January 1913, Bradford on Avon's County School was on firmer ground. It was housed in a building that was still comparatively new and that had been designed for educational purposes; two important additions had been made; where experience had indicated that modification of the accommodation was required, modification had been undertaken; although its budget was tight, it had the inestimable advantage of having a wealthy and interested patron who was unfailingly generous in his gifts; and it had a stable and committed staff of both full-time and visiting teachers – Hallett and White, Arthur Baker and Miss Blake, and John Crompton himself being its core. Somehow, however, things had not yet gelled as they should have done. Either because of managerial complacency, competition from neighbouring towns, or a lack of ambition on the part of local parents, the County School was failing to progress. After a start that had been slower than might reasonably have been expected, progress had ceased altogether, with no growth at all in its roll over the previous ten years. But things were about to change.

For the rest of the decade – the whole of which, of course, was overshadowed by the First World War and its devastating effects on so many people and virtually every aspect of national life – pupil numbers rose quite dramatically, and the number of girls overtook that of the boys. From 48 in the summer of 1913, the roll rose to 57 in September, the elusive 60 was attained for the first time in February 1914 when 63 pupils appeared on the books, there were 81 in September of that year, 90 in 1915, and then the roll showed a steep rise to 129 in 1918, to 133 early the following year, and then to 150 in September 1919. So in six years the number of pupils almost tripled. One, but not the only, reason for this was the opening of a Preparatory Department at Easter 1917. Its life was short and perhaps its history can be detailed here.

The Prep Department was a mistake from the start. And it was a mistake that was to be repeated in subsequent years. Whether, in introducing it, the Governors realised that pupils in that Department would not be eligible for a grant is not clear, but it soon became evident that it had to be self-supporting and pay for itself entirely – its teacher, its books, its equipment – from fees levied directly on the parents. It opened with 15 children (12 new boys and girls and 3 who were already at the school) in April 1917, qualification for entry being that the child would attain the age of 8 during his or her first term and that he (or she) was sufficiently able. Fees were initially 5 guineas a year (rather less than in the senior school), but were later raised to £6 and then, just before its closure, to £9.

A teacher trained for junior children, Evelyn Elliott, from St Margaret's High School in York, was appointed to take specific responsibility for these youngsters, and she made a good impression. At any rate, when the Department was disbanded because of its financial non-viability, successful efforts were made to retain her on the permanent staff of the senior school. But it all ended in tears. The cost of running a Department for which the school received no grant from public funds was just too great, and Bradford's Prep Department ceased to exist in July 1921 after a life of just over 4 years. Somewhat earlier, a similar venture had been tried at the two Trowbridge High Schools, and there also it had caused problems, lurching from crisis to financial crisis until, considerably later than in Bradford, it too was disbanded.

The appointment to the County School of Miss Elliott because of the starting of a Prep Department was an addition to the staff; another addition, because of increased pupil numbers, was Dorothy Vine in 1918. A teacher of general subjects, she did not stay long. She left in order to secure a degree at university, but died within a few weeks of leaving Bradford. Her replacement, Dorothy Burgoine stayed for the next 34 years. Aged 28, she had taught at Kimbolton and Ashby de la Zouche before coming to Bradford on Avon, also to teach general subjects and, from the time of Mr Hallett's resignation in 1922, art throughout the school.

George Breen left for promotion at Newquay County School at the end of 1914. (He died at the Star and Garter Home in Richmond in 1933.) And, in line with the recommendations of HMI at their last inspection, a lady was sought as his replacement. This was to be Ethel Barnes who taught French, with some history and some girls' games. Breen's duties in drilling the boys were taken over, first, by a Peter Cottle, and then by Sergeant Chapel, who continued until Easter 1917 when he left to rejoin the army. Sergeant McDonald from the Cadet School in Trowbridge followed, giving help in physical exercise with both the boys and the girls.

Tragically, Gideon Norton White died suddenly in 1917, and, although he was only a part-time (or "visiting") teacher, he had been very much a founding member of the school whose loss was keenly felt. John Martin, Head Master of the Adcroft Elementary School in Trowbridge, and Reginald Culley, followed by Alfred Gorvett, replaced him on a part-time basis as teachers of woodwork and handicraft. The system at that time was for the workshop to be used principally by elementary school children, with only the first year boys from the secondary school being taught practical subjects. Les Hills joined the school in 1925 and particularly remembers the man who followed Gorvett – Henry Chappell. "He was a big man who hated us secondary school boys, and he used to lash out at us with his ring-covered knuckles."

Misses Rhodes (1914-1917) and Hurry (from 1918) can be added to the list of part-time teachers who assisted the school, both of them giving instruction in Swedish Drill to the girls, a discipline much in vogue at this time. An endless list of young women came to teach cookery and needlework, most being engaged for a term or, perhaps, two at the most. And there was Thomas Isaac Hallett for art.

But the most interesting staffing development of these wartime years involved Arthur Baker. He had been senior science master at the school since 1905, and he had had a year away in 1913-1914 through his winning a national scholarship, tenable at the Royal College of Science – a signal distinction. A man called Arthur Plowman had stood in for him temporarily at the school. Now, at a time of national emergency Baker volunteered for a commission in the army. With the loss of Breen, however, the school was in some difficulty, so representations were made and his papers were returned marked, "Required at home on government work". The respite was short. Six months later, he was called up as a 2nd Lieutenant in the Wessex Engineers, granted leave of absence for the duration of the War, guaranteed his job back when (or if) he returned, and allowed £30 a year in lieu of salary to augment his army pay.

In the short term, he was replaced – and very satisfactorily replaced – by Frederick Booker, an Old Boy of the school who had been deemed medically unfit for military service. Unfortunately the army changed its mind, and Booker, in his turn, received his call-up papers in mid 1917. A Peter Walsh took over for a few weeks, but he was not really competent in secondary science, and the Rev A T Richardson, vicar of Holy Trinity and one of the school's Governors, stepped in for a while to take some of the senior classes and also to cover for Miss Blake during a period of illness. But these were all makeshift arrangements as an adequate replacement was simply not to be found in wartime. John Crompton, therefore, decided to take the science classes himself and to appoint a junior Mistress to fill the vacancy left by Arthur Baker. Kathleen Jowett was selected. She stayed for a year and was then replaced by W H (Harry) Brosnan, an elementary school teacher from West Twerton School, Bath, who joined the County School after being discharged from the army, having been wounded twice in his 3 years' service. He was to remain until 1945.

The Head later admitted that he found these changes stressful and difficult to handle. He was keenly disappointed at Miss Jowett's decision that a career in the Air Force was more to her liking than teaching, but he felt that a corner had been turned with the appointment of Dorothy Vine and Harry Brosnan.

These changes all sound quite neat and logical. In reality, they were anything but that. The crises and shortages of wartime led to improvisation and the adopting of expedients which, if not desperate, would scarcely have been acceptable in more normal circumstances. Nevertheless, at the end of the War, the teaching staff at Bradford was: John Crompton (1897-), Miss Blake (1902-), Arthur Baker (1905-), Miss Barnes (1915-), Miss Elliott (1917-), Miss Burgoine (1919-), and Harry Brosnan (1918-). To these can be added six part-time teachers who gave specialist help for a few hours a week, as and when they were needed and could be afforded.

Two positions which, year after year, remained unchanged were those of the Chairman and Vice Chairman of Governors. Lord Edmond Fitzmaurice was regularly returned unopposed for the one, Dr Flemming for the other. The Vice Chairman, however, was perhaps more involved than he would like to have been. Lord Fitzmaurice was for many months unable to attend Governors' meetings in person because of illness, and at this time a number of meetings were actually held at his home at Leigh so that he could personally take the Chair and actively participate in discussion. At the other end of the social spectrum, Mrs Farr had been replaced as Caretaker, and in the period 1913-1920 a succession of local ladies took on the job, most failing to give anything like total satisfaction to their employers. Miss Blake seems to have been the vehicle of communication of the school's dissatisfaction with its Caretakers to the Governors; time and again we hear that Mrs Walton or Mrs Ford or Mrs Brown was expected in future to perform better, with a warning, formal or informal, given to this effect. Mrs Mullings managed to escape censure, but possibly only because of the brevity of her tenure of the post!

Of course the War was felt in ways other than simply changes to, and losses of, teaching staff. The great outburst of pride and hope that marked its opening was reflected in the singing of the British, French, and Belgian national anthems at the start of the Prizegiving ceremony in 1914. But as time passed, a realisation of the horror of the situation on the ground replaced the fevered jingoism of the early days. The first school casualties were announced; Roland White was lost in the sinking of the *Niger*, and Wallace Lees was killed in France. Pupil attendance became much more patchy, with boys in particular missing school in order to do jobs that were normally done by men who had joined the armed forces. A tolerant view was taken of this; and it was also a lack of qualified men to act as instructors that prevented the school from forming a Cadet Corps, as it was invited to do. It was felt that there was a danger of the buildings in Junction Road being damaged by enemy action, and so the Governors were moved to insure them against "aircraft". More positively, the boys and girls of the school joined together in the practical exercise of furnishing and fully equipping one of the wards at the Red Cross Hospital at Avoncliffe to which, in 1917, the workhouse had been converted. Other schools in the town also helped in this way.

Money nationally had become tight, and there was a feeling anyway that in those difficult times it was inappropriate to spend on things that could be seen as non-essential or frivolous. Consequently, the annual sports became very low key events, the public not being invited as had been the case in happier days. And although the tradition was continued of recording the names of those who were prizewinners or who had gained County distinctions on an honours board, the Chairman of Governors felt it right to pay for this himself. In the black days of 1916 it scarcely seemed right to charge such a frippery to public funds. A Roll of Honour of those serving in the forces was, perhaps, different. By 1915, there were over 40 former pupils in the services, and their names were inscribed on a document which was framed and displayed in the school.

Some years later, the County School benefited from the War Office's generosity by accepting from it a trench mortar as a tangible reminder of the destruction wrought during the years of conflict. One supposes that it was received with gratitude; it was certainly put on display at the front of the school for passers-by in Junction Road to marvel at. Les Hills confirms its presence there, and recalls one memorable occasion when the boys managed to unleash it so that it ran away down the slope to finish up entangled in the railings at the bottom. A great inquiry and rumpus ensued. Later it was removed from public view. "Mortar, because of its odd wheels and unsightly condition, to be moved to the rear of the building and left there until next year," say the Governors' minutes.

The school's premises were modestly enhanced just before the outbreak of War by the creation from a redundant storeroom of a comfortable rest room for the female members of staff. The girls' cloakroom accommodation was also extended and better lighting provided for the woodwork room, these too being simple and relatively inexpensive alterations, and once again the school was indebted to Lord Fitzmaurice for a personal contribution towards the cost. A year or two later another minor improvement was the enlarging of the cycle sheds so that they would take 30 rather than the 15 cycles originally accommodated. Both were an indication of the school's growth in this decade. It was in 1917, however, that a really significant addition to its facilities was made.

Lord Fitzmaurice made two purchases of land, both of which he immediately gifted to the Foundation. The first was a strip of land, or a Paddock, at the back of the building which he bought from the executors of a Mr Crisp and added to the Endowment on 31 December. The second was the field known as Pound Close (excluding a small piece of land in one corner owned by Mr Selfe) which he acquired from the executors of Sir Charles Hobhouse and transferred on 28 December 1917. This latter contained a pavilion and a quantity of dilapidated corrugated iron fencing that belonged to the Town Football Club. There was also a right-of-way through it to Mr Chard's farmyard, and Lord Fitzmaurice felt that thought should also be given to providing access across the field to the Tithe Barn, which in 1917 was in the new ownership of the Wiltshire Archaeological Society. This was agreed. And though not a condition of his gift, he expressed the wish that the field be made available to the children of the town when it was not required by the school.

The Paddock was a rectangular strip of about half an acre, bounded on its longer sides by the school itself and by Poulton field, and on its shorter by the gardens of the houses in Trowbridge Road and by the Gas Works in Frome Road. Its immediate use was to be for instruction to the pupils in gardening, so the playground fence was removed and the school's boundary extended to take in the new ground. Some old huts were removed, it was ploughed and harrowed, a part of it was dug, and a gardening instructor – a Mrs Kosyleski – engaged. By the summer of 1918, the project was going well; at least two classes were being instructed and it was planned to put more ground under cultivation. The following year, however, Mrs Kosyleski resigned and Harry Brosnan took over briefly. But gardening as a subject was abandoned shortly afterwards when need for it disappeared and increased pupil numbers necessitated additional accommodation that was to be built on the new land, and in 1920 all the gardening tools that had been acquired were returned to the County Council as being surplus to requirements.

Pound Close was to be used differently. Since its very inception, the County School had struggled to find suitable fields and courts for its games teams. Hubert Bowyer had supplied such a field for the girls in 1914; Spencer Moulton's sports field had been sought on various occasions for girls' tennis and, later, for football and for both girls' and boys' cricket; tennis courts in particular seemed always to be in short supply. This was an inconvenient and expensive business. The acquisition of Pound Close which measured almost four acres, therefore, was a most timely addition to the school's property. This change in ownership provoked a certain amount of conflict with the local football club which suggested that the school should purchase the pavilion that stood in Pound Close. When this proposal was rejected, it offered the pavilion to the school provided the Governors take over the debt (of £130) that was outstanding on the building. This offer, too, was refused, negotiations not being helped by the club's alleged trespass on the site and its unauthorised removal of fixtures. Mr Burbidge proved to be a more satisfactory neighbour. He was granted grazing rights on the field for his sheep, provided he removed them at 12 hours notice when it was needed for games. A notice board was put up at the entrance indicating the field's new owners.

Shortly after these acquisitions, the Great War came officially to an end – on 28 June 1919. To mark the declaration of Peace, Pound Close was renamed Victory Field, and it was there that a United Service of Thanksgiving was held a few days later. Celebrations were nation-wide, and the school was granted an extra week's holiday. The notice board was altered to display the field's proud new name; it was announced that Sports Days would resume in all their prewar glory; a one-ton roller was purchased, a mower accepted as a gift, and the pavilion bought and repainted; on his return in September, Arthur Baker was congratulated at having been mentioned in dispatches; he celebrated by getting married. And the football club was refused permission to use the field; they moved shortly afterwards to Poulton. So all was back to normal and everything was very satisfactory.

Academic success for the boys and girls of Bradford's County School, it has to be said, was modest. Few actually sought it at this time, the drop-out rate being considerable in what was, at any rate officially, a five-year course. Boys and girls with free places were expected to complete at least three years, but many were not complying. The majority of pupils left for work in the local factories, in retail outlets, in clerical positions, and in agriculture and other manual work at a relatively early stage. This situation was exacerbated during the years of the War, with regularity of attendance also suffering because of the need for children to take on jobs that had previously been done by adults. Nevertheless, the work of the third, fourth, and fifth years was geared to the demands of the Oxford Local Examinations, first the Junior and then the Senior examination, though few attempted, let alone surmounted, that final hurdle. (The Oxford Senior Examination was also deemed to be the leaving test for Pupil Teachers when, in 1916, the school was asked by the Board of Education once again to act as a Pupil Teacher Centre, Phyllis Ostler being accepted as a student.)

Boys and girls joined the school at (about) the age of 11 from the elementary schools in the town and the local villages. By the 1920s, admission was unashamedly by academic ability, social status, and a degree of affluence, but children from poorer homes who aspired to a better education could gain entry through the selection examination and the free place system. Even within the school there was a social division between scholarship children and fee payers, but it was nothing like the divide that existed between County School pupils in general and humbler members of the peer group who either failed to gain entry or who chose to remain unselected. In this, Bradford on Avon was typical of many places up and down the country, with rivalry, or sometimes downright hostility, existing between the chosen few and the lumpenproletariat. Scholastic success for their children was the aim of some parents; more often they were looking for an extended education in what they saw as respectable company. High academic achievement, therefore, was not necessarily all-important.

1913 had been a good year, but the best results so far were produced in 1915. In that year 6 pupils passed the Oxford Senior Examination, one with 1st, one with 2nd, and three with 3rd class honours, and there was one pass. G E Hewett and K M Archard were both exempted from London University matriculation because of their success. Four pupils passed the Junior Examination, and seven were successful in the Bursar Examination for qualification as student teachers. 1918 was another good year, with 7 Senior passes. The Head Master's son, J R Crompton, achieved 1st class honours, with a distinction in English, at the age of 15, and the following year, 1919, he gained an unusually brilliant County Scholarship which led him eventually to the Government Records Office. But these were exceptional successes. Results were usually more pedestrian.

If examination success were elusive and a cause for anxiety, another on-going worry for the Head Master and his Governors was the level of teachers' salaries. In 1912 HMI had said, "The salaries offered are not high, but it is understood that a scale of salaries is now under consideration by the Governing Body." It might have been under consideration, but no formal scales were forthcoming; it was left to the individual teacher to exercise what professional muscle he might have and obtain the best terms for himself that he could. Applications were made to the Governors; some were agreed, others refused. Miss Blake's position, in particular, was peculiar. When she joined the school in 1902, her salary was set at £120 a year, plus a capitation allowance of £1 for each girl that she brought with her. This latter element was dropped in 1904 when the Dual System ceased. As Vice Principal of the County School she was awarded £140, a figure maintained without increase for the next 9 years. Now, in 1916, it was raised to £150 with the promise of a review of her position. A couple of years later, she made something of a fuss when Ethel Barnes's salary was raised to a point not very much short of her own, but she explained later that it was only because she feared that her position in the school was being threatened by the narrowing differential.

The General Education Committee made its views on salaries known, those at Bradford on Avon being very much on the low side, and it promised a County scale as soon as possible. In the mean time, the teacher shortage that was the product of the War spawned a number of requests for more money that were hard to resist. Undeniably, however, none of the teachers at the County School was being over-generously treated, and the Governors introduced an improved interim scale of salaries – based on qualification, experience, length of service, and value to the school. The County scale, brought in in 1919, indicated a higher rate still and added considerably to the Governors' financial worries, but, henceforward, salaries were much less the subject of local negotiation. John Crompton, the Head Master, was placed on £450 a year, rising by annual increments of £25 to £500; Miss Blake was on £210, rising by £30 increments to £270; Arthur Baker initially received £240, but his salary soon rose steeply as, though a non-graduate, application was made for him to move to the graduate scale for salary purposes because of his academic distinction and his value to the school. It was determined, too, that Miss Blake, like Mr Baker, should be regarded as a graduate because of her long and excellent service; and the other full-time staff were rewarded somewhat more modestly. Visiting teachers continued to be paid by the hour. The Governors' Secretary, solicitor Alex Wilkins, benefited too by having his stipend almost doubled between 1915 and 1919 – to £60 a year.

The school's income from Board of Education and County grants rose from time to time as these were increased to meet increased costs, but fees had remained stationary at £6 since 1904, and they had included within that sum the cost of gym shoes, cap or hat band, books, and a contribution for PE and games. In 1921 a standard fee of £6 guineas was adopted for all County schools, with parents being expected to meet the cost of uniform and equipment, and the school allowed to keep back a small sum (5/-) to defray the cost of organised games. The 1920s, however, proved to be a time of financial stress that was to tax the resources of many schools to the limit.

Despite these serious matters, gifts continued to flow to the County School from Lord Fitzmaurice. Many, particularly to needy individuals, were anonymous or given quietly, others were a matter of public record. Again and again he donated books to the school library, and, in 1913, a Stuffed Heron; the following year, he paid the difference in price between the cost of a new piano and what was received from the sale of the old one; then, again in 1914, he gave six pictures to the school – *Earl Grey – As a Boy, A Florentine Musician, Cornelius de Lyon, Queen Mary of Norway, Desiderio da Cettignano,* and *A Pastel*; in 1915 he subsidised the girls' hockey team, which at the time was particularly successful, to enable them to travel to away matches; and in 1917 he paid for a cabinet to house a collection of fossils. (This was a particularly fine collection that had been gathered by Dr Adye and that was now given to the school by Mr Collins of St Margaret's St.) His most significant and most valuable gift, however, was that of the Paddock and Pound Close, mentioned above, that was made in the same year.

Credit went to Julia Blake when the County School won the Challenge Shield,

First Class, at the Wiltshire Music Festival on the third consecutive occasion in 1913 and, as a consequence, were allowed to keep it. (In 1914 they won it again!) Carpenter and Murphy, however, brought no credit to the school, being expelled for "misconduct". (What did they do?) Signs of the times were the requests that now began to be made for the setting up of a Wireless Telegraphy Club on school premises, and, from 1914, the use of the gymnasium by the yeomanry billeted in the town.

As the War finished and pupil numbers continued to rise – 129 in 1918, 150 in 1919, 167 in 1920, 171 in 1921 – additional teachers (Miss Burgoine and Mr Brosnan) and classroom space were needed, the latter being temporarily solved by the division of the art room into two spaces by means of a curtain and screen, and, in 1919, by the use of the Congregational Sunday Schoolroom. Unfortunately, this "bulge" in numbers coincided with the start of the financial problems of the 1920s, and so a legitimate demand for more teachers and additional accommodation continually ran up against the need both locally and nationally to economise. Expansion in any form was simply not the order of the day. Even so, Donald Saunders was added to the staff in 1919 for junior work, and Alfred Gorvett arrived at the same time as a visiting teacher to take woodwork; he gave way to Henry Chappell in 1923.

Evelyn Elliott, who had originally been appointed to take charge of the short-lived Prep Department, had become a valued member of staff, so it was hoped that she could be taken on as a permanent employee when her particular responsibility was disbanded in 1921. The local authority agreed with some reluctance, as it did to a further additional teacher, but only on the condition that the County School got rid of all its visiting teachers, of whom there were, as there always had been, many. Wisely this condition was soon dropped. Even so, the General Education Committee wanted the Governors to move in that direction so that "arrangements can be made for all the school work to be conducted by all the permanent members of staff". Ethel Barnes (1915-1921), who had been at the County School for 6 years and who had just graduated, left for the Girls' High School in Trowbridge and was replaced by Hannah Bird from Dublin. Arthur Percival, a 30-year old historian and future Acting Head Master, was recruited as the additional teacher.

After the War, economy and a tightening of belts became the watchwords; a foretaste of what was to come was given by an Education Department memo to all secondary schools in May 1922. Not everything it threatened was eventually put into practice, but what it suggested was that from September normal school fees should be doubled, except in the case of non tax-payers; that free places should not be awarded to the children of tax-paying parents; that the number of free places should gradually be reduced to 40% of the number of children in any school; that the award of junior scholarships should be discontinued; and that Governors of secondary schools should be asked "to reconsider the staff employed with a view if possible of reducing the number of teachers". This was heavy stuff, and at Bradford, as elsewhere, the memo was not exactly met with enthusiasm. The Governors, however, agreed to make gestures of cooperation.

The services of Mr Saunders (1919-1922) were dispensed with at Christmas, and it was decided not to continue to employ part-timers Baber (cookery), Hurry (Swedish Drill), and Hallett (art). But Hope Hurry was a survivor. Despite the threat to her job, she continued to teach at the school, was told again the following year that her post would go, was immediately re-engaged, set about re-equipping her department, and was taken on to the permanent staff of the school in 1923, leaving eventually in 1927 after almost 10 years of service to girls' gymnastics. Thomas Isaac Hallett (1897-1922) was rather different. He had taught art at several institutions throughout the area for many years, and latterly, certainly, his work had been characterised by competence rather than flair or imagination. He resigned from Trowbridge Girls' High School in the summer of 1921 following an adverse inspectorial report, and offered to do the same at Bradford. In fact, he retired at the end of 1922 after more than a quarter of a century at the school, albeit part-time. His length of service was recognised by the school's Governors when he left by the presentation of a silver tray and coffee pot.

So, for the period 1912-1923 the County School's full-time staff were:

Head Master:	J Crompton (1900-),
Vice Principal:	Miss J Blake (1902-),
Assistants:	A H Baker (1905-), G T Breen (1907-1914),
	Miss E T Barnes (1915-1921), Miss H Bird (1921-),
	Miss E Elliott (1917-), Miss K Jowett (1917-1918),
	W H Brosnan (1918-), Miss H Hurry (1918-),
	Miss D Vine (1918-1919), Miss D Burgoine (1919-),
	D Saunders (1919-1922), A B Percival (1921-).

The Education Department memo quoted above makes mention of "free places". The free place system was introduced by the Education Act of 1907 and its purpose was to give the brightest children at elementary schools a chance of secondary education even though their parents would not normally have been able to afford it. All grant-aided secondary schools had to reserve such places, for which they were reimbursed, to a number of not less than 25% of the previous year's intake. To establish who was worthy of a free place, an annual examination was held. Those with the highest marks were the winners; the losers either had to pay fees or give up their hopes of a secondary education. For the first ten years or so after 1907 the number of free places awarded annually at Bradford's County School was in single figures; in the 1920s it tended to be somewhere between 11 and 15. To take one particular year, of the 167 pupils on roll in 1920, 100 paid fees whilst 67 had free places. By 1926, there were 75 fee payers and 62 with free places. But there was another smaller category of pupil – those who held Free School Exhibitions. These boys and girls were also taught without charge to their parents and they, too, were identified by the annual examination, their expenses being paid from the Trust that administered the estate of the old, and long defunct, Free Grammar School. This free place system survived until 1932 when it was replaced by a means-tested scale of fees.

The doubling of the fees that was also mentioned in the memo never actually happened. There was much discussion about it in the months that followed, much disagreement, much heart-searching and hand-wringing, but in the end all remained as it was with the threatened cut in grant not materialising.

And Peace had brought a welcome impetus to things. A new prospectus was issued; a school troop of Girl Guides was formed under Miss Barnes and this flourished for several years; the local Wireless Association was given permission to erect a mast in the school's grounds and to use a room for use in wireless instruction; further, they put up a hut and an aerial, by the canal, at the far end of Victory Field, paying rent of 1/- per year in pursuit of their hobby; Sir Arthur Elton presented 3 Elton Ware vases to the town and it was decided to house them in the school museum; Harry Brosnan's 3 years in the army was recognised as counting towards his seniority; and there were murmurings about the need for more rooms to accommodate the extra numbers that there now were in the school as compared with (say) 20 years ago.

This requirement for more room had by this time become a constant subject for debate. The building in Junction Road had been designed as a Technical Institute and adapted somewhat later to meet the need for a mixed secondary school, and the tiny number of pupils initially accommodated was dwarfed by those on roll a quarter of a century later. This failure of the Governors to provide properly in terms of bricks and mortar for the town's secondary boys and girls led from these years onwards to increasingly acrimonious exchanges between them and the authorities, both local and national, and, eventually, to the ultimate threat of closure. But this degree of crisis was for the future.

In the 1920s, so tight was space that preference was for a time given to parents who agreed, in writing, that their child would stay on at school until he (or she) was at least 16. They were reminded that the *laissez faire* attitude to attendance that had been tolerated during the years of the War was no longer acceptable, and, as far as the quality of their work was concerned, individual boys and girls were warned about the thin ice on which they were skating. Pupils whose parents were tardy in settling the bills for their fees were actually threatened with suspension, a pervasive cash crisis combined with a shortage of resources forcing the school to be much more pro-active in protecting its interests.

An additional building on the main school site was needed and investigated, but early in 1920 Mr Pullinger persuaded the Governors to accept a hut. A stone-built structure would have been expensive and subject to delay. A hut, however, as luck would have it, was to hand immediately. This was not any old hut; it was a Superior Hut, measuring 109' x 18' which had been put up for hospital purposes during the War. Its cost was £107, plus the same again for transport and erection. And so it was agreed. Sited in what had been the Paddock, up on the bank immediately behind the main building, by the end of the year it was up and in use, providing 4 new classrooms, 2 cloakrooms, and a room allocated to the assistant Masters – a smoke-filled den at the right-hand end. Heating for this Hut was always a problem. Initially it was by Tortoise stoves. (Handfuls of maize scattered on these stoves, it was found, could be roasted and turned into popcorn.) When they wore (or were burnt) out, heating was by radiators connected to the school's central system, but they had to be supplemented by more stoves in the colder weather. And as the Hut was being installed, so too was a new boiler and heating system for the whole school, the old system creating so many problems after 25 years of use that it had to be replaced. In summer, ironically, the Hut was too hot and classes had to be taken out-of-doors. Perhaps the relative values of various bits of school property is indicated by the insurance costs put upon them in 1922: £11,500 for the main building, £1,000 for the woodwork room, £1,000 for Clifford House, and £700 for the Hut.

This Hut was known locally as the "Gallipoli" Hut, though it had no connection at all with that particular military disaster. Perhaps it was thought at one time that it was originally destined for use in Turkey. Whether or not, it was one of a number that were acquired by Wiltshire schools (there was another, the "Black Hut", much in evidence at Trowbridge Girls' High School) and they were rescued from post-war superfluity on Salisbury Plain, where they had been put up as hospital accommodation for soldiers, to become integral and very well remembered components of the various schools which they came to grace. One elderly member of the clan was reported on television news only last week (May 1998) as still being in use at a primary school in Swindon some 80 years after its "temporary" erection.

In 1922, most unusually the Caretaker was commended, and Mrs Brown's wage was accordingly raised. A year later, strangely, her work was heavily criticised, this dissatisfaction conveniently coinciding with the idea that it might be possible for the same person to keep both the school buildings and the games field across the road in good order. Mrs Brown was consequently given notice, and Mr Sims, a former Petty Officer in the RNR, was appointed in her stead at £2 a week to act as Caretaker, Cleaner, Groundsman, and Stoker.

That same year – 1922 – was more notable for the school's receiving a most handsome gift. This was £10,000 worth of 4% Funding Stock from an anonymous donor. Even at the time, the identity of this benefactor was not difficult to guess, but anonymous he wished to be and the stock was transferred on 7 June to the Official Trustee of Charitable Funds upon Trust for the Foundation. The annual interest from this stock of some £400 was added to the school's income and, together with an income from rents of about £30, gave an additional £430 to what was received from official sources. This, of course, was a truly magnificent gesture, particularly so when what £10,000 in 1922 would be at today's values is calculated, and it was the basis of the Endowment Fund from which the school thereafter benefited in very many ways year in and year out.

In June 1923, the County School enjoyed another visit from HMI – Miss Baster, Mr Battiscombe, Capt Parker, Mr Trice Martin, and Miss Schooley on this occasion.

They found that the number of pupils had fallen from the maximum of 171, achieved in 1921, to 138, partly because of "local trade conditions" and partly because of the discontinuance of the Prep Department. A further fall was feared, but the greater concern was for the large number who left before the age of 16. At the time of the inspection, only three had reached that age, with 25 pupils in the first year, 45 in the second, 32 in the third, and 36 in the fourth. They were organised in seven forms – II, IIIA and IIIB, IVA and IVB, VA and VB. It was expected that, the following year, there would be one first year, one second, two third, and (probably) only one fourth, with parallel forms in any age group in danger of disappearing. The principal thrust of the inspectors' remarks, however, was concern – real concern – about the number of pupils who continued to leave before the age of 16 (81% in 1920-21) and the Board of Education warned that, unless this trend were corrected, its recognition of the school would be at risk. And if the pupils were a bit of a worry by virtue of their fewness, the brevity of their stay, and their age range, so too were the staff because of their lack of relevant qualification. Only two of the assistant teachers were graduates and one of the masters "cannot be said to have any adequate qualifications for teaching in a secondary school".

Of the subjects on the curriculum, science, history, geography, art, and Latin (re-introduced in 1921-22) were found to be in a satisfactory state, or better. English was a thing of bits and pieces, taught by five different teachers and with no one properly in charge. French was "far from a strong subject" and in mathematics "the standard reached [was] by no means good".

But it was the accommodation, the capacity and suitability of the buildings, that, less than 30 years after the school opened, were of the greatest concern.

> "Since the last full inspection [in 1912] the accommodation has been increased by the erection of a block of huts containing four classrooms, two small cloakrooms (one for boys and one for girls), and a room for Assistant Masters.
> The cloakroom accommodation for girls, which was extended after the last inspection, is somewhat limited; a further enlargement was intended but not carried out.
> Generally speaking the buildings and equipment are good, but the staff room accommodation is inadequate. The Head Master shares a room with the Principal Mistress, and the Assistant Mistresses have to use the library; the usefulness of this latter room for the purpose for which it was intended is thereby seriously curtailed. Office and lavatory accommodation for the staff is very restricted. An additional staff room, with cloakroom and lavatory accommodation for Mistresses, is wanted and should be provided when circumstances allow."

This was the mild overture to the storm of criticism that arose in future years when the inadequacy of its buildings was to call into question the school's very existence.

A senior citizen of the town, reflecting on the County School as he knew it in the mid 1920s, summed it up like this:

> "If you were a boy at the school, you were almost bound to be in the football team because there were so few of us. In every way it was a very small school. It was more like a large family than a school. Everyone knew everyone else and the atmosphere was relaxed. This was taken from Mr Crompton who was a gentleman and very fair in everything he did."

But if it was comfortable and caring, taking its tone from its ageing Head Master, Bradford's secondary school was also unchallenging and becoming somewhat complacent.

Date	Name	Form		Offence	Punishment	Signature
April 29th	Stevens I.	IIIB	F	Work not learnt.	Do work set.	M.H.T.
" "	Watts R.	IIIB	F	Homework neglected.	" "	M.I.W.
May 3rd	Dyer	Va	C	Homework not given in	Geography question written	B.J.
" "	D. Dyer	Va	B	" "		
May 24th	Crossman	IIIB	F	Inattentive in class	Do set exercise	M.I.W.
" "	Hopkins	IIIB	F	" "		M.I.W.
May 26	M. Moore	IIIA	?	Homework not learnt.	Written answer	D.B.
" "	Watts	IIIA	F	" "	" "	D.B.
May 27th	S. Rivers	IIIA	B	Homework not learnt.	Do question set	D.B.
"	R. Watts	IIIA	F	" " done	Do work set	M.I.W.
"	J. White	IIB	C	" badly written	" "	D.B.
May 31st	E. Gerrish	IIIA	B	Homework not learnt	Do question set	M.B.
3rd June	Crossman W.	IIIB	F/M	Persistent laziness.	Complete Chemistry notes.	M.H.T.
" "	B. Elkins	IIIB	P	Unsatisfactory homework	Rewrite	B.J.
June 7th	Crossman H	IVB	F	Persistent laziness	Complete Chemistry notes	M.H.T.
"	Alford R.	IIIB	F	Laziness & Carelessness.	Do given exercise	M.H.T.
"	Lowe V.	IV	C	Talking in class	Write out proposition	J.W.J.
"	Coleman R	IV	F	" "	"	J.W.J.
"	Sheppard	IIa	F	Homework badly done.	Do work set.	M.I.W.
June 14th	Crossman W	IIIB	F	Homework neglected	Do work set	M.I.W.
"	J. Kellen	Ia	B	Talking in class	Do work set	M.H.T.
" 17th	Slade R.	Va	F	Wilfully damaging school property	Do 4 arithmetics.	S. Riddick (Captain)

A page from the Detention Book of 1926.

112

Under New Management
The County School:
1924-1935

THROUGHOUT THE PERIOD 1924 to 1926 drawn-out negotiations were conducted about what was needed and what could be afforded by way of major building additions to the County School. Plans had been drawn up, discussed, discarded, and alternatives considered even before the visit of the Inspectors, but momentum was added to the process by the criticisms of HMI. The provision of toilets, in particular, came under the spotlight, but the Head Master's room, the library, and the art room were also problem areas. From this time onwards, shortage of accommodation was a preoccupation for all those charged with the management of the County School and its successor, the Fitzmaurice Grammar School.

In January 1925, there was a Public Enquiry into the Bradford elementary schools, and it looked as though, as a result of that Enquiry, a new Cookery Centre might be set up in the old Boys' School building at the top of Church Street. If that were to happen, it would mean that young girls from the elementary schools would no longer have to go to the County School for instruction in cookery, which had long been the case, and it would also mean that no new provision for cookery need be thought about for the secondary school. On these grounds, therefore, decisions about what was needed in Junction Road were deferred pending the results of the Enquiry. A sum of £2,100 was put into the Authority's estimates to cover the cost of new buildings for the secondary school, but almost a year later plans were again put off because of the serious financial situation that then prevailed. Finally agreement was reached. At the end of 1926, it was decided that new lavatory accommodation was to be provided, and some cloakroom conversions were to take place as the inspectors had recommended, but thought of continuing with any kind of provision for elementary school children at the County School was abandoned.

These were significant decisions at the time, but all traces of what, in their day, were important alterations have now disappeared, former usage having been totally obliterated in the revamped internal layout of the old building that took place in the 1980s. The attractive facade of the 1897 Technical Institute remains, of course, but internally it is now quite different and its out-buildings have long been swept away.

Speech Day in 1925 took place, as was usual, just before Christmas. On this occasion it was on 18 December, and, with the Honourable Mrs Hanbury Tracey as principal guest, it was unremarkable except in two important respects. First, of course, it was to be Johnny Crompton's last formal prizegiving and the end of an era as he shortly afterwards gave notice of his resignation from the summer of 1926 of the post that he had held for 26 years. This, at the time, must have been quite momentous news. Secondly, he announced that the words *Esse quam Videri* ("To be rather than to seem") were henceforth to be added to the school badge. And so they were. And so they remained as the school motto for the next 55 years.

But before he left the scene a few interesting developments took place.

Mr Christopher presented the school with a telescope. A nice cinder path was laid to the Gallipoli Hut. Miss Blake and some of her girls were given permission to level an area in Victory Field in preparation for the laying of a tennis court; if voluntary labour were used, the cost would be in the region of £26. So a start was made, but this was to be a very long-term project indeed! Better lighting was installed throughout the school. At the instigation of HMI, a new flag pole was bought and set up in the same place as the old one, just by the front steps. The art inspector very much liked what he saw of Miss Burgoine's work, she having succeeded Mr Hallett as teacher of art. Miss Barnes, who had left the school in 1921, remembered it four years later by presenting a valuable encyclopaedia to the Library. Sports Days continued in summer, and the annual Prize Day was always just before Christmas. And life went on peaceably and fairly predictably at the County School, Bradford on Avon, until "Johnny" Crompton, who had been there as long as the school itself, finally retired. Despite the adverse criticism to which he had been subject in his early days, there is no doubt that credit for the esteem in which the County School by this time stood was his.

Born in 1866 in Rochdale, he was the son of a methodist minister, growing up in a Welsh manse and receiving his early education in Wales. At Oxford, he had been a sportsman, having a particular interest in football, cricket, and rowing, and he became a leading figure in the Oxford Union, that nursery of budding politicians. He received his BA in 1889 and MA (Cantab) in 1907. After his teaching career had brought him to Bradford on Avon, John Crompton proved to be a many-sided figure, not only respected for his professionalism, but prominent as a lay preacher, a loyal supporter of the Baptist Church, a leading participant in various musical societies, a County chess player, and a member of the Conservative Club and the Volunteer Militia; and, as we have seen, he maintained his sporting interests.

During the First World War, for a time, he virtually ran the boys' side of the school single-handed, and thereafter, as a colleague of those days put it, "he saw the school grow and grow until it was far too large for its clothing". In retirement, he and his wife moved to Cambridge, believing that the academic atmosphere there would give him scope to develop his interests, but among those who knew him it was felt that this severing of his connections with a town to whom he had given so much was a mistake. And so it proved. He never really settled. Nor did he ever recover from his wife, Isabel's, death in 1932. His health deteriorated rapidly; he died on 31 March 1933 and is buried at Sutton in Surrey. The school flag was flown at half-mast in memory of this "quiet and retiring" man whose creation the County School at Bradford on Avon effectively was.

Two tributes sum up his character. Arthur Baker, writing many years later, said:

> "No words can adequately describe Johnny Crompton. He was first and always a Christian gentleman. His scholarship was profound, and his kindliness to, and concern for, all his pupils a model for all time. I owe him as much as one man can owe to another, and even now his smile comes back to me as a living thing."

And:

> "Things did not always go smoothly, but in sunshine or shadow he maintained that same quiet serenity, loving patience, and confidence in the future that endeared him to one and all."

There were 375 applicants for his job, these being whittled down to a short-list from which 3 were selected for interview. Successful at that interview was H S Rosen, MA, a modern linguist and Housemaster at High Pavement School, Nottingham. Rosen would be expected to live at Clifford House, next to the school, for which he would pay £35 a year rent, and his salary would be £600.

Henry Rosen made changes – inevitably. His impatience with what he found at Bradford contrasted sharply with the tolerant, easy-going regime of Johnny Crompton, and Arthur Baker, many years later, recalled the restlessness and ferment of those few years during which he had charge of the school:

> "He came from a large school in Nottingham. It was his first headship, and he was filled with a burning desire to introduce new ideas, and enthusiasm. He was most anxious to enhance the reputation of the school. To speak of it as the Tech

was to render him apoplectic with indignation. He certainly shook us all up a bit....For three years we had no failures in the School Certificate. The House system was introduced and many new activities started. Years later he admitted to me that Bradford on Avon exercised on him its powerfully soothing influences, and he mellowed rapidly."

Les Hills, who was a pupil from 1925 to 1930, said that Henry Rosen had a galvanic effect on the school. At his first morning assembly he announced to cheers that he was doing away with corporal punishment, but an uneasy silence followed his next words – that "things were going to change and become much tougher". A tall, ex-army officer who had been wounded in the right arm, so that he had to support it when he wrote on the blackboard, he is remembered by Les Hills as a very strong personality with the ability to exercise a remarkable control over his pupils, and Betty Wayling, Arthur Percival's daughter, recalls the atmosphere at home brought about by the change in her father's Head Master:

> "I don't think Pa liked him. He was dark and hawk-like, and whereas in the past staff conversation had been, 'Dear old John said today....', it now became a curt, 'Rosen said....' Things had perhaps got rather too comfortable as Mr Crompton approached retirement, but the view was that Mr Rosen was just using Bradford as a springboard to bigger things."

Rosen had been a Housemaster before he moved to Bradford, and shortly after his arrival a stimulus was given to internal competition by the creation of a House system for both sport and work. This was not simply a device to encourage competition on Sports Day, but embraced every aspect of school life and, like the pastoral system in the later comprehensive schools, ensured that the progress and welfare of every pupil was watched over by at least one senior member of the teaching staff.

> "In order to ensure that full attention is given to the mental, moral, and physical needs of the pupils, the school is being reorganised on the House System. This is an attempt to reproduce, so far as it is possible to do so in a day school, that completeness of care and control of the individual pupil obtained in the great Public Schools by the allocation of each boy to a particular House, and to the care of a particular House Tutor....This sectional control will supplement, but not replace, the present supervision of all pupils by the Head Master and Vice Principal."

Blake and Pinckney Houses were for girls, Crompton and Fitzmaurice for boys. Miss Burgoine (in charge of Blake) and Mr Percival (of Crompton) served in those positions for many years, but Pinckney and Fitzmaurice Houses had a constantly changing list of mentors.

To mark and give meaning to this innovation, in 1927 House cups were presented for competition. Helen Blake of Belcombe gave the Blake Cup for girls' games, and she was followed by Captain Erlysman Charles Pinckney JP, of Wraxall Lodge, who gave a magnificent cup, the Pinckney Cup, for girls' work (from 1960 it was awarded to the champion House); the Frankell Cup for boys' work was given by Alfred Frankell; and F J F Cowlishaw of St Margaret's Street, son of the Master of the old Free School, presented the Cowlishaw Cup for boys' games. The 4 cups were thereafter displayed in a specially designed showcase. Never one to be left behind, Lord Fitzmaurice gave 2 prizes for Public Service, to be awarded to the Head Boy and Head Girl annually. The County School was conscious of, and eager to give a public face to, the quality of its work and play, and in that spirit, as by this time (1927) the school flag through constant use was past repair, a Governor, Mrs Scratton, presented a new one to be flown proudly when occasion warranted.

The arrival of the new Head Master saw a burgeoning of school clubs, particularly (but not exclusively) of sports clubs, with badminton, boxing, and rowing among them. J H Finney became the boxing instructor, with, by June 1927, 41 boys engaged in the sport. A school Boat Club, with 12 members, was affiliated to the town's Rowing Club, and in 1931 (after Rosen had left) the County School entered a crew in the Saltford Regatta for the first time; the following year the Old Boys rowed in the Jamaica Cup in that Regatta. In 1927, too, work began on the preparation of a hard tennis court on Victory Field as per the resolution of 5 years earlier; the levelling of the ground was done by pupils under the supervision of the Groundsman, but the eight-year saga was not destined to end until 1930 when a mere £35 was needed to complete the job. Cricket received due recognition with a Mr Leatham employed as coach, and in 1928, through the kind offices of Colonel Palmer of Berryfields, professional coaching in Trowbridge was obtained for the boys for the first time. A pupil of the school, H E W Slade, school captain from 1927 to 1929 and destined for ordination (as the Rev Father Slade of the Oxford Mission House), presented a silver cup for cross-country running, and in 1931 the Bradford on Avon Swimming Club, on being wound up, also presented a cup to the school. The following year, the school won the County Football Cup. Sport of all sorts was clearly important, Sports Day always an event of note, ending with tea in the Gymnasium by wish of Lord Fitzmaurice. The occasion was unspoilt by the annual list of those injured by accident or over-exertion.

Henry Rosen also revamped the teaching week. Four full days of schooling, from 9.00 to 12.30 and 2.00 to 4.00, with half days on Wednesdays and Saturdays had formerly been the pattern, but this had created travelling difficulties for those who came from a distance, with a return journey within a short space of time on two days a week. He moved, therefore, to a more conventional five full-day week. Morning assembly changed, too. Under Mr Crompton (who, to Les Hills, looked very old, with his white hair and white moustache) it had been a fairly free and easy affair, with teachers dressed informally or, indeed, casually. The new Head, "The Boss", as he was called, required higher standards all round that were epitomised by the academic dress demanded of the staff.

Another innovation that came rather later, under Mr Farrar rather than Mr Rosen, was the establishing of *The Gudgeon*. It first appeared in 1930. More will be said of the school magazine later, but volume 1, number 1, was a modest enough publication, printed on coarsish paper and with a buff cover bearing its title, the school badge, the date and the price (6d). It and its immediate successors carried the usual editorial, small items of school news, House and sports reports, perhaps a longer article, and a number of contributions in verse and prose. Advertisements appeared for the first time in 1931, and for today's reader these are as interesting as the magazine's literary and factual contents, recording, as they do, the commercial life of the town in the early 1930s. Messrs Pugsley (boots and shoes), Edwards (butcher), Christopher (chemist), Goodall (outfitter), Nichols and Bushell (grocers), Rossiter (radio and electrical), and Alex Brown (ironmongers) rub shoulders with less likely advertisers such as the Bradford on Avon Scholastic Trading Agency, the Gas Company, and Moore's sports shop in Bath. A magazine of 1933 has a young French girl who was on a pupil exchange in Bradford, Simone Bonnet, writing in French of her impressions of the town, the school, and the house in which she was staying. It is a lengthy piece. The reader, having struggled through the French original and not noticing what follows, is then faced with an equally lengthy, literal translation of the same article in English. In the next magazine, Mireille Dubois kept up the tradition!

The full-time members of the teaching staff of the school when the new Head Master arrived in 1926 were: Henry Rosen (1926-1929), Miss Blake (1902-1930), Arthur Baker (1905-), Harry Brosnan (1918-), Miss Hurry (1918-1927), Miss Burgoine (1919-), Arthur Percival (1921-), Miss Wray (1925-1928), and Miss Skinner (1926-1928). Miss Blake was coming to the end of her 28 years of service to the school, but, as can be seen, 4 of the staff still had many years ahead of them in Bradford.

A Miss Claxton and a Mrs Vincent were employed successively to teach the girls swimming, whilst Harry Brosnan looked after the boys. Thus was the tradition of swimming instruction as part of the curriculum continued. Marjorie Wray joined the school in 1925 to replace Miss Bird (1921-1925) who had died in office, and there was the small drama of the appointment of Miss Skinner. This was sparked by the decision of Evelyn Elliott (1917-1925) to leave in order to marry at the end of October. Her husband was Frank Panzetta who was on the technical staff at Spencer Moulton's and a young man much sought after by the unmarried ladies of the town. She returned for another couple of months after her wedding, her replacement the following January being Miss Ereline Skinner, an English specialist. The Chief Education Officer, Mr Pullinger, was apparently taken by surprise by this flurry of changes and he wrote in some embarrassment to John Crompton asking whether Miss Skinner's appointment could either be aborted or held in abeyance. The Board of Education in London had asked for every possible economy to be made, so serious was the financial situation, and perhaps Miss Skinner could be dispensed with? He received a dusty answer; Ereline Skinner started in January 1926.

For the period 1924-1935, then, the changes in the permanent staff of the school can be listed as follows:

Head Master: John Crompton (1900-1926), Henry Rosen (1926-1929), Sidney Farrar (1929-);
Vice Principal/) Julia Blake (1902-1930), Bessie Jones (1930-1933),
Senior Mistress:) post abolished;
Science: Arthur Baker (1905-);
Art: Dorothy Burgoine (1919-);
History: Arthur Percival (1921-);
General subs: Harry Brosnan (1918-);
French/Latin: Hannah Bird (1921-1925), Marjorie Wray (1925-1928), Agnes Allwright (1928-1931), Mary Williams (1931-1933), May Priestley (1931-);
English: Evelyn Elliott (Mrs Panzetta) (1917-1925), Ereline Skinner (1926-1928), Aileen Farrell (1928-1929), Mona Lynn (1929-1932), Leslie Kernutt (1931-);
Geography: after Misses Blake and Jones – Ruth Watts (1933-);
Girls' PE/games: various, including – Hope Hurry (1918-1927), Doreen Goodwin (1927-1930), Esther Robinson (1930-1932), and Ruth Watts;
Dom Science: Nora Moroney (1923-1929), Mrs Molly Glasspool (1929-1931), Marjorie Taylor (1932-1933), Anne Phillips (Mrs Rees) (1933-);
Prep Dept: Marion Cargill (1933-1935), post abolished;
Maths/physics: new post – Herbert Robinson (1928-1931), John Jenkins

	(1931-1932), Robert ("Johnny") Otter (1932-);
English/history:	new post – Joan Yates (1935-).

And at the end of the period – in 1935 – Sidney Farrar had as his staff: Baker, Brosnan, Burgoine, Percival, Priestley, Kernutt, Watts, Rees, Otter, and Yates.

Betty Percival (now Mrs Wayling) was a pupil at the school from 1930 to 1937 and she remembers those who taught her with great affection:

> "Mary Williams came from the north, and May Priestley, a Quaker, was attractive, had red hair, and dressed very well. Poor Mr Robinson had a stammer, but he seemed to get on all right with Miss Allwright. And Mr Kernutt was tall, alert, bright eyed, and looked just like a bird."

And she was not above indulging in a little gossip brought home by her father of the days before she was old enough to attend the secondary school – such as the unlikely incident of John Crompton's exercising corporal punishment on a boy who had gone too far even for him. The culprit was a Tommy Loram, and it was his desire to get to a football match that started before the end of school that led to his undoing. Encouraged by like-minded friends, he advanced the school clock by some 45 minutes, thus bringing lessons for the afternoon to a premature end. Unfortunately his ruse was discovered, and in the privacy of the Head Master's room he paid the penalty.

As far as pupil numbers were concerned, by the mid 1920s they had stabilised at around 150 – a few more or a few less from time to time.

By this time, of course, Henry Rosen had also gone. He stayed a mere 3 years before departing for Chippenham Secondary School, a much larger establishment than Bradford's County School. (In 1929, the two Trowbridge High Schools contained almost 500 pupils; Devizes with 285 and Chippenham with 270 came next; and in the third division were Bradford on Avon with 160, Calne with 150, Marlborough with 138, and Warminster with 120.)

Isabel and John Crompton just before his retirement.

His successor was Sidney Farrar, a man much more in the Crompton mould than the ambitious Mr Rosen. There were 206 applicants for the post; 4 were invited for interview, with the 33 year-old Farrar, Senior English Master at Sheffield's Central Secondary School for Boys, successful; should he have refused the job, Arthur Baker was second choice.

The above list of teaching staff is marked by the number of young men and women who only stayed two or three years at the school. The County School was a very small institution in a small town that was something of a backwater, and professional advancement had to be looked for elsewhere. Either that, or one stayed for life! Of course, there were other reasons, too, for some of the changes. Miss Lynn left to become Mrs Nott; Misses Wray, Allwright and Skinner all had breakdowns of health; Miss Farrell came from, and left to return to, the United States; Miss Jones achieved a headship in New Brighton; and poor Miss Cargill's job simply disappeared.

Periods of staff illness, and consequent absence from school, seemed to be endemic, and a faithful band of stand-in teachers was employed with unusual frequency. Mrs Panzetta, Mrs Iles, Misses Howse, Clark, Griffith, Sturgis, and Mr King were all used because, in addition to routine absences, Miss Blake was frequently and lengthily away, Miss Jones suffered a nervous breakdown, Miss Skinner took a trip to South Africa from which she did not return, and Miss Allwright was to have been dismissed because of a lengthy absence when she resigned anyway.

Julia Blake (Vice Principal) actually resigned at the end of April 1930. Like John Crompton, she had become a fixture and her going came as something of a shock. She herself said: "I had hoped to stay at the school for some years longer, but I find that is impossible." Ill health had dogged her all her life and the time had been reached for her to give up what was increasingly becoming an unequal struggle. Almost a founder member, after 28 years at the school she had just bought a house, Belcombe Croft, with a view to eventual retirement when events overtook her. She was a "character". Respected, and, perhaps, feared, her grip on naughty boys was apparently as effective as the hold she had over her girls. Les Hills thought her "a tartar" who peered at one fixedly through a lorgnette, and it was clear to him and his pals that when she worked with Johnny Crompton it was she who ruled the roost.

Much was made of her going. An advertisement was placed in the *Wiltshire Times*, and a formal evening was held in the Gymnasium with the presentation of an Autograph Souvenir, a bouquet, and a handsome cheque. Sadly, she was taken very seriously ill only a couple of years later, and, after seeking medical help in Bradford (Yorkshire) and Bath, she died at the Forbes Fraser Hospital, not unexpectedly, in early January 1934. What she had done for the County

School was recognised in the tributes paid to her at her funeral at Holy Trinity Church. A link with the very earliest days of the school had been broken.

Miss Blake's successor, Bessie Jones, was officially designated Senior Mistress, and that is what she was – the senior female member of the teaching staff. The Senior Assistant Teacher and the Head's Deputy was Arthur Baker, officially designated such in 1930, and he it was who stood in for the Head from time to time when this became necessary. When Miss Jones in her turn departed, the teaching of geography was taken over by a junior appointee, Miss Watts, and the money saved by doing away with the senior post was allocated to the 2 House Mistresses of the newly formed girls' Houses, Blake and Pinckney.

Two rather humbler figures and one un-humble figure also deserve mention for the places they held in the school's development at this time. The first humble figure was Caretaker Sims. He had been in post since 1923 and remarkably seems to have remained free of criticism. In 1928, however, he threatened to resign because of the excessive work-load to which he was subject – a threat that he rescinded when he was given an assistant. Leonard James was the helper from 1929 to 1933 at 15/- a week, and in 1933 first a lad called Morris and then Cecil Bigwood took over. Sims himself retired the following year, staying on as Groundsman, to be followed as Caretaker by Edward Adams, a former Sergeant's Mess cook, who replaced both Sims and the school cook, Mrs Smith, accepting £2.12.6 for the combined posts. Hard upon these changes came the abolition of the job of Caretaker's Assistant and the appointment in his place of a Charwoman. The other humble figure was Marion Palmer. At the suggestion of HMI, she was appointed the school's first Lab Assistant in 1927, but she was so adept and flexible and willing to tackle tasks beyond the strict limits of her brief that, a couple of years later, she became the Head Master's Secretary at a starting salary of one guinea a week.

Alex Wilkins was in a different league. He had become Secretary to the Governors in 1910. A quarter of a century later, his knowledge of the school in all its aspects was encyclopaedic and his contacts with Governors, local tradesmen, parents, and national bodies all-embracing. He must have been a rock of reliability to the Chairman in particular, but on occasion he could be waspish and direct even to someone as distinguished as Lord Edmond. When the latter suggested yet another meeting of the Governing Body, Wilkins, writing from his office at 10 Masons Hill, indicated that he could well do without such a meeting and the work that it generated. "I have not had a straight week's holiday for the past 20 years," he snapped. And to a parent who had not paid his fees by the due date, he "demands peremptorily" that the money be forthcoming. His crony seems to have been a man called Gough, another solicitor who occupied the same position at Calne as Wilkins did in Bradford. In the early 1930s, the National Economy Campaign saw all teachers taking a salary cut of 10%, a move contested by the teaching unions. Alex Wilkins did not approve of this dissent. He wrote to Gough, telling him that he was thinking of taking a cut in his personal salary "as a gesture against the unpatriotic attitude of the teachers through their Union in the present crisis". He appears to have been meticulous, professionally tidy, enormously hard working – and, perhaps, somewhat difficult and testy when things did not go his way!

Sidney Farrar's arrival as Head was marked by the issuing of a new school prospectus. Dated 1930, it largely reflects the views of his predecessor and gives interesting sidelights on the ethos and organisation of the County School at that time. We have, for example, the praise lavished on the facilities afforded by the gymnasium (quoted elsewhere), and we learn that the games offered were football, cricket, athletics, and rowing for the boys, hockey, tennis, stool-ball, and cricket for the girls. School uniform is carefully described: for the boys a navy-blue blazer, grey flannels (or shorts), black shoes, a school cap, and a blue and gold tie, and for the girls, a tunic, navy-blue serge knickers, white blouse, black stockings and shoes, the school hat, and a girdle in House colours (purple for Pinckney and green for Blake).

The various punishments available (as created by Rosen) were also clearly delineated: detention of 30 or 45 minutes, according to age, for minor offences; having one's name entered in the Appearing Book, with information about the offence being sent to parents; having one's name entered in the Black Book (a far more serious matter that resulted in expulsion should it happen a second time); being On Report to the Headmaster that required teachers to write weekly reports on the quality of work achieved over a period of not less than four weeks; and a warning on the termly report of one's apparent inability to profit from secondary education (failure to improve again proving terminal). There was no corporal punishment. The merits of the Historical, Scientific, Debating, and Dramatic Societies are extolled, and there is mention of the Twenty Club (a badminton club for senior girls to which one could be elected, to a maximum of 20 members), the Boat Club (each boys' House having a boat of four, with four reserves) which was affiliated to the town's Rowing Club, and the Hobbies Club for boys which met twice a week. It is an interesting, clear, and very firm little document.

From the school's opening in 1897, pupil numbers had struggled up from single figures into the 30s, and then from 1902 to about 1913 they remained steadily in the 50s. During the years of the First World War they tripled – to 150 by 1919 – and after a peak of 171 in 1921 they maintained a plateau of about 150 throughout the 1920s. The early 1930s again saw a significant increase which created difficulties for the school. From 162 pupils in 1929, numbers rose to 186 in 193, to 213 in 1934, and to 222 in 1935 – an increase of 27% in 5 years, with a slight annual balance in favour of boys as against girls. This rise was halted in 1935 by the Authority's attempted insistence (by no means always successful) on a maximum intake of 30 annually, and total numbers then fell back somewhat so that in the late 1930s and early 1940s the school roll stabilised at between 170 and 189.

The National Economy Campaign of 1932 brought about the demise of the free place system. In that particular year, 19 free places and 2 Free School Exhibitions were awarded at Bradford on Avon, a pattern that had been set long ago and one with which everyone was comfortable. However, the following year saw the introduction of the County Entrance Examination, with County Junior Scholarships awarded to a number of pupils who had no fees to pay at all. They were not to number more than 30% of the previous year's admissions. In addition to the Junior Scholarships, there were Special Places. These were essentially means tested places for pupils who had performed satisfactorily in the examination, fees being 3, 6, 9, or 12 guineas according to the circumstances of the parents. There were also Travelling Exhibitions (expenses towards the cost of transport) for some of the pupils who lived 3 or more miles from the school.

What sounds in this abbreviated form to have been a relatively simple arrangement was complicated by an arcane system of passes in the Entrance Examination at Classes A, B, C, or D. The benefits for which one was eligible diminished as one dropped from the excellence of a Class A pass to the humiliation of Class D. To be eligible for a Junior Scholarship, for example, a child had to pass in Class A and be assessed at 3 guineas. A lower grade pass allowed one a Special Place, to be paid for according to the parent's income, but Class D pupils were not to be admitted at all. And it was over Class D pupils that the Governors found themselves in hot water in 1933, the first year of the new system. They had the effrontery to offer places at the school to 4 Class D pupils – the most goatish of the goats from whom the sheep had been separated by the examination. Moreover, they foolishly tried to justify their action by sensible argument – a move generally felt to be illogical and totally outrageous. "The 4 Class D pupils were accepted on the evidence of their school records, personal qualities, and the recommendations of their Head Masters", not simply on the results of a written examination. As a consequence of this outlandish concession to good sense, the Governors were rapped over the knuckles and had to promise not to repeat their offence.

The new arrangements for entry to the school began in September 1933. At that time 12 pupils entered on a Scholarship and 34 started as Special Place holders. This new cohort of 46 joined 97 who were already there on free places and 66 who paid the standard fee.

The County School still had the problem of persuading parents to allow their children to stay on to complete the full course and take the School Certificate at the end of it. So, in the period 1926 to 1935, though numbers actually taking the examination increased, it was only from figures in the mid-teens to those in the low 20s, and the number of pupils who passed (the School Certificate being, of course, a pass/fail examination) remained consistently below 20 – 16, 13, 11 in 1927-1929 and 13, 14, 18 for the years 1933-1935. Beyond School Certificate, higher education beckoned. But, in Bradford on Avon, not too assertively. In 1927, for example, the free place of a boy called Greenland was transferred from Bradford to Trowbridge because he wished to prepare for university entrance, and Trowbridge was the place from which that transition could be achieved. It was immediately thereafter that the decision was made to establish a proper Sixth Form at the County School, with Higher School Certificate as the objective. So, in 1929 there were 2 HSC passes from the 4 who entered, 1 more in 1931, 3 out of 3 in 1933, and 1 out of 2 a year later. Such small numbers must have been difficult to accommodate economically, but by 1935 the Head was able to tell his Governors that the school now included a Sixth Form of 18.

Unfortunately, the Preparatory Department must be mentioned again. The establishing of such a class had been tried, and had failed, just after the First World War. There was a further flirtation with the idea in 1927, the rationale for the venture being spelled out clearly in the *Wiltshire Times* in that year:

> "The demand for Preparatory Departments is partly educational and partly social. It should be solely educational. No distinctive curriculum is necessary to prepare children for admission to the County secondary schools, and there would be no educational need for Preparatory Departments if the elementary schools were organised as they should be. But there are serious flaws in organisation, some of which are at present inevitable in many schools in the County, and until better plans are adopted there will remain an educational want for Preparatory Departments in some areas. The social demand is based rightly or wrongly on standards of speech, manners, and habits. In these matters, all elementary schools should be placed beyond criticism, but while the parents of some children are convinced that this has been accomplished they will seek alternative schools. Where the right type of private school does not exist the education of these children will be prejudiced unless Preparatory Schools are maintained."

The article misguidedly cited Trowbridge, Devizes and Chippenham as towns in which Prep Departments had been, it thought, successfully tacked on to the secondary school, and it made clear that such departments must be self-financing.

The fees paid by parents had to cover salaries and maintenance costs, plus £1 per term per child required by the Education Committee for books, apparatus, fuel, light, and use of premises. At Bradford on Avon, this could be achieved if 25 children aged between 8 and 10 each paid 4 guineas a term.

The Governors liked the idea. The precedent of 1917 seems not to have been remembered. Room could be found for such a class when, or if, the town's elementary school children stopped coming to Junction Road for cookery lessons – a practice of many years standing but one that might cease after the elementary school reorganisation that was planned for January 1928. Indeed, if a financial short-fall occurred, perhaps the Foundation could help. All the speculation was abortive, however. By the summer of 1928 only 5 parents had expressed an interest, and the idea was dropped.

But the Prep Department refused to lie down. Four years later, it reared its head for the third time when one of the Governors, Mrs Scarisbrick, again suggested the creation of a junior class as though the notion were new minted instead of the tired old discredited idea that it was in reality. This time, it generated a head of steam that drove it on to realisation within the space of 3 months. Accommodation was a problem. Where could these small children be fitted in? The Congregational Church schoolroom seemed a possibility. Unfortunately, the church's terms (£52 a year, plus rates, plus provision of a Caretaker and of collapsible furniture) were not acceptable. The unhappy solution was that the Prep class was put into what had been the Head Master's room (between the gymnasium and the cookery room), he moved into Miss Jones's room, thus displacing the Senior Mistress, and she had to lose her privacy and make what she could of sharing the Mistresses' room. Marion Cargill from Westbury was appointed from January 1933 to take the class that, at its inception, numbered 11.

On this occasion, the Prep Department lasted for 8 terms, Miss Cargill having to be dismissed in August 1935 when it closed down. And they were 8 terms of the strongest criticism from all quarters – from the Board in London, from HMI, and from the County authorities. Nevertheless, there were 16 in the Department by September 1933 and it was claimed that it was self-supporting. Sadly, the signs were not propitious. The Board of Education's unhappiness with the venture was clearly articulated, as were the views of 2 HMI who visited the class at the end of its first year:

> "[Mr Bridge and Miss Pearson] did not wish to conceal that they did not view the experiment favourably, considering all the circumstances of the case, especially the curtailment of the accommodation of the secondary school itself which it could, and must, involve."

Hilary Chard was a member of the class.

> "I remember Miss Cargill as being quite strict. There was a formal atmosphere for all the lessons, with the emphasis being on the 3 Rs, and there was little or no play. We were separate from the rest of the school, not going into morning assembly and taking our morning break at a different time from the older pupils. Mr Farrar's son was in the class, but he didn't go into the senior school when he was 11."

Numbers fell; the situation was reviewed; vacancies in the class were advertised; numbers fell further; and as early as the autumn of 1934 a conference of parents was called to discuss the future of the Department. The following spring, closure was hinted at, and numbers fell again. And the Prep Department was finally wound up in July 1935, its effects being sold for £2.10.0, and Miss Cargill's dismissal being the occasion for expressions of regret at the sad circumstances of her going. It was a failed experiment that, in the light of history and the school's on-going difficulties over accommodation for senior pupils, should never have been attempted. The little boys and girls did not fit in (literally) – not even on Sports Day:

> "It seemed hard that tumbles in the trials led to the under-eights being excluded from the Blind Ponies."

That, at least, is how *The Gudgeon* reported one obscure Preparatory disaster. It is impossible over half a century later to know how much the Governors' mishandling of this situation, in which the issue of accommodation – rooms and teaching spaces – was central, contributed to the crisis about buildings and the school's viability as a recognised institution which came to a head in 1935. But a crisis is what arose.

The school was already hard pressed before this swelling of numbers in the 1930s. For some time it had consisted of the attractive-looking but small and inconvenient main building, with a number improvements effected, that had opened in 1897; the gymnasium of 1901 and woodwork block of 1905; and the Gallipoli Hut of 1920. This accommodation was quite inadequate for the number of pupils on roll, and the school now found itself in considerable difficulties. Urgent discussion, therefore, with both HMI and the Local Authority about what to do were entered into as early as 1930, the consequence being a sort of mini-inspection of the school in March of that year. In the published report of the inspection, the promising start made by Sidney Farrar was mentioned, Bessie Jones was thought to be "a considerable addition to the strength of the staff", the number of pupils was expected to increase because of the hoped-for development of the Sixth Form, the disbandment of the three year course of Latin-for-all in favour of its being confined to a selected group was approved, and nothing too worrying was found in the few subject areas examined. The inspectors' principal concern, however, was the buildings.

> "The premises present rather a difficult problem. The teaching accommodation in the main building is not very extensive. and the greater part of the classroom accommodation and one staff room are in the hutments. The provision for science work is quite inadequate, the utility of the domestic subjects room is seriously diminished by its use in connection with the school dinner, and the library is also a classroom.
>
> The replacement of the hutments by a permanent building would involve a scheme of some magnitude. The hutments are in good condition and were it merely a question of classroom accommodation they would serve for some years yet, but the best solution of the other questions of accommodation seems likely to be to extend the main buildings so as to include the teaching accommodation and to utilise the hutments for the dining room, kitchen, and manual room, the building now used for manual instruction being converted into a library, a use for which its appearance and size would make it very suitable. How the main buildings can be extended would be for an architect to determine, and it would seem advisable for the Governors to take expert opinion on this matter."

One or two minor improvements to the site had been made in the late 1920s. A new metalled path had been laid to the Gallipoli hut in 1927, and throughout that year discussions had taken place about the building of a new "sanitary block" for the girls at the north east end of the school. Built by Selfe and opened in 1928, this proved to be a useful addition to the facilities. It was a substantial, separate building, close to the back and to the left of the gymnasium, and it left the boys' cloakroom facilities as appearing even more desperately inadequate by comparison. Official stimulus was given to rebuilding plans by the findings of the inspection in 1930, but seven years were to go by and another full inspection take place before the professional help that had been advised was actually sought.

By 1932, what was needed as a replacement for the hutments was estimated as 6 classrooms, a chemistry lab, 2 staff rooms, 2 prefects' rooms, 1 refectory, a boys' dressing room, a book store, and a woodwork room. All that happened on the ground, however, was the erection in that year of an additional cycle shed behind the girls' cloakrooms. The favoured site for the new library had always been the Head Master's former room, but, as we have seen, this was for a time given over to the Prep Department and the provision of a more spacious library had to await that Department's demise. Across Frome Road on Victory

Field, certainly, a new Pavilion was planned and opened, but at Junction Road the accommodation available for the teaching of a rapidly increasing number of pupils was clearly becoming less and less adequate.

In the February of 1935, a letter was received from the Director of Education (Keith Struckmeyer by this time, William Pullinger having died in 1931) asking for a date when representatives of the General Education Committee could meet the Governors to discuss the future of the school. At this meeting, the Local Authority's concern about the state of the County School at Bradford on Avon was made clear. "There was no immediate intention of closing the school," it was said, but something really significant had to be done about its buildings. And it is from about this time that the future of the County School – indeed, its continuing existence in any form – can be said to have been in serious doubt. Everything was put on hold for a time, of course, by the military and political crisis in Europe and by the Second World War, but the need for hard decisions to be taken about the County School, apparent from about 1935, was postponed rather than removed. And this issue re-emerged as a matter of major importance as the War drew to a close.

The Governors had for some time regarded a peculiar advantage that the school possessed, the Endowment, as a Building Fund, but cold water was poured upon this idea. The GEC felt that it could more appropriately be used "to supplement staff, and for other educational purposes" – a sort of occasional amenity fund rather than as a source of funds for new premises. In any event, the Authority saw the school's future in the short term as being one-form entry mixed selective, and it urged that steps be taken to review the whole of the provision so that adequate accommodation, long overdue, was available for such an organisation. As an earnest of good intentions, extensive repairs and redecoration were carried out to the existing buildings, including the Head Master's house, in mid 1935.

More cheerfully, an Open Day was instituted. This was an initiative of Sidney Farrar in the spring of 1933. Parents and friends of the school – many more than had been expected – were welcomed to an exhibition of the school's more visually arresting work and activities. The boys, under Johnny Otter, put on a display of physical exercises, and in the afternoon tea was served and inter-school matches were played.

To go back a year or two in time, things other than worries about the buildings had occupied the school in the Rosen and early-Farrar days. The battle with the Town Football Club continued, their request for the use of Victory Field on Saturday afternoons being (predictably) turned down. Indeed, because of the creation of the House system, the school actually needed more football and hockey pitches itself, and possibilities were investigated. A solution was

Above: Football 1st XI, 1933-1934, winners of the County Cup. Back row, left to right, M Herring, J Gerrish, O Summerell (captain), R Edwards, F Hopkins, B Rowley; front, R Fricker, S Morris, R Comley, I Gerrish, R Gornall.

Below: Principal guests at a meeting of the Old Bradfordians at The Swan in the early 1930s. Seated, left to right, Mrs Farrar, Mrs Scarisbrick; standing, Dr Flemming, Mr Farrar, Mr Edwards, Mr Holbrow, Capt Pinckney, Mr Otter, Canon Clarke.

eventually found by the renting of pitches on the Recreation Ground behind the school from the Committee responsible for their management. And the Old Pupils' Association, moribund at this time, was revived as the Old Bradfordians Association. Lord Fitzmaurice, Miss Blake, and Messrs Crompton and Rosen were given honorary positions, Arthur Baker was busy in its reconstitution and acted as MC at most of its functions, and well attended whist drives and flannel dances were held, with badminton, tennis, rambling, and play-reading attracting their own enthusiasts.

The late 1920s and early 1930s were a depressed time nationally, but, as the above activities suggest, they were years of change and development at the County School.

New technology was welcomed. The Head Master had a wireless. By 1927 the school certainly needed one too, but, until its acquisition in 1929, the pupils had to make do with Mr Rosen's which from time to time he carried over from his house. Then, in 1928, electric light and a telephone were installed. The cost of running power to the school was £69.10.0, with another £25.6.0 for the fittings. The electric supply was extended to the Head Master's house, but the Governors balked at letting him also have a telephone. That was a step too far. His successor got it 6 years later. And the purchase of a school gramophone had to wait until 1931. (A new wireless set and gramophone combined replaced the older machines in 1934!) There is a quaintness today about mention of these ancient pieces of equipment, and electricity, of course, is taken for granted. The impact of its introduction 70 years ago, however, must have been huge, and that first provision of a radio, a gramophone, and a telephone must have altered life dramatically.

With the reorganisation of Bradford's elementary schools from January 1928, speculation arose about whether or not the town's younger girls would continue to trek to Junction Road for their cookery lessons or whether the proposed Cookery Centre at the old boys' school building in Church Road would actually come into being. It did, and the attendance of pupils from the elementary schools at the County School ceased late in 1928. This was a matter of some importance for a school chronically short of room, and it simplified future discussion about extensions which no longer had to be planned for use by very young children. At the other end of the age-range, and harking back to the school's original role as a Technical Institute 30 years earlier, all evening classes were halted in 1928 because of lack of numbers. A half-hearted attempt to restart them in commercial subjects and cookery was made in the autumn of the following year, but with an average attendance of 7, 8, 10, and 10 at the 4 classes the portents were not good and the experiment was abandoned. The educational scene had moved on.

School trips, both recreational and educational, became the norm in these years. The boys, for example, visited the Austin Motor Works at Coventry in 1928; there was an excursion to Windsor which included a viewing of the state apartments at the Castle; the Head, together with Baker, Percival, and Miss Allwright took 21 pupils and 5 former pupils to Paris at Whitsun, 1931; Johnny Otter and Arthur Percival went camping to Conway with a group of boys; and a different sort of trip was that enjoyed by 2 pupils who went to Geneva to the League of Nations summer camp in 1935. This was a direct result of May Priestley's forming a Junior Branch of the League of Nations Union which soon boasted a membership of 100. The Governors assisted pupils' ability to travel by voting a grant for the poorest to enable them to take part in foreign exchange visits.

Dinners were introduced in 1930 at a cost of 9d a head, and by 1933 some 35 pupils each day were availing themselves of the facility in the cookery room. A further 85 a day preferred to bring their own lunches from home. The number of accidents occurring at school, however, was becoming a matter for concern. Within a very short space of time in this latter year, Meta Mattock, Mary Moore, Harold Coupland, and a boy called Booker had all come to grief and there was concern that parents were tending to look to hold the school liable when, legally, there was no such liability. Poor Booker "fell under a car whilst cycling round the corner of Trowbridge Road" but neither the severity nor the nature of his injuries was specified.

Concern of a different sort was raised by a rumour, heard by Mr Farrar and reported officially to the Governing Body, that "the reputation of the old pupils employed in the County Offices was a very low one and that they were slovenly and unable to express themselves coherently...." (This has a satisfyingly modern ring to it!) The Head Master fought back, and with commendable initiative contacted the County Treasurer, the County Medical Officer, and the County Surveyor, all of whom saw former pupils of the County School as giving "excellent service" and showing "a high standard of efficiency". The rumour was effectively scotched. Continuing success in the Wiltshire Music Festival, and individual distinction like that earned by Michael Cousins in the Civil Service Examination, were more typical of the school's standing in those years just before and after 1930.

Indeed, positive things were happening on many fronts. The Chairman, for example, at his own expense, had New Forest gravel laid over a swampy part of the girls' playground to make it more usable. He also gave a number of water colours for corridor and classroom decoration, and Alfred Frankell donated a complete *Encyclopaedia Britannica* to the Library. The school prefects became noticeable for their newly designed badges; a further Honours Board was purchased, the old one being full, and this necessitated the removal of a collection of war trophies which were offered to the British Legion; and (a sign of the times) the boxing instructor, Mr Finney, was allowed to put on a course in the Gymnasium one evening a week for the local unemployed.

Henry Rosen was Head until 1929, and Sidney Farrar thereafter. The real power, however, lay with the Governing Body, the Chairman of whom was Lord Edmond Fitzmaurice. In 1935, he began his 31st year as Chairman of Governors (or, more accurately, his 30th as for one year he had been Chairman of the Technical Education Committee). As a young man of 29, he had had a serious accident, the consequences of which were to affect him in later life. Illness caused him to abandon his career in national politics in 1909, but throughout the rest of his long life, increasingly racked by physical infirmity, he exerted a beneficent and liberal influence in local government, and on education in particular, his work on behalf of individual Wiltshire boys and girls often being undertaken without publicity.

His Deputy and close friend on the Governing Body of the County School for a long time had been Dr Flemming; John Thornton in 1929 and Canon W H M Clarke in 1934 succeeded Flemming. Though Lord Fitzmaurice never ceased to interest himself actively in the affairs of the school, as age and sickness overtook him the Deputy Chairmen had increasingly to involve themselves in day-to-day matters of school management. His death in his ninetieth year, therefore, was no real surprise, but it caused great sadness to all who had known him in his many roles – local, national, and international. He had been ill for a long time, very ill indeed for three weeks, and unconscious for several days when he died at 2.30 a.m. on 21 June 1935 at his home at Leigh, Bradford on Avon.

At the final Speech Day, held on 30 November 1979, the guest of honour was the Earl of Shelburne, and he used the occasion to speak of the life and work of the man who founded the school. There can be no better way to conclude this first part of its history than to quote from what he said.

> "Edmond Fitzmaurice was born the second son of the 4th Lord Lansdowne in 1846; he died only 44 years ago in 1935. His great-grandmother married Napoleon's son. Therefore, within one man's lifetime, a bridge spans a period of over 200 years, and the distant past of the French Revolution becomes almost as yesterday. As second son, he had the advantage of choice of any career, but the disadvantage of limited means. He was educated at Eton and won a scholarship to Trinity College, Cambridge. At Cambridge he revived the University Football Club and followed Sir Charles Dilke as President of the Cambridge Union. At this point, he was at the cross-roads of life…. Torn between taking silk at the Bar or entering politics, he chose the latter, and in 1869 and for the next 16 years represented Calne as its Liberal MP.

On being elected, he moved from his family home, Bowood, and bought Leigh House above the town.... His first political appointment was Private Secretary in the Home Office, and it was during that time that he briefly fell out with Gladstone (who was a close friend throughout their lives) on the abolition of university tests.... Before the Gladstone government fell in 1885, Edmond Fitzmaurice was appointed Under-Secretary of State for Foreign Affairs under Lord Granville, the Foreign Secretary. During these 16 years, his main interests were foreign affairs, local government, and education. Particularly, being a scholar, I suspect he appreciated his good fortune in having had a first-class education and wanted everyone else to have the same chance. He was not only a generous benefactor, but was also an extremely shrewd politician.

For the next 13 years, due to ill-health, Edmond retired from national politics. But although not able to compete at Westminster, he turned his energies towards local government. County Councils were created in 1884. By 1896 he had succeeded Mr Fuller – whose family still lives at Neston and Charfield – as Chairman of the County Council, a position he held until 1906. It was during his first year as Chairman of the County Council that [this] school was founded.

In 1898 at a by-election at Cricklade, he was returned as Liberal MP, and so once more entered national politics. The Liberal Party was still out of office and remained so until 1905."

The Earl of Shelburne then goes on to explain how Campbell-Bannerman, the Prime Minister, surprisingly felt unable in 1905 to offer Edmond Fitzmaurice a Cabinet post in the new Liberal government but offered him a peerage, his proposal being for a purely courtesy title as, of course, Fitzmaurice was a second son. ("I must decline. My modest fortune, that of a younger son, is not sufficient to warrant acceptance.") But after much to-ing and fro-ing, he accepted both the peerage and the responsibility for answering on foreign affairs in the House of Lords. Three years later, in 1908, Asquith, who followed Campbell-Bannerman as Prime Minister, made him Chancellor of the Duchy of Lancaster, and he became a member of the Privy Council. Unfortunately, ill-health again forced his resignation a few months later.

Shelburne then closed his account of his great-uncle like this:

"Whilst in retirement, during the ravages of the First World War, he received two letters which I should like to quote. One was from Private Heavyside, Hut 24, Camp 7, Codford, Wiltshire. It was dated 10 October 1916:
'My Lord: You will see by the above address that I am now in the army. I have been successful in joining the Royal Army Medical Corps and I am stationed at Codford. It was largely due to the fact that I possess the certificate for rendering

first aid that I was able to join the Corps that I most desired. I attended a class under Dr Flemming last winter in your school, and this is only one of the many proofs of the usefulness of your magnificent gift to the town. I am most grateful to you, my Lord, for your kindness to me in the past, and your school has been most useful to me to help me carry out my duties to my King and country. Yours respectfully, Private Heavyside.'

A second letter, of December 1916, was from 2nd Lieutenant Stanley A Moore, who was in the Second Signal Corps of the Royal Engineers:

'I find the French that I was taught at the Secondary School extremely useful to me. If one is able to speak French, it obviates many difficulties and makes things very much easier for one. My work at present is cable laying and laying telephone lines. I am with the Signal Corps and I like the work immensely. Here again, my knowledge of electricity and magnetism which I gathered at school is extremely useful. I motorcycled about 20 miles, which journey took 2 1/2 hours through the mud to see my brother Howard, who was a clerk with Mr Compton, the solicitor. He is a sergeant in the 6th Wilts Regiment. I was just in time to see him before he left for 10 days' leave in England.'"

So Lord Shelburne's account not only draws attention to his ancestor's distinguished career in national politics but also, and rather poignantly, highlights the practical value of his later involvement in education to the young people of Bradford on Avon.

Left: Canon W H M Clarke, Chairman of Governors, 1935-1936. This portrait used to hang in the entrance hall of the school.

Below: Speech Day, 1937. Dr Flemming (Chairman of Governors), Mr Farrar (Headmaster), and the Bishop of Salisbury (principal guest).

Mainly About Buildings
The Fitzmaurice Grammar School:
1936-1938

A SUB-COMMITTEE OF THE GOVERNORS was formed on the death of Lord Edmond Fitzmaurice to discuss ways in which funds could be raised so that his name could be permanently commemorated and linked with the school. The first decision it made was that from 1 January 1936 the County School should be renamed the Fitzmaurice Grammar School, Bradford on Avon. A further decision was that a bronze tablet recording his services and benefactions should be placed in the school's hall over the front entrance. And both these decisions were implemented.

The tablet, cast by the Frome Metal Workers Guild, was unveiled by the Marquess of Bath on 17 June 1936, and read:

> In grateful memory of the Right Honourable Lord Fitzmaurice of Leigh, Chairman of the Governors of this school for thirty years until his death, in his 90th year, on June 23rd 1935.
> By his initiative the school was established, by his generosity it was extended and endowed, and by his interest and counsel its growth was guided and its traditions founded.
> *How high a lot to till*
> *Is left to each man still.*

Sadly, this large tablet, with its quotation from Matthew Arnold (and containing an odd inaccuracy), was lost and probably destroyed during the conversion of the old school buildings into retirement homes in the 1980s.

From the money raised for the Memorial Fund, enough remained to buy a clock for the school library and a portrait of Lord Fitzmaurice enlarged from that taken by Mr Lambert of Milsom Street, Bath, in 1911. The clock has gone, but the portrait, after hanging for many years in the entrance hall of the school, is now in the vestibule of the Fitzmaurice Suite at Leigh Park Hotel, Lord Edmond's old home.

The new Chairman of Governors was Canon W H M Clarke, but within a year he too had died and he was replaced by Dr Flemming to whom the guidance of the school fell yet again. Dr Flemming, with his Vice Chairman, who from 1940 was G C V Holbrow, saw the school through the wartime years to the reconstituted Governing Body of 1947.

Lord Fitzmaurice's death in 1935 caused the postponement of Speech Day for that year, thus breaking a tradition going back beyond the start of the First World War. Always held in the gymnasium just before the school broke up for the Christmas holidays, it was Prizegiving in the early days, and Lord Fitzmaurice was expected to preside. Unfortunately, he missed many of those celebrations because of illness, but when he was able to be present he always spoke lengthily and authoritatively about some aspect of the educational scene, nationally or locally. The Head Master then gave his annual report – on both the school and the technical institute initially, though the latter soon dropped from consideration – and the Guest presented the prizes. Year by year the list of those thus honoured was a roll-call of the wives of the local gentry: Mrs Moulton, Mrs Hobhouse, Lady Cairns, Lady Guillamore, Mrs Kennard, Mrs Littleton Webber, the Hon Mrs Hanbury Tracey, Lady Alexandra Palmer, Lady Methuen, Lady Gatacre, Miss Talbot of Lacock Abbey....They always distributed the prizes with grace and assurance and followed this with an address on some wholesome and improving theme. Votes of thanks directed at the principal participants followed, and the proceedings closed with music and song. The pattern was unvarying, except in two respects. In 1936 the event moved to March, before reverting to Christmas again in 1943. Indeed, in that year there were two Speech Days, one in March and another in December so that the pattern for the future could be set. The second change was the invitation of guests who were more nationally significant figures, like the Bishop of Salisbury and A G Street, or personalities from the wider world of education and the universities.

In the years immediately prior to the Second World War there were a few staff changes – but not many. Leslie Kernutt who was in charge of English went off to Harrow Weald County School in 1936 and was replaced by Wilfred ("Tom") Eastwood (taking the name of Tom, according to Jo Uncles, from that of the Fool in *King Lear*); Misses Yates and Watts left in order to get married, their places being taken by Miss Munford (who later became Mrs Courtney) and Doris Gare; and May Priestley moved to a teaching post in Huddersfield, leading to the appointment of Margaret Capon. She stayed at Bradford until early 1939 when (another loss to the profession through matrimony) she was replaced by Phyllis Holder. French, girls' physical education and games, geography, and English were the subject areas affected. And Sidney Farrar was taken seriously ill during the summer holidays of 1936, eventually recovering fully but allowing Arthur

Baker to act as Head in his place for the first term of the 1936-37 school year.

There were other changes of personnel, too. Mrs Hazell and Mr Hayter, as Cook and Caretaker respectively, took over from Adams, who had combined the two jobs, in 1936, and the long-serving Marion Palmer, after 2 years as Lab Assistant and 10 as Head Master's Secretary, gave way to Constance Dallimore in 1939. More exciting was the storm of protest that arose over the decision of summer 1937 that, as from that September, pupils from Melksham were not to be admitted to the grammar school at Bradford. The same ruling applied to the Boys' High School in Trowbridge. Melksham children would "for the present" have only the option of the Trowbridge Girls' High School or the secondary school in Chippenham. Much agitation resulted, especially from the Melksham parents, and after a great deal of huffing and puffing the Authority relented in time for the 1938 intake again to have its full range of options. (The Fitzmaurice Governors noted with satisfaction the admission of 5 pupils from Melksham in that year!) Atworth pupils suffered in a rather different way. Again from the September of 1937 "no conveyance" was to be provided for them. They were to get to school by bike, or, if physically unable to do that, a lodging allowance would be considered. How, and when, this restriction was removed is not clear.

Overshadowing all else in these immediately prewar years, however, was the uncompromising report of the three HMI who visited the Fitzmaurice Grammar School in March 1937. General inspections were events dreaded (quite unnecessarily) by pupils and anticipated with some apprehension (reasonably enough) by the teaching staff. They provoked a spasmodic tightening of the grip, a (sometimes belated and forlorn) attempt at efficiency and enthusiasm, a tidying of the books, and they provided in their reports a useful snapshot of how a school looked at a given moment in a ten- or fifteen-year span. At Bradford on Avon there had been full inspections in 1901, 1904, 1908, 1912, 1923, and now again in 1937, and if it is remarkable for anything the report on this latter inspection is unusual in the frankness of its remarks about the buildings that formed the Fitzmaurice Grammar School.

In other sections it was a most positive report. Sidney Farrar received generous praise. "He has served the school well in every direction, and in doing so has earned the confidence and high regard of parents, staff and pupils." The teaching staff, too, passed muster, despite, in several cases, their lack of experience. "Youth predominates, six being between twenty-three and twenty-eight years of age." And it is remarked that "it is quite in accordance with modern practice that well qualified young teachers in rural schools, after serving for two or three years in their first posts, should seek greater responsibilities elsewhere." The specialist teaching in almost all subjects was commended, a consistent problem being the necessary handing over of some classes to non-specialist teachers. Maths in particular was mentioned as having made great strides since 1923.

By 1937 there was a small Sixth Form, but HSC and university entrance was only possible on the arts' side, the restricted lab facilities not permitting it in science. In theory, a fast, four-year track was possible for the most able up to GCE, but in practice those who followed it were very few indeed – only 8 in 3 years – and the recommendation was that it should be dropped. Another curricular difficulty was the place of Latin. It was offered as an alternative to physics in the third year of schooling, the result being that the boys generally did physics and the girls Latin. Otherwise, the science offered for GCE was general science for all, covered by a five year course. Jo Uncles was in the Sixth Form at this time, and she says:

> "The Sixth Form was very small, perhaps five or six of us, and we lived in the Library that was between the cookery room and the gymnasium. I think that though the school itself was also small, we were quite up-to-date, with girls unusually being able to study physics after the 4th year split into science and arts subjects. Mr Otter was very popular. He was an excellent teacher and, in between his spells of throwing chalk at people, he made the lessons come alive by the way in which he presented things. He later married a girl from the school – Edwina Dean."

The number of pupils admitted to the school annually had, by 1937, tended to vary rather significantly. In 1933 and 1934 two forms were accepted, but experience had proved that not all the pupils thus admitted had been able to profit from the academic education offered by a selective school. In 1935 and 1936 there was only one form of entry, not because of the experience of previous years but simply because there was no room in the building for more. The conclusion reached by the inspectors, therefore, was that "a substantial two-stream school could not be expected". When they left, the boys and girls of Fitzmaurice, about half of whom came from the town itself, tended to find work locally in clerical posts, engineering, "and a variety of useful trades", with an average of about one every year going on to university and one more going to training or agricultural college.

When they came to describe the accommodation in which the above activities were carried out, however, the inspectors were frank and uncompromising in their condemnation. They said:

> "The best impression of the school is obtained from the outside. Of solid stone construction and dignified well-balanced design, the main building is set back

Girls' hockey XI in late 1930s. Back row, left to right, Priscilla Rawlings, Pat Brosnan, Evelyn Gregory, Joan Webber, Miss Munford, Joan Hitchcock, Margaret Ralph, Enid Sealy; Front, Margery Hobbs, Alma Comley, Marion Falkner, Enid Dainton.

from the street and approached by a flight of steps. Behind this the ground rises, and a further flight of steps and covered way give access to the hut-classrooms, built as extensions some time before the inspection of 1923.

Inside the building, no close scrutiny is needed to reveal its defects. It would be both unjust and unnecessary to compare it with more recently built or extended secondary schools. The only fair criterion is its adequacy for the secondary school education of the pupils, and here it is defective in several directions."

This was a pretty fair description of Fitzmaurice Grammar School in 1937 (and, indeed, it would have been appropriate at any time between 1920 and 1945), and the inspectors then went on to enumerate the school's shortcomings in depressing detail. In summary:

a) there were insufficient classrooms;
b) the four hut classrooms were small, old, and badly ventilated – the three others were small and old-fashioned – there was no classroom

The School Laboratory

for the Sixth Form which lived in the library;
c) there was only one, inadequate laboratory;
d) the gymnasium doubled as a hall – as a gym it was gloomy and inadequate – as a hall it would hold the whole school – it acted as a passageway to the hutments;
e) the domestic science room was small and ill-equipped – it also served as a kitchen and a dining room;
f) the Head Master's room was too small;
g) the Mistresses' room was formerly part of the art room with access only via the art room – the Senior Mistress had a small compartment off this room;
h) the Masters' room was a shabby section of the hutments;
i) the boys' toilets were sub-standard – the girls' were newer but too small.

The conclusion the inspectors reached after this dismal catalogue was that, in spite of the great difficulties under which they taught and learnt, both staff and pupils were doing far better in all sorts of ways than might have been expected. Nevertheless,

"Various sections of this report make it clear that the school is heavily handicapped by inadequate buildings.... There are....definite limits to mastery over adverse surroundings, and these limits have been reached. In the present state the school may go on, as an institution, for some years. But it is no longer moving with the times. The inspectors are fully aware of the dilemma confronting the Governors, and sympathise with them in their desire to provide the amenities which are lacking and thus preserve the traditions which have grown up around their school."

Prior to the official report's being published, the inspectors met the school Governors in the presence of Keith Struckmeyer and his officers, and the senior Inspector, Mrs Parkes, "addressed [them] at considerable length, outlined the nature of the report HMI would make in about two months time, and stressed the inspectors' opinion as to the insufficient and unsuitable building accommodation". The school "was hardly a fit place to ask staff to work in". To their credit, the Governors moved quickly – though perhaps they had little choice. Within 6 months, a Special Buildings Committee had been formed; Dr Flemming had discussions with HMI which persuaded him that the school's continuing existence was very genuinely in doubt; meetings took place between the Governors and education officers about ways in which an escape could be effected from the accommodation cul-de-sac in which the school now found itself; and a report was commissioned by the Buildings Committee on what was needed either a) to convert the existing buildings to a two-form entry school which would meet the Board of Education requirements, or b) to create an acceptable one-form entry school capable of eventual extension to two forms of entry. This report was the professional advice first suggested all of seven years earlier.

W H Watkins FRIBA from Belcombe Court, himself a Governor, drew up the required report. It, together with associated drawings and plans, was presented to the Director and the GEC and, apart from a few minor criticisms, was accepted in principle. The scheme was for the creation of a mixed secondary school with accommodation for 240 pupils (that is a single-form entry, with 8 classes of 30). The existing building would be retained in its entirety and a substantial new wing built at the rear of the site, facing SSE. The alterations planned to the existing buildings were:

a) an extension to the library;
b) the provision of a larder and a store for the Domestic Science room;
c) the conversion of the classroom at the front to the Head Master's room;

d) the conversion of the existing Head Master's room to a waiting room;
e) the ending of the use of the gymnasium, effectively by now an assembly hall, as a gymnasium;
f) the demolition of the boys' lavatories and cloakrooms;
g) the extension of the chemistry lab on the first floor and the provision of a prep room and store;
h) the extension of the girls' cloakroom and lavatory accommodation; and
i) the demolition of all the temporary buildings on the site.

The plan also envisaged a new wing containing a gymnasium with associated changing room and showers, four classrooms, and a handicraft room, and there would be a new boys' cloakroom and lavatory block, with staff rooms and lavatories on the first floor. Because of the rising ground, the floor of this new block would be between the ground and first floor levels of the existing building and it would be connected to it at both levels. And Mr Watkins listed the advantages of the layout as follows:

a) there would be minimum interference with existing permanent structures;
b) there would be no interference with specialist rooms like those for art, chemistry, and domestic science;
c) easy circulation was allowed for, with proper supervision of the pupils possible in any part of the school; and
d) the best possible use had been made of the high ground at the rear of the site which was not suitable as a recreational area.

It was a bold plan, but not perfect. The sloping site was not ideal for such a development, but without fiddling about with huts or temporary buildings, it provided all the accommodation needed for a small mixed secondary school. Perhaps, as Mr Struckmeyer pointed out, some of the classrooms were too small, plans for the library, cookery room, and hall were still inadequate, and there was no secretary's room, but, these points apart, everybody liked the proposals.

So, by April 1938, a year after the inspectors' traumatic visit, a plan for the rebuilding of the Fitzmaurice Grammar School existed and was, in large part, accepted. Unfortunately a quick implementation of the plan was impossible as the GEC already had expensive commitments elsewhere, and three years at least was going to be needed before the scheme could be considered. But with political tension building throughout Europe and with only little more than a year to go before war was actually declared, everybody soon had far more to worry about than the rebuilding of the secondary school at Bradford on Avon. A resolution of this particular crisis, therefore, like many others, was postponed for the duration and nothing more was heard of major building developments until hostilities ceased. Watkins was congratulated on the acceptance of his plans for the rebuilding of St George's Hospital, but his plans for Bradford secondary school were put away to mature.

They were briefly dusted off in 1943 when the Governors were reminded of the still urgent need for refurbished and extended boys' toilet accommodation, better laboratory facilities, and a new kitchen and dining room. These were the three areas of acutest need, the boys' toilets, tucked away towards the back of the main building, being ludicrously and noisomely cramped, with the single laboratory on the first floor an unarguably gross underprovision. The kitchen and dining room, in fact, materialised shortly afterwards, but discussions had to be re-opened on the other matters after the War was over.

It is a reflection of the sort and size of the concerns that the school had over very many years that an account of its history should be so dominated by a dissection of the problem of its buildings.

Aerial view of the school showing, from left to right, the girls' cloakroom of 1928, the gymnasium of 1901 added to the main building, and the woodwork room of 1905, with the Gallipoli hut of 1920 and the dining room of 1945 in the background.

The Second World War
The Fitzmaurice Grammar School:
1939-1947

THE GREAT WORRY FOR PARENTS, staff, and Governors from the 1920s onwards was failure of the buildings to match the number and needs of the pupils enrolled at the school. This overshadowed all other considerations.

A much less crucial problem was that of the number of pupils opting to stay for school dinners. They were falling, and the lower they fell the more expensive did the dinners have to be to cover the full cost of their preparation. In 1938 they cost 8d. The problem was County-wide rather than local, and there was a danger of the service collapsing altogether. One consequence of the War, however, was a huge increase in the demand for the provision of meals at school and so the problem solved itself within a year or two. Another, purely local, difficulty centred on what to do about the Free School Exhibitions. These had been awarded for many years but by 1937 had outlived their usefulness. They were, therefore, converted in 1938 to Maintenance Awards (4 in this first year) and in 1939 this help was extended to cover the actual payment of fees where individual cases warranted it. (Six pupils benefited initially.)

With the imminence of War with Germany, the Director of Education, Keith Struckmeyer, became Keith Innes. For Hilary Chard (now Mrs Lywood), however, the national crisis meant the dashing of a long cherished hope. Cricket was one of the girls' major games, and traditionally they had held an annual match against the girls of Stonar, the highlight being the cream tea given to all the participants by Sir George Fuller afterwards at his home at Great Chalfield. Hilary's future happiness depended on her selection for this match, but the War, which put an end to so many good things, came too quickly for her. Such frivolities were abandoned for the duration and her dreams remained unfulfilled.

Sidney Farrar left in 1939. He had been at Bradford for a little under 10 years. Perhaps the smallness and the uncertain future of the grammar school persuaded him to look for something more challenging; at any rate, he went at Easter, like his predecessor, to the secondary school at Chippenham. He was followed as Head at Fitzmaurice by Geoffrey Rowntree – "Gummy" Rowntree. There were over 400 applicants for the post, one of whom again was Arthur Baker, but on this occasion he was not shortlisted. Rowntree was Senior History

Master at Derby School and his headship at Bradford on Avon ran for the duration of the Second World War and just beyond. He received the assurance (which was important in view of the the then current uproar about the viability of the school's buildings) that "the new Head Master might feel safe in his position for a period of 5 years at least". Sidney Farrar was presented with a portable typewriter in recognition of all he had done for the school, and he in turn gave three water colours by contemporary artists to mark his headship.

Geoffrey Rowntree's staff stayed remarkably stable for the whole of the War. Arthur Baker, Harry Brosnan, Arthur Percival, and Dorothy Burgoine were, of course, fixtures. Phyllis Holder, Doris Gare, and Winifred Munford (Mrs Courtney), also remained throughout. Johnny Otter and Tom Eastwood were called up, but their replacements – Mrs Stein and Megan Williams (Mrs Yelland) – proved to be durable. Only Mrs Rees left (in 1941), to be replaced by Dora Collins (Mrs Neathey).

Perhaps it was not quite as straightforward as this. Baker actually rejoined his regiment, at the age of 57, at the outbreak of War, but returned to teaching because of ill health a year later. Miss Collins stood in for him for that year before (as Mrs Neathey) she took over from Anne Rees in Domestic Science. And when Otter went into the RAF in 1941, the post in maths was taken, first and very briefly, by Loeb David Maier ("a refugee"), and then by Elise Stein for virtually the duration of the War. Two more very short-term appointments followed when she left in 1945 before Johnny Otter was able to secure his release from the services in June 1946.

In full, then, the staff changes for the period 1936-1947, with married names for the ladies, were:

Head Master:	Sidney Farrar (1929-1939), Geoffrey Rowntree (1939-1947);
Science:	Arthur Baker (1905-1945), Ellis Darby (1945-);
Woodwork and PE:	Harry Brosnan (1918-1945), Cyril Copland (1945-);
Art:	Dorothy Burgoine (1919-);
History:	Arthur Percival (1921-);
Maths:	Johnny Otter (1932-1947);
English:	Leslie Kernutt (1931-1936), Tom Eastwood (1936-1947), Megan Yelland (1947), Catherine Proudlock (1947-);
Dom Sci:	Anne Rees (1933-1941), Dora Neathey (1941-1947), Minnie Rhodes (1947-);
French:	May Priestley (1933-1936), Winifred Courtney (1936-1945), John Smith (1945-);
Geography:	Ruth Watts (1933-1937), Margaret Capon (1936-1939), Phyllis Holder (1939-1946), Margaret Prince (1946-);

Eng/PE/French: Joan Yates (1935-1936), Doris Gare (1937-1945),
Jean Davis (1945-1947), Barbara Foulds (1947-).

Mrs Stein's daughter, Ilse, was a pupil in the school when her mother taught there and she remembers her teachers very clearly.

> "The Senior Mistress was Miss Burgoine, whom my mother and all the staff called Burg. She was by far the oldest of the seven women – gentle, kindly, quirkily humorous. She taught art with skill and patience. Because I was a real flop at copying clusters of deadly nightshade, I was allowed to drop art [for German], so my appreciation of Miss Burgoine did not happen until the Lower Sixth....There the history of art classes were brilliant. I still cannot see paintings by Cimabue or Giotto without drawing on those early talks illustrated not by slides but by picture postcards passed from hand to hand.
> Miss Burgoine lived at The Old House in Silver Street with Mrs Courtney, who was my mother's closest friend on the staff. She had been Winifred Munford until she married Gerry Courtney who was then in the Royal Air Force and the object of her constant anxiety. She was an excellent French teacher.
> The other person who taught French was Miss Gare, whose main responsibility was for girls' games and gym. She was not my favourite person because I was an inordinate physical coward; she clearly knew, and was merciless. Tuesdays and Thursdays were clouded by the dreaded horse and wallbars. On the hockey pitch I managed to devise strategies to disguise the fact that I was running away from the ball and not after it. Tennis was much better, but not till the Fifth Form.
> Boys' games and gym were taught by Mr Brosnan who also took woodwork. It must have been hard on the boys, in that non-egalitarian age, to be taught entirely by women and elderly men....On the other hand, it made for a very stable staff. During my four years at the school, nobody left, though three of the women did get married.
> Mick Williams, a sparkling, attractive, diminutive Jessie Matthews lookalike, who taught English, married a very tall, thin man, also in the Air Force, whom she described as 'yards and yards of nothing', and thus became Mrs Yelland. He came back after the War and they moved to Plymouth.
> Miss Holder taught geography. After a long friendship with one of the town's doctors, Dr Gibson, she married his partner, John Gilpin, and together they moved down to a new practice for him in Exeter at the end of the War.
> Miss Collins who taught domestic science married a garage mechanic called Peter Neathey, who joined the army, and (I think) did not come back. But if I am right and he was killed, it must have been towards the end of the war, because I clearly remember him around on leave in his khaki for quite a while. My own relationship

with Mrs Neathey was clouded by the fact that I once lied to her in the matter of having scrubbed a table, which was plainly dry and therefore unscrubbed, after cookery. I could never look her in the eye again, which was awkward because she and Miss Holder lived next door at 28 Newtown, to our 30, and they and my mother were friendly, in and out of each other's houses.

The remaining men on the staff were Mr Percival and Mr Baker. Mr Percival taught history. I suppose we must have done some written work – essays and such – but I don't recall. What I do remember is that he was a brilliant raconteur who made history lessons into a tapestry of extraordinary events and eccentric people. We sat and listened, entranced, by the hour."

(Howard Neathey, known to his friends as Peter, was taken prisoner at Arnhem and repatriated after the War.)

The years during which Ilse Stein was at school were the wartime years when everything was subject to change. But in the last year of peace many things that happened in, and to, the school had a familiar ring. The guest at Speech Day, which was in March, was HMI Mrs Parkes, standing in at the last minute for A G Street who was ill. The statutory 30 pupils had been admitted in September – of whom 12 had passed at Class A, 11 at B, and 7 at C; of these, 9 were awarded County Junior Scholarships and 21 Special Places; 3 were assessed at 12 guineas, 1 at 9 guineas, 2 at 6 guineas, and 24 at 3 guineas. There were 172 pupils on roll; 14, typically, were in the Sixth Form which had been established some years earlier, with a few aiming for HSC. The boys wore their grey flannels, blue blazers and pullovers, and the girls their felt hats, navy blazers and regulation navy overcoats. Blue was the school's colour. Roma Alexander, age 11, began at her new school in September 1939 and well remembers the uniform:

> "....white blouse, navy gymslip – the lovely school badge with the gudgeon on it sewn on the front and, yes, navy blue interlock knickers, black woollen stockings with sensible black shoes and a horrible felt hat with the school band round it....My satchel was on one shoulder and (here the war is already intruding on my reminiscences) my gas mask, in its awkward cube-shaped box, on the other."

Because the gymnasium had been blacked out, evening Keep Fit classes became possible again in the winter months, taken by Mr Otter for the men and Miss Whitehouse, a visiting instructress, for the ladies, and a little genteel haggling went on about the cost of continuing to hire the hockey pitch behind the school. £8 was extortionate; the pitch must be given up unless the Trustees of the Recreation Ground would consider something like £5; well, £6 was settled on, and everyone was happy. And school dinners sank deeper into debt.

For everyone, War meant air raids and gas masks, sirens, shelters and pillboxes, sandbags, black-out, conscription, and camouflage, evacuees, the ARP and Home Guard, shortages of almost everything, the requisitioning of buildings, GIs, Digging for Victory, and Spitfire Weeks. Bradford on Avon experienced all these novelties, with some more than others affecting the boys, girls and staff of the Fitzmaurice Grammar School.

A young entrepreneur, Joe Lucas, did his bit to raise funds for the local Spitfire Week by organising an aircraft recognition competition, but he recalls, over half a century later, that it was not a success. Despite a prize of one dozen eggs at a time of food rationing, he attracted only one entrant.

The organisation of air raid precautions took place as early as 1935, with an Act to give them official validity two years later, and in 1938 the staff of the school were lectured on procedures by the ARP Officer. Late that same year, the school was closed for 2 days so that preparations could be made for the reception of children from London during the Crisis. 1939 saw blackout fitted to doors and windows, walls of sandbags erected to give added protection to the building, and 2 stirrup pumps purchased to deal with incendiary bombs. Brigadier Kelly was the County ARP Organiser, and he visited the school to give his advice. Trenches and shelters were not needed, but in the event of an air raid "children were to be distributed in the ground floor rooms and made to sit on the floors with their backs to the walls, and such children as could reach their homes in five minutes were to be sent home". However, this proved to be impracticable. Disruption to the work of the school was huge. At the end of 1940, therefore, a different plan was adopted. Work was to continue after the air raid siren had sounded, no pupils were to be sent home, and they only moved to positions of safety when warning of imminent danger was given. This was by arrangement with Mr Chrystal, Works Manager at Spencer Moulton. He had a spotter on the roof of Abbey Mill who raised a red flag, visible at the school, when danger threatened.

Betty Knowles remembers these comings and goings. She was a pupil from 1940 to 1947 – and then went on to teacher training college, later becoming one of the last Pupil Teachers to practise at Christ Church Junior School.

> "The war brought various shortages; clothing coupons were introduced and uniform regulations were relaxed a little – out went gym slips, large hats, and black stockings, to be replaced by pinafore dresses, berets, and a choice of socks or stockings. The St Trinians look disappeared during war-time, never to return....During my first year we were allocated 'safe' areas in which to shelter during air-attacks. Our first post was sitting on the floor under the windows in the Head's study with our backs to the wall. As there were only ten girls, we had just enough space. Where the boys went, or, indeed, the rest of the school,

Fitzmaurice Grammar School
Bradford-on-Avon, Wilts.

Report for Term ending **April 4th.** 1939

Name of Pupil **Benjamin John** Form **II** House **Fitzmaurice**

Age of Pupil **11.9** Average Age of Form **11.6**

Number of Half-days absent, up to **Mar. 17th.** 1939 ; **0**

Subject.	Class. (See note below)	Remarks.	Initials of Subject Teacher.
English	C	Quite good.	D.G.
History	C	Very fair.	A.P.
Geography	C	Works well	M.C.
Scripture			
Mathematics	C	Good.	H.W.B.
Trigonometry			
Gen. Science	C	Good but erratic	A.H.R.
French	C	Fair	W.R.M.
Manual Work	C	Good	N.W.B.
Domestic Science			
Art	C	Fair. Has tried hard.	D.L.B.
Physical Training	C	Good	J.O.
Swimming			
Games	C	Fairly good.	H.W.B.

GENERAL REPORT:

Very fair.

J. Otter .... House { Master. / Mistress. }

S. Tanar M.A. .... Headmaster.

Next Term begins **May 2nd.**

NOTE.—The pupils' work in each Subject is assessed by one of five letters. These letters and their interpretation are given below:

A Outstandingly and unusually good.   C Average.
B Good—above the average.   D Below average and not altogether satisfactory.
E Very poor and of unusually low standard.

A and E will be given only in unusual cases; in the interpretation of the other letters regard should be paid to the pupil's actual achievement and aptitude, and to the teacher's comments.

THE FITZMAURICE GRAMMAR SCHOOL

John Benjamin, age 12 – probably prouder of his catch than of his report!

The teachers' comments on his report (opposite), typical of their time, would not be acceptable today by virtue of their complete meaninglessness.

remains a mystery to this day. Fortunately, we only had to take shelter there once, in September of October 1940 whilst a dog-fight was in progress; it happened just before the lunch hour and we were allowed home after the all-clear siren had sounded. The action, which lasted only ten minutes or so, must have been almost overhead because some of the boys found pieces of shrapnel in the road afterwards.

School dinners were only for out-of-town pupils. They were cooked and eaten in the cookery room, so domestic science lessons were timetabled for afternoons only. We who lived within walking or cycling distance usually went home for lunch."

Evacuees came to Bradford on Avon in large numbers. One estimate is that, between 1939 and 1945, 3,500 women and children sought sanctuary in the town from urban areas – in particular, from the East End of London, Bristol, and, at one stage, Bath – though many stayed only for a short time, returning to their homes when the immediate danger seemed to have passed. And so the Fitzmaurice Grammar School, as well as being a Reception Centre, welcomed throughout the War a small but shifting population of boys and girls who stayed for a week or two or for much longer periods. It was also the Home Guard

Attack Headquarters and Place of Assembly, which meant that the Directing Officer for the area, Arthur Baker, could, in an emergency, requisition the buildings and use them as a Home Guard Centre.

A request was received for the release of Geoffrey Rowntree should a time of national emergency arise, but this was refused as being impracticable because he was the only one left to run the school; all the other men on the staff had military duties, or quasi-military duties, of one sort or another. After his brief recruitment to the army at the start of hostilities, Arthur Baker had returned to teaching and in early 1941 became Directing Officer for Bradford on Avon, with responsibility for leading and coordinating local ARP services. Harry Brosnan commanded the 4th Wiltshire Home Guard at Winsley in which he was a lieutenant, Arthur Percival was also a lieutenant, in the 5th Somerset Home Guard in Bath, Johnny Otter was in the RAF from January 1941 to June 1946, and Tom Eastwood served in the RASC from 1941 to 1945. With the exception of Geoffrey Rowntree, therefore, all the male staff were actively engaged, and the strong connection that the school had with the Home Guard was reflected in the gift it received as hostilities drew to a close – a letter of thanks for the use of its facilities and a framed photograph of the local Home Guard platoon.

Dig for Victory was one slogan of these years, and, as had happened in the First World War, gardening and food production found its way on to the timetable. Tools were bought and areas of ground set aside for cultivation. An official fire-watching rota, on the other hand, was not at first thought to be necessary for the buildings, though it became a requirement in the middle of 1942 when 3 people had to be on duty throughout the hours of darkness. A third stirrup pump was therefore bought, and Alex Wilkins had the ignominy of being cautioned by the police because of an unscreened light that had been seen shining one night from the school premises.

Hilary Chard lived at Barton Farm during the War and she was a pupil at Fitzmaurice Grammar School proper (as opposed to the Prep Department) from 1936 to 1942. The foibles of many of her teachers are still fresh in her memory. She remembers Sidney Farrar as a fair and approachable man, his successor, Geoffrey Rowntree as more aloof and far less popular. Johnny Otter and his affairs were of consuming interest to the girls whilst it was Miss Williams' fate, she recalls, to be worshipped from afar by the boys. Miss Burgoine dealt severely with any girl guilty of unladylike behaviour (being seen walking arm in arm with a boy, for example, as happened to Hilary); Mr Percival could often be hurtfully sarcastic; and Mr Baker's Sixth Form science lessons seldom aspired to anything more adventurous than verbatim readings from the text book. His curious way of speaking (also mentioned by Ilse Stein) which seemed designed to keep his pupils at a distance has stuck in her mind, too. Endless posters had to be painted in art lessons urging people to Dig for Victory or reminding them that Careless Talk Costs Lives, but more exciting was the morning when she and her friends stood in the playground and watched a dog fight between aircraft of the warring nations.

The Baths at Bradford on Avon had been requisitioned early as a First Aid Post, and although the girls were at first allowed to go to the baths in Trowbridge, effectively it was 1945 before swimming returned to the timetable. And other signs of the times were a relaxation, and then an abandonment, of uniform requirements for both boys and girls for the War's duration when clothes rationing was introduced, the release of boys to allow them to help with essential jobs like harvesting, the opening of the school during holiday periods for voluntary attendance, and the digging of a trench in Victory Field by the military. The purpose of this was not clear. And equally mysterious was the purpose of the wire that the army strung around Victory Field in 1941. Having received permission so to do, the Groundsman removed it some 3 years later. Further visible evidence of these being unusual times was the removal from the site of all metal "railings, gates, chains, bollards, and fencing", these being needed for melting down for the production of munitions.

Graham Hayter was in the same class as Ilse Stein and Roma Alexander, and he remembers how sport and games in general suffered as a result of wartime conditions:

> "Mr Brosnan had been appointed after the Great War; he taught woodwork, junior maths, and boys' PE and games after the young sports master had departed. He was old and limped, so we had minimal PE and never learned sports' skills. Games lessons were usually a cross-country run along the road to Avoncliffe, and then a return to school via the canal tow-path. Part of the problem was that clothing coupons had to be used for everyday garments, so none were available for football boots and sports wear, though we were loaned school daps for the year. No interschool sports tournaments were possible. I remember just one summer term of rowing; the local Rowing Club had two Fours, so it was possible to have an inter-house regatta, and this was great fun. The small Town Baths were used by army personnel during these war years, so there was no school swimming. I would have loved sport, but War denied us a chance to participate. The girls were more fortunate since Dot Gare, our youthful French teacher, also taught girls' PE and games. They played tennis in summer and hockey in winter, all enthusiastically, but even for them there were no inter-school tournaments."

Late in the War, the school was liaising with the Parish Invasion Committee about the movement of pupils should a sudden emergency arise; Colonel Rocke left a bequest to benefit boys and girls financially if their fathers or grandfathers had served in the 1st, 2nd, or 7th battalions of the Wiltshire Regiment; and the early release of Flying Officer Otter from the RAF was sought on the grounds of the general shortage of teachers and the imminent retirement of two of the few remaining male members of the school's teaching staff – a request that was refused. However, the most poignant reminder of how long and how draining the War had been was found in the lengthening list of casualties. In its final form, it read:

J L Angell (1927-33)	*W/O rear gunner RAF killed 1941*
R C Bray (34-38)	*Flt Sgt RAF killed 1944*
E J Brown (33-38)	*Sgt Observer RAF killed on air ops Oct 1943*
N B Darch (28-34)	*Sgt City of London Yeom.killed in Sicily July 1943*
L F Gill (32-36)	*P/O RAF killed March 1944*
S G Hill (18-25)	*died in internment 1945*
K H King DFC (34-39)	*P/O RAF killed 1945*
Reg Miller (32-36)	*Sgt RAF killed in action 1940*
L B Mortimer (34-38)	*A/C RAF lost at sea July 1941*
R P D Perkins (33-39)	*P/O RAF killed on air ops 1944*
C Read (18-?)	*Liverpool Constabulary killed by enemy action 1941*
N H Webb DFM (27-32)	*Flt Lt RAF killed over France 1940*
B K G Willmer (31-36)	*Sgt RAF killed whilst flying 1941*

Constance Dallimore, as has been noted, became Head Master's Secretary in 1939, and the wartime years saw this particular post changing hands with increasing frequency. She was replaced by Irene Coudray, who was followed by Mrs Dotesio, Miss Watts, Miss Burton, Miss Fox, and Miss P Russell in 1947. Mrs Hopkins who came as Cook in place of Mrs Hazell in 1940, soon saw the number of pupils taking school dinners double. Consequently, her wages were increased and the price of the meal fell from 8d to 7d. In early 1942, 50 meals a day were being served, so Mrs Leslie (the new Cook) was given a scullery maid to help her. By the end of the year, numbers had risen to 95 – still in the same room as when 17 or 18 had been accommodated – so agitation began (which was distinct from the clamour for long-term, major improvements to the school buildings) for a new dining room and kitchen. The school's all-time bargain dinners cost 5d in 1942, 1943, and 1944, but at this price they were making a loss, so up they went again to 6d, with the threat that, unless new facilities were speedily forthcoming, the number being served would have to be restricted.

The school's caretaking passed from Hayter to Burbidge, and after that there was a gap during which the cleaning and stoking was done by pupils – evidence of yet another wartime shortage. Mrs Burbidge and her son followed, then her son on his own, and he, in 1945, once more combined the job with that of Groundsman. By October 1946 P J Hunt was Groundsman, and shortly afterwards Mr Green and his son became Caretaker and Assistant Caretaker respectively. Sims had been appointed both Caretaker and Groundsman in 1922; he retained the former job for 10 years, the latter for 21. During the War he had been very seriously ill, retiring on grounds of ill health in 1944 with a gift of £15 from the Governors to mark his long service to the school. He died the following year.

Two other names of these years were Alex Wilkins (again) and Dr Griffiths. By 1943, Wilkins had been Clerk to the Governors for 32 years, and he now announced his intention to resign. At the Governors' request he reconsidered his position, but eventually decided to stick to his guns, taking with him Mrs Hardy (formerly Miss Foster) who for the last 6 years had assisted him and attended meetings with him. She was offered the post but refused it, the new Clerk and Correspondent to the Board of Education from 1 April being F G Overy. (To complete this particular chapter, Overy remained until 1947, stepping down at that time because of ill health and being replaced by Lt Col H T Russell.) Dr Griffiths was rather different. He was a Harley Street specialist who came to Wiltshire in 1942 to speak at a number of schools. Mrs Ryder (formerly Ilse Stein) remembers him well.

> "We had a sex educationalist called Dr Griffiths who came annually to give talks to groups of boys and girls of different ages, and then to co-educational groups, to show that the subject was not taboo in mixed company. This was amazingly progressive in the 1940s. What was less advanced and more a sign of the times was that Dr Griffiths, who also saw individuals, either at their own or the staff's request, was asked to counsel my friend, A.... B...., because she was often seen in the company of black American soldiers. Bradford was then a Black GI zone, while nearby Trowbridge was White. A.... met her blokes, innocently enough, at the weekly dances held in the Town Hall, which was then in Market Street. It was thought (by whom, for heaven's sake!) that a talk from Dr Griffiths might solve her 'problem'."

These "blokes" were presumably from Abbey House which was requisitioned for the billeting of Afro-American GIs.

And so, in 1945, this period of turbulence – with constant change, deprivation, the ebb and flow of hope, its tragedies, and its pervasive spirit of making the best of things – finally ran its course. Shortages and hardship continued, but stability and a returning in many aspects of life to a sort of normality took the place of flux and uncertainty.

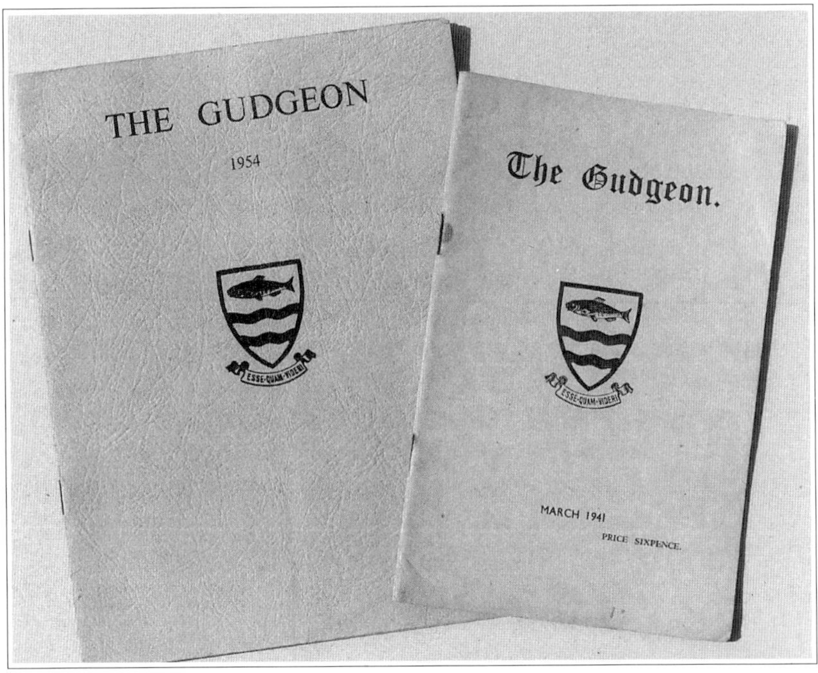
THE GUDGEON
1954
ESSE QUAM VIDERI
The Gudgeon.
ESSE QUAM VIDERI
MARCH 1941
PRICE SIXPENCE.

*Above: Class VA in the girls' playground outide the girls' cloakroom, July 1944;
left to right, rear, John Matthews, Eric Gerrish, Norman Sartain, Terry Sleightholme, David Huntley, Michael Baker, Robert Pepler, Raymond Tiley;
centre, Jean Vallis, Monica Bull, Iris Cooper, June Mumford, Mrs Courtney, Jean Uncles, Patricia Austin, Mary Turner, Joan Lywood, Margaret Wood;
seated, Graham Hayter, Jean Watts, Roma Alexander, Ilse Stein, Eric Rogers.
(John Wicks was absent.)*

*Above left: Teaching staff, July 1944;
left to right, back, Mrs Courtney, Mrs Stein, Miss Holder, Mr Brosnan, Mr Baker, Mr Percival;
front, Miss Gare, Mrs Neathey, Miss Burgoine, Mrs Yelland.*

Below left: **The Gudgeon** - *small and large versions.*

Right: Dr C E S Flemming, Chairman of Governors 1936-1947. This portrait used to hang in the entrance hall of the school.

The Fitzmaurice Grammar School acquired a new dining room and kitchen. The possibility of this was first mooted in 1943 when, after years of stagnation, school dinners rather suddenly became popular. Plans were drawn up early in 1944, a start was made on the buildings late that same year, and they were up and running in May 1945. This prefabricated building, erected by Messrs Carter and Co at the rear of the school, intended only as a temporary structure that would last for about 5 years but that survived for 35, provided at its opening about 140 meals daily. A late sophistication dreamed up by the Governors as a desirable embellishment was a verandah linking the dining room to the main building. This, however, was not allowed. An internal embellishment that was sanctioned was the decoration of the building with murals of local scenes, renewed from time to time over succeeding years.

And minds began to turn again to major development. At the same time as the idea of a new dining room was conceived, it was suggested that land at the rear of the school should be purchased so that, when the time was right, an extension to the old building could be considered and new life breathed into the proposals that had been so enthusiastically floated just before the War. Wiltshire County Council agreed. Negotiations were entered into with the owner, a Mr Jackson, who was an Agricultural Engineer and who used the land in connection with his business. By 1945 it had been bought and leased back to the vendor until such time as it was needed, so once again it was possible to look to the future rather than live simply from day to day. This was so not only in terms of buildings and land but also of people. Wartime stability (or stagnation) was crumbling.

The Irishman, Harry Brosnan, retired at the end of the summer term after teaching at the Grammar School (and the County School before it) for 27 years. He had hoped to retire to Bridport but was thwarted in this as he was almost immediately taken seriously ill and died just over a year after leaving Fitzmaurice. Appointed in 1918, he had been in charge of boys games and athletics for the whole of his career. In the 1930s, he had been responsible for the football XI that won the County Championship four times in five years and for the cricket XI that won the County Cup. He also taught junior maths and woodwork, and, in his earlier years, boys PE. Up to his retirement, which should have been in 1942 but which he delayed in order to help the school out, he organised the annual Sports Day and the Swimming Sports. Mrs Roma Challis remembers him.

> "He taught maths and one day he asked me why any one side of a triangle was always shorter than the other two added together. It was quite clear to me that this was bound to be the case, but I could not think what he expected me to say.

> He seemed so angry and shouted that wasn't it obvious that 'a straight line is the shortest distance between two points'. I was only eleven and it was my first experience of being taught by a man, so from then on I was terrified of him. He was the teacher who issued the new exercise books, but not before he had checked that you had used every single page of your old one, and, woe betide you if there was evidence that any pages had been torn out. But we were at war and everything was in short supply and nothing should be wasted."

At the same time, Mrs Courtney went to Malmesbury Grammar School, Doris Gare to Southend High School for Boys, and Elise Stein to Greenford County School in Middlesex. Mrs Stein was a Czech refugee with degrees from Vienna and Prague who was taken on to the staff of this English country grammar school, one feels, with some hesitation. In the event, she is remembered as an inspirational teacher, commended for her skills by the Head to the Governors and granted a special allowance for her qualifications and work in mathematics. C C Copland was appointed to replace Brosnan, Miss Jean Davis came for Mrs Courtney, John Smith for Miss Gare, and Otter and Eastwood returned from the services to displace Mrs Stein (and two very temporary fill-ins, Fritz Gutman and Eric Phillips) and Mrs Yelland respectively. Baker, too, finally went in October 1945, though he was soon to be found back on the Governing Body.

Arthur Baker stayed on into the Christmas term for a few weeks to suit his pension plans; at his leaving he recalled his starting at the school in 1905 when he taught all the science, most of the maths, some geography, boys' games, and (his particular delight) girls' hockey. He had served in the army throughout the First World War and was offered a permanent commission just prior to being demobilised. However, he returned to the County School, to be remembered still, almost 100 years after his appointment, by many ageing Bradfordians and neo-Bradfordians. Roma Challis recalls him as a somewhat Patrick Moore-ish sort of figure who loved to chat about astronomy, whilst for Ilse Ryder

> "Mr Baker was the Senior Master and taught what was laughingly described as science. He and Mrs Baker lived in one of the modern villas along Belcombe, beyond Newtown, with their little daughter, Jennifer – a bright, pretty, chirpy redhead. At school, though, Mr Baker seemed old and timid. He was affectionately known as Uncle Ben. In a school of small classes and biddable, country children, he simply could not keep order. Because he was desperately shy, he devised a method whereby he never had to address us, but spoke entirely in infinitives. The one exception, caused only by the vagaries of the English language, was his regular parting instruction: 'May go, when ready'.
>
> The format of each lesson was the same; he dictated notes into our rough

books, which for homework had to be copied into neat. You got a detention if you were found writing straight into neat. The neat books were then taken in and marked, I presume for presentation, because he must have known the content to be sound.

Although we were nominally doing general science, he liked mechanics best, and each year began with the same text, regardless of what level he was teaching. 'The Principle of Inertia states that a body will continue at rest, or in uniform motion in a straight line, unless acted upon by an external force.' (When I started teaching mechanics to Maths Sixth Forms, it took a conscious effort of will to re-think definitions and not lapse into Baker-ese.) He must have taught us biology and chemistry at some stage because we passed the general science exam, but I really can't remember anything at all except mechanics. We were taught in the so-called science lab, but there was no sign of equipment or, perish the thought, practicals."

Ellis Darby followed Arthur Baker in science, Margaret Prince was appointed for geography in 1946 when Miss Holder left to get married, and in another small spate of changes in 1947 Dora Neathey left, Tom Eastwood married Jean Davis and they moved to Yorkshire, Eastwood taking a post at the Technical College in Huddersfield. Minnie Rhodes succeeded Mrs Neathey in domestic science, Barbara Foulds followed Miss Davis, and Mrs Yelland (again) and Catherine Proudlock joined the school to teach English. Hilary Chard had helped out in the period between school and university and she also returned from time to time to assist with science as and when her attendance at college allowed. For this she was given an honorarium as no salary could officially be paid.

An appointment of 1947 that should be mentioned was that of Mrs Anne Rees. She had previously taught domestic science in the school. A well qualified scientist and a first-rate teacher of physics, she had given private coaching in that subject during the War to some of the more ambitious pupils at her bungalow on the hill behind the Three Gables. Now she was re-appointed in a part-time capacity. After leaving Bradford, she went on to teach physics with distinction at Trowbridge Girls' High School from 1954 to 1969.

From 1944 Miss Burgoine had been officially recognised as Senior Mistress. When Baker left, she was also designated Deputy Head, but in 1950/51 it was Arthur Percival who became Acting Head when Avery was granted leave of absence for a year.

A clear sign that normality had been resumed was the reinstatement in 1947 of rowing as a school activity after a seven years' lapse, but, somewhat earlier, and as Peace loomed, the question of the school's status and of its possible rebuilding, indeed, the whole question of its future and its place in Wiltshire's pattern of secondary education under the new Education Act of 1944, was raised again. The matter of a new dining room had been dealt with; now (in 1945) urgent discussions took place about the need for additional cloakroom space for the boys, the provision of another laboratory, and improvements to the girls' cloakroom facilities. But as plans that were much more radical and comprehensive and far-reaching had been drawn up prior to the War and then mothballed for the duration, the Governors could be forgiven for asking rather plaintively how these short-term and long-term plans fitted together.

They therefore formalised their thoughts. Three points were important, and they were that the Governors recorded their wish that:

> a) in any future plans for reorganisation, the Fitzmaurice Grammar School should continue to exist as a separate school and as a grammar school; and
> b) the Fitzmaurice Grammar School should be organised so as to have an annual entry of two forms; and they indicated a preference that:
> c) should a completely new secondary school be built, that school should be the Fitzmaurice Grammar School as they had no view that would prevent the present school's transference to a new building.

That was all pretty clear, but by way of reply they received an outline plan from the Education Department to which they were not exactly hostile but lukewarm rather than enthusiastic. This ignored Mr Watkins' prewar scheme entirely, and suggested a school rebuilt in two blocks some distance apart. What had happened to the earlier plan? they wondered. Why were two separate blocks now being suggested? Why was there no prefects' room, visitors' room, medical room, Caretaker's room, Sixth Form room....? Before these questions could be answered, a further plan was hatched. The Fitzmaurice Grammar School was to be built as a completely new school of a single unit on the site of the junior council school nearby, it would be two-form entry taking pupils from a wider geographical area, and the present building would be given over to Further Education for adults. £53,000 was floated as being the cost of the new school, but the excitement generated by these heady ideas was matched only by the vagueness and uncertainty of the proposals.

Running alongside these deliberations about buildings and sites was the matter of the school's status. Under the 1944 Education Act, formal application was made for it to be a Voluntary Controlled School, which application was granted on 28 September 1945. As a Voluntary school it was maintained, but not established, by the LEA; as a Controlled school, the management, curriculum,

Miss Burgoine with an Art class, 1947.

and staff appointments were conducted in accordance with the Act.

Under the same Act, the Governing Body was reconstituted and met in its new form for the first time in June 1947. Its composition makes interesting reading: Dr C E S Flemming, Lady Gurney, Mrs E H Daniell, Mrs A Swanborough, Sir Hubert Young, Messrs A E Angell, A H Baker, J F Beaven, T Y S Blease, G C V Holbrow, H W Slade, and S C Tucker. Four of the twelve were Foundation Governors; Dr Flemming was elected Chairman and Mr Holbrow Vice Chairman. But in doing things in this way an error was committed.

There should have been two quite distinct bodies. One was the Board of Governors of the Fitzmaurice Grammar School as constituted above, and its function was the management of the school. The second, which was unfortunately forgotten about, was the Board of Foundation Governors, the function of which was to administer the Foundation and its Endowments but with no part to play, after the 1944 Act, in the management of the school. From 1947 to 1966, therefore, this Board ceased to exist, and it was only in the latter year, when the omission was recognised, that the Foundation was again properly set up at a meeting of 19 May.

But 1947 was a time for a breaking of links with the past. Mr Holbrow died almost immediately and was replaced by Mr Slade, a long-time Governor of the school, as Vice Chairman. Dr Flemming stepped down as Chairman before the year was out, and G C Rowntree resigned as Head Master to take up the headship of Huntingdon Grammar School.

In writing both about Geoffrey Rowntree and the Fitzmaurice Grammar School during those wartime years, Ilse Ryder combines accuracy, affection, and whimsical comment.

> "Mr Rowntree was a Quaker, an enlightened, liberal man, young to be a Head at that time. He lived in Junction Road, where the school was, with his wife and young children, Susan and Simon (Sarah was born after the War), and so was very much part of the local community. Although there were clearly defined boundaries, he was a democrat both with staff and pupils. We had a School Council, with elected representatives from each form, which met and discussed school matters and policy. Where he inherited traditions, as, for example, the House system, he put them to novel use by instituting annual school competitions – a kind of mini Eisteddfod.
>
> On a personal level, Mr Rowntree was a boon for my mother because he knew about 'abroad' – he had even been there! – and therefore managed to persuade the Governors that a PhD from the University of Vienna did count as a degree. When I was sent to him for persistent lateness, he made me learn Goethe's *Glocke* as a punishment. (I can't say that I was never late again, but I do still know the poem by heart.) Although the school didn't offer German as a subject, he entered me for School Certificate and coached me in the lunch-hour once a week. I was bilingual anyway but had had no written German since the age of 10 and needed to acquire the skill of translation, which he taught me.
>
> As regards general education standards at the school, I think that in English, French, and maths to School Certificate I could not have had better teaching anywhere. Beyond that, I am not sure.... With the end of the War in 1945 and the imminent return of Mr Otter, my mother's job ended and she was appointed to Greenford County School in Middlesex. I, of course, moved with her.... The teachers there did me proud. I was taught physics in a real lab with equipment and with regular exposure to practicals. I certainly owe it to the education at Greenford that I was offered a place at both Oxford and Cambridge. I wouldn't have made it from Bradford. *But it is my time at Fitzmaurice that I look back on as being the halcyon days.*"

John Weeks (1938-1943), like Ilse Ryder, also mentions Rowntree's introduction of the mini-Eisteddfod and the School Council, the latter being a bold attempt at the democratic representation of pupil opinion in a way that

The school dining room in use shortly after being built.

was years ahead of its time. It was "with the idea of encouraging widespread thought and discussion by pupils on school affairs". To begin with, the whole school met twice a year for these discussions, and from these meetings a successful School Club for social activities, such as table tennis, badminton, and ballroom dancing, was formed. Sadly but inevitably, idealism gave way to more pragmatic considerations. For some, these gatherings were intimidating, and soon they were replaced by twice-termly form meetings followed by a School Council composed of representatives – 2 pupils for each form above the first year, 2 members of staff, and the Head Master. In 1946-47 it met 3 times; however, the apathy displayed was "disappointing", and shortly afterwards the idea was dropped.

A footnote should be written on the very remarkable lady who for a few years taught maths at Fitzmaurice Grammar School during the Second World War. Mrs Stein was really Dr Stein, a Bohemian Czech and a German-speaking Jew with a doctorate in mathematics from Vienna. From 1928 to 1938 she was Visiting Lecturer at the University of Prague and Statistical Expert at the Institute of Market Research in Vienna. With the imminence of war, her daughter, Ilse, was brought to this country by the Barbican Mission to the Jews, her mother following shortly afterwards on a domestic permit. All her family except Ilse – her husband, mother, father....– had to be left behind and all died in the concentration camps.

In this country, Dr Stein rebuilt her life, working first as a chambermaid, cook, and governess, and then taking what teaching jobs she could. One, in 1940, was teaching chemistry at a school called Thornbank at Malvern-Wells, her only equipment being pieces of litmus paper. From September of that year until July 1941 she was maths mistress at The Red Gables School in Carlisle, a slight improvement upon Thornbank. And then, after being interviewed by Geoffrey Rowntree on Derby railway station, she came to Bradford on Avon. (Greenford County School and, eventually, higher education in London followed.) Speaking heavily accented English, one feels that she was initially taken on to the staff of the small country grammar school in Bradford on Avon with some hesitation, but everyone who knew her at Fitzmaurice (1941-1945) speaks of her as having been an inspirational and highly respected teacher. She was later awarded the Golden Doctorate, an Honorary Doctorate, of the University of Vienna.

Elise Stein's is an extraordinary story which remained largely unknown to those whom she taught.

Above: School prefects, 1950; below: Fitzmaurice 1st crew on the Avon, 1951.

A New Team
The Fitzmaurice Grammar School:
1947-1954

IN SEPTEMBER 1947, GEOFFREY ROWNTREE was replaced as Head by Geoffrey Avery. Educated at King's College, Cambridge, Avery had taught at King's School, Canterbury, before the War, and came to Bradford on Avon "with an excellent record in scholastic and military spheres". But his assumption of office was only one of several important changes to excite the school at this time. Within a few weeks two senior members of the school staff, Johnny Otter and Ellis Darby, resigned, the latter to take up the headship of the local secondary modern school. The Chairman of the Governing Body, Dr Flemming, stepped down, though he remained a Governor of the school, and the Vice Chairman, G C V Holbrow, died, their replacements being the Rev W D Galsworthy, the newly appointed vicar of Christ Church, and H W Slade, as Chairman and Vice Chairman respectively. F G Overy retired from his post as Clerk to the Governors because of ill health, Lt Col Russell taking that position. A Miss Russell replaced Miss Fox as Head Master's Secretary, and F A Kranz became Groundsman. And in December the venue for Speech Day moved from the old school gymnasium, which it had long outgrown, to the more spacious and comfortable surroundings of the Alexander Cinema (today's St Margaret's Hall) for which there was a charge of two guineas. So, all in all, the transition from War to Peace very quickly brought a new look to many aspects of management and life at Bradford's grammar school.

Some things, of course, never changed. Both Dorothy Burgoine and Arthur Percival were regarded as having always been at the school, though Miss Burgoine was to retire in 1953 after 34 years of service. By 1955, John Smith (in French) and Albert ("Ted") Jelfs (Senior Science and Maths) had assumed mantles of comparative seniority, and Geoffrey Avery himself stayed for a respectable eight years. Elsewhere, however, change was pretty well constant – particularly among the women teachers. Few even of those who were permanent and full-time stayed for more than two or three years, and in subjects like domestic science, physical education, music, and the new separate sciences – chemistry and biology – part-time and temporary teachers came and went with bewildering rapidity. The permanent teaching staff for the period of Geoffrey Avery's headship were:

Head Master:	Geoffrey Avery (1947-1955);
History:	Arthur Percival (1921-);
Art:	Dorothy Burgoine (1919-1953), Cicely Cox (1953-1955);
Science:	Ellis Darby (1945-1947), Albert Jelfs (1948-);
English:	Catherine Proudlock (Mrs John) (1947-1952), Lilian Oakman (Mrs Brown) (1953), Kenneth Revill (1953-);
French:	John Smith (1945-);
Maths:	Johnny Otter (1932-1947), Sydney Corby (1948-1951), Sidney Johnson (1952-);
Woodwork:	Cyril Copland (1945-1949), George Rice (1949-1955);
Geography:	Margaret Prince (Mrs Malpas) (1946-1950), Arthur Heamon (1951), Mona Boden (Mrs Cole) (1951-1953), Kathleen Hyde (1953-);
English:	Barbara Foulds (1947-1949), Mrs Yvette Roblin (1949-1952), Roy Day (1954-);
Dom Sci:	Minnie Rhodes (1947-1952), Sylvia M'Quhae (Mrs Adams) (1953-);
Biology:	Nora Lawson (1952-);
Girls' PE:	Betty Cummins (1953-1954), Mrs Day (1955);
Boys' PE:	Harry Haddon (1954-);
Boys' Games:	Richard Hope (1951-1952).

But a few embellishments can be added to these bare statistics.

Miss Burgoine, whose appointment at the school went back to the close of the First World War, retired in the summer of 1953. As can be imagined, much was made of her going, and she was presented with a cheque (preferred by her to a present) to mark her many years of service. At Christmas the following year, she was invited back – a nice touch – as principal guest and distributor of prizes at the annual Speech Day. She was a link with the past, and, on her retirement, she recalled some of her earliest memories – of Lord Fitzmaurice, for example, who invited every newly appointed teacher to his home at Leigh, and of Julia Blake: "I visited her when she was dying and, perhaps, the most precious of my memories of her lies in her last words to me. 'I am glad,' she said, 'that you are going to take my place at the school. You will love it, as I have done.'"

Miss Burgoine's retirement left the school with only one out of the five women on the staff with more than one year's teaching experience, this being a part-time teacher, Anne Rees. And so Mrs Rees assumed, albeit unofficially and unremuneratedly, Miss Burgoine's disciplinary and pastoral oversight of the girls, as well as acting as House Mistress. The position of Senior Mistress remained formally unfilled. This situation lasted for one term only, however, as Mrs Rees herself left in December 1953. There had been some discussion between her and Mr Avery about her conditions of employment; she had made a suggestion which proved to be unacceptable; and so she left. Anne Rees's going was unfortunate, but Bradford's loss was Trowbridge's gain, and she went on to become one of the mainstays of Trowbridge Girls' High School over the next 15 years.

Fitzmaurice Grammar School's other long-serving teacher, Arthur Percival, saw out Geoffrey Avery's headship, as he had the headships of Crompton, Rosen, Farrar, and Rowntree before him. But he needed a bit of help. Mervyn Comrie stood in for him for a term in 1949 when, for a time, he was seriously ill; John Cannon took his place for the whole of the 1950-51 academic year when Percival was Acting Head, Avery having been granted leave of absence to take up a Fellowship at Bristol University; and Nevill Boyd-Maunsell did the same when, in 1955, Percival was again Acting Head for the one term's interregnum between Avery's leaving and Bradshaw's arriving. It had been his intention to retire in July 1955, but at the request of the newly appointed Head he stayed on for a further year to ease the change in leadership.

Dorothy Burgoine and Arthur Percival had been the twin rocks upon which the school was set for more years than most could remember. No one could replace them, though Albert Jelfs and John Smith naturally assumed the roles of senior assistant teachers both by length of tenure and by the importance of their teaching responsibilities. After the retirement of Miss Burgoine and the going of Mrs Rees, Miss Lawson became the senior woman teacher on the staff and the official Senior Mistress from September 1955, three years after leaving Reading University. (She, in fact, had been appointed as a replacement for Mrs Roblin, Roy Day joining the school somewhat later as an additional teacher to accommodate the extra number of pupils that by then were on roll.) As has been said, others came and went very rapidly, and for a variety of reasons – Copland, for example, for promotion in further education in Berkshire, Minnie Rhodes in order to look after a sick mother, Miss Cox to get married, and Miss Foulds to move to Bradford Girls' Grammar School in Yorkshire.

A matter of singular unimportance but of some interest as a social comment on the times is the fact that, of all these teachers, only Geoffrey Avery himself and George Rice, both family men, owned a car in the early 1950s – or so Sidney Johnson believes. (Today, of course, staff cars still tend to be few and modest whilst the problem of the number and size of the vehicles parked on school premises by Sixth Form students grows more and more intractable.)

The rather fluid situation in girls' games and PE stabilised somewhat with the arrival of Miss Cummins in 1953, her immediate predecessors having been

Misses Turner, Jordan, Briggs, and Davis, and Mrs Blakeney. Mr Haddon was a part-time teacher and Sylvia M'Quhae spent one day a week at the Victoria Institute in Trowbridge.

The Governing Body was in something of a similar state of flux. After stepping down as Chairman in 1947, Dr Flemming resigned as a Governor the following year because of increasing deafness. He had been on the Board from the school's very earliest days and for many years had been Vice Chairman under Lord Fitzmaurice. He resisted all attempts to persuade him to stay, and, in making a presentation to him, his colleagues paid tribute to his huge contribution to the school's development. Death also removed the Vice Chairman, H W Slade dying late in 1949. The new team – the Rev W D Galsworthy, vicar of Christ Church, and the ubiquitous A H Baker – provided an interesting interlude. It was interesting because first there was the matter of the Clerkship, secondly that of the Political Activities, and thirdly the Resignation. All were somewhat intertwined.

The Clerk to the Governors from 1947 to 1949 had been a Colonel Russell. In that year he resigned ostensibly on grounds of ill-health, Mrs Betty Edwards taking his place. The next six months or so saw numerous meetings held (some at Christ Church Vicarage and most with auditors and representatives of the Treasurer's Department present, and with the Director of Education himself involved) and many letters written to try to sort out the problems that had arisen over Col Russell's book-keeping. It was a matter of some delicacy, the precise details of which are no longer clear. What is clear is that Mrs Edwards had been handed something of a poisoned chalice for which she received extra remuneration. The Governors disclaimed all responsibility "for the £60 incurred in taxi hire [and] the charge for electricity" that appeared in the account books, and the Chairman asked the County Authority to take whatever action it deemed fit to secure full restitution from Col Russell. It was a cause of great worry and concern, Mrs Edwards having to bear the brunt of the unpleasantness and all the extra work involved in clearing up the mess. The short period of Col Russell's clerkship, therefore, turned out to be something of an embarrassment.

The Political Activities were those of two of the members of the teaching staff. They were politically very committed and there was a concern that their extra-curricular interests might have spread to the classroom. This matter having been noted earlier, it was again brought to the attention of the Governors as a matter of urgency by the Rev Galsworthy who, in October 1951, had been voted out of office as Chairman and been replaced by Arthur Baker. There was genuine concern that something might be going wrong, and this was heightened when Galsworthy, "having had information come to his ears", requested a special meeting of the Governing Body to discuss the situation. A thorough investigation was instituted, discrete inquiries were made (including a questioning of the previous year's Head Boy) and other inquiries that were perhaps more direct, but no evidence was forthcoming that any member of the teaching staff had done anything that could be considered in any way unprofessional. The matter was therefore dropped. Even so, with the Director of Education again involved, it was all rather disquieting.

Galsworthy received no satisfaction over the above matter about which he had felt strongly, and he had also been replaced by Baker as Chairman in 1951. He was clearly in a minority in his opinion about what was going on, and possibly he did not handle it too well. Whatever the nuances of the situation, his letter to the Clerk, dated 10 October 1951, set out his position.

> "I have for some time been vaguely aware of a certain amount of thinly veiled hostility towards me on the part of some of the Governors, and, in view of the fact that this hostility, although unexpressed in words, was made only too apparent at the last meeting, I feel that it is better for the general harmony of the Governing Body that I should resign my position as a Governor of the Fitzmaurice Grammar School. I rather hesitate to do so at this particular moment, as I was, I suppose, responsible for suggesting to the Governors a line of action which may well have serious consequences for the school, but no doubt exists in my mind that they will be able to deal very adequately with any situation that may arise from such action."

He replied peevishly to his colleagues' attempts to get him to change his mind and then failed to reply at all to a further placatory letter on the subject, so it was made known that he had resigned from the Governing Body because of illness. His resignation was accepted, but it was all very unsatisfactory and unpleasant. He left Christ Church four years later to go as Head Master to Kingwell Court (later known as Old Ride) School. So from late in 1951 the Chairman of Governors was Arthur Baker, with S C Tucker as Vice Chairman.

Mention should be made of one or two other people during these years. Miss J H Bethell became Head Master's Secretary in 1949, this position causing upset a little later. As an economy, the Local Authority came up with a plan to replace the full-time secretary with a part-time helper or a young girl, a suggestion which Geoffrey Avery unsurprisingly thought "outrageous". It was quickly dropped. Dr Griffiths and his lessons in sex education have already been mentioned. He was succeeded by Dr E R Matthews who spoke to both parents and pupils, and very well regarded he was. By 1950, however, the plan was for him to train the teaching staff to do this work. All were therefore asked if they would be willing to participate in the venture, but to a man (and a woman) they declined, so Dr Matthews had to continue to plough his lone furrow.

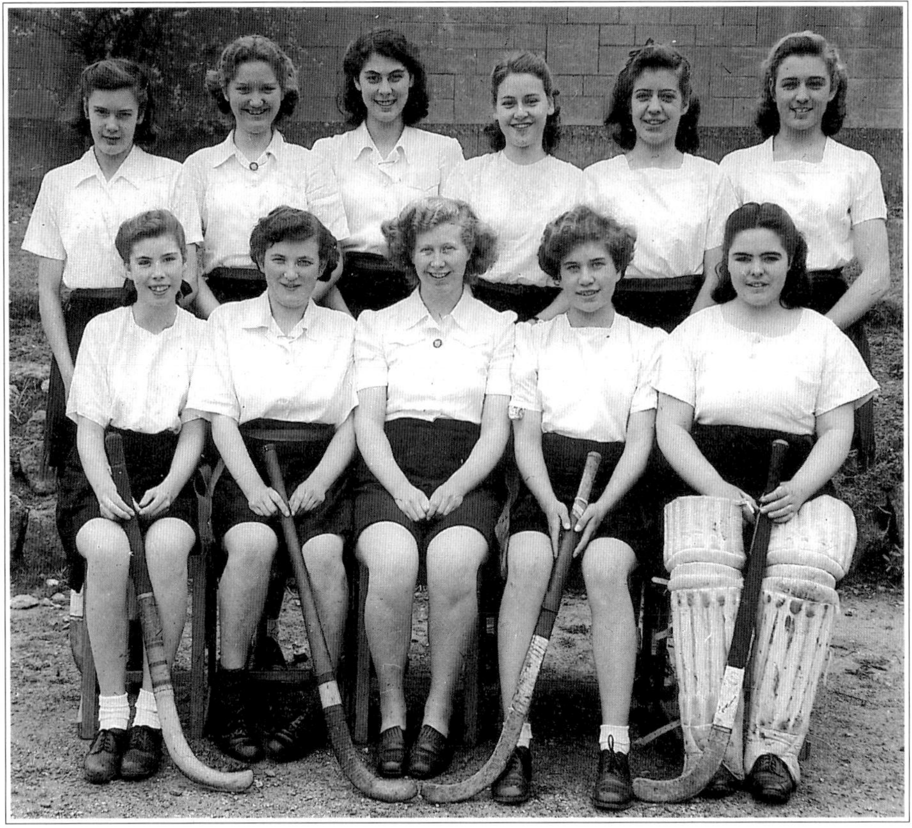

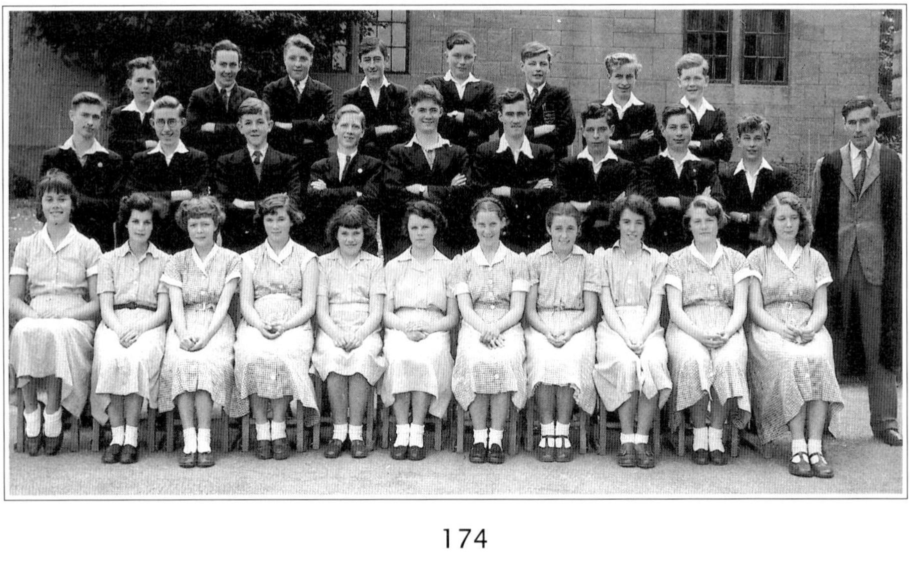

Above: Mrs Rees with a Cookery class, 1948.

Opposite above: Blake House hockey team, 1950. Back row, left to right, W Wadsworth, J Gay, M Hawkins, P Thorne, T Tiley, A Hillier; front, G Niblett, J Abbott, J Washford (captain), M Maggs, D Rees.

Opposite below: Mr Johnson with his class, c 1953.

Right: Miss D Burgoine, Mistress 1919-1953.

However, by 1952 these lessons were having to be subsubsidized from the Endowment Fund, and a year later it was voted, probably as a consequence, that they should cease.

Caretakers were a problem. Between 1950 and 1951 there were Mr Green, Mr Ellery, Mr Harrison, Mr Jenkins, and Mr Collins, their wives often acting as Cleaners. Some, like Jenkins, died; others found the work uncongenial; and a constant factor in the school's inability to recruit the right sort of man was the lack of a Caretaker's house. There was a suggestion for the building of such a house in the school grounds but, fairly quickly, the idea was dropped. Amid these comings and goings, Mr Kranz continued as Groundsman. And finally in this chronicle of non-teaching staff, the death was reported in 1955 of Alex Wilkins, long-time Clerk to the Governors who had resigned from that position some 12 years earlier.

So this was a period of change, with alarums and excursions aplenty to prevent those in authority from sinking into complacency.

Before the War, inconsistencies had begun to appear in Fitzmaurice's admissions policy - inconsistencies of which it was aware and which were forced on it, like so many other things, by the limitations of its buildings. As has already been said, two forms of entry were admitted in 1933 and 1934; this reduced to one in 1935 and 1936. The War years saw much greater fluidity, with pupils, particularly evacuees, coming and going irregularly, but with a recognisable pattern of larger alternating with smaller entries. After the War, however, the former fluctuation between one and two forms of entry more clearly reasserted itself - two in 1947, one in 1948, two in 1949, and one in 1950. A few years later, the inspectors saw it this way:

> "In theory, there is in alternate years either a one-form or a two-form entry, but in practice this system is not easy to operate both when pupils enter the school and during their progress through it. A prime difficulty is that the existing form rooms and practical rooms are so limited in size that only small classes can be housed there. Thus more pupils may offer themselves at entry in any particular year than can be accommodated in one form. In addition, a single-entry form may later through transfers and other causes become so enlarged that sub-division is inevitable."

The Head Master put it more simply: "The school is a 1.5-stream school, taking in alternate years one stream of 30 and two streams of 20-25 pupils."

It was a very clumsy and unsatisfactory system, and the difficulties it posed in practice were spelled out by Geoffrey Avery in 1954:

> "Last summer a single entry was due. Sufficient pupils offered for a class of

33 which, together with 1 pupil to be kept down, made 34. It is agreed that classes of this size are frequent in a grammar school, but in this school space is the problem. There is no classroom in which we can take more than 34 desks; 30 means overcrowding. During the holidays I was asked by the Education Authority to take 2 transfers and by the Headmaster of the Secondary Modern School to examine, with the possibility of accepting them, some 6 pupils completing their first year at his school. At the same time, we were uncertain whether 2 pupils on the normal admission list now at independent schools would or would not take up the places offered.

The question of a single or a double entry thus hung on all these factors and on these in turn hung the question of finding an additional member of staff. Negotiations continued throughout July and August and it became clear towards the end of August that we must take 2 classes and seek an extra member of staff [Elvin Day]."

In another *cri de coeur* on the same subject, Geoffrey Avery put his difficulty rather more colourfully:

"The present 4th year began as a double entry of 41; the present 3rd year was too big for the single bed of Procrustes at 36. The feet of the previous year were chopped off by retaining 8 pupils, and the new victim stretched to become a double entry."

These boys and girls came in almost equal proportions from Bradford on Avon, from Melksham, and from the villages and other West Wiltshire towns. Those who were local tended to walk, cycle, or use the service bus; a school bus served some of the villages to the north and east – Monkton Farleigh, Atworth, South Wraxall, Holt, and Broughton Gifford; and from Melksham and Dilton Marsh they came by local trains, hauled, probably, by little GWR tank-engines. (Sidney Johnson recalls actually having to interrupt Speech Day proceedings on one occasion in order to extract the train pupils for Melksham who, had they missed the 4.15, would have been stranded.) And by Geoffrey Avery's time, both the number of pupils who completed the course they had embarked upon and the length of those courses had improved considerable. On the other hand, though the courses provided for advanced study were carefully tailored to the needs of individual students, the Sixth Form remained comparatively small with, on average, two boys or girls going on to university every year and twice that number continuing with some other form of full-time further education.

Avery's headship began in September 1947, and he had quickly become aware of the problems facing the school. The chief of these was, obviously, the inadequacy of the premises, and sadly, the promise of a "new" school, to be built in the 1949-51 period, became increasingly unlikely of fulfilment with every day that passed. Another matter to occupy him was the failure rate of his girls in the most recent School Certificate examination; only 5 out of 15 had passed, and this matter required attention. A School Cadet Corps had been mooted, but there were practical difficulties militating against this innovation as well as against the hoped-for acquisition of the playing field immediately opposite Victory Field. It was all very frustrating.

More positively, however, rowing as a major school activity (in abeyance since the War) was revived and the association with the local Rowing Club renewed. A new notice board was erected at the main gate so that matters of interest to the public at large could be posted, and a most successful Speech Day was held in 1947 at the Alexander Cinema. As had been the immemorial custom, subject and form prizes were awarded together with the various House Cups – the Blake and Pinckney (for girls' work and games), the Frankell and Cowlishaw (for the boys), the Athletics and Swimming (for both boys and girls), the Cross Country and Rowing Cups for the boys, and the Boys' PT Shield. A year or two earlier, little Roma Alexander had found herself allocated to Blake House.

> "We were put into Houses, with no choice in the matter. I was placed in Blake so must wear a green tie and girdle in winter and a dress of that colour in the summer with – horror of horrors – a panama hat! Other girls were allocated to Pinckney House; those poor souls had to wear mauve. The boys were divided between Fitzmaurice (blue) and Crompton (maroon). From then on we knew where our loyalties lay. At all times I would support, cheer, encourage and applaud the girls in green be it a hockey match, netball, tennis, or cricket. Those were the games in which we were given instruction on our beautifully kept sports field which was just down the road. The groundsman was named Mr Sims and he was a friendly, kind man, very conscientious, always making the school look smart with neatly manicured grass banks on either side of the main gate. The rather shabby huts at the rear of the school could not be seen from the front. The school playgrounds were on either side of the main building, girls on the left, boys on the right."

In 1947 there was a new prize to be won. To mark his very long association with the school, Dr Flemming presented a shield for public speaking. It was made from wood that had been a part of the priest's door at Farleigh Castle, and was doubly appropriate in that the donor was himself a witty and lively speaker and the Castle had belonged to the first Speaker of the House of Commons. Obtained during restoration work some years earlier, the wood was at least 600 years old; the trophy was designed by Miss Burgoine, made by Mr Copland, and presented on this first occasion by Dr Flemming himself. The first winner of the Flemming Shield was P Wells (with G Smith and C M King winners in 1948 and 1949). A reciprocal gesture was the presentation to Dr Flemming of 6 volumes of Churchill's wartime speeches

This rather thoughtful and unusual occasion was echoed four years later when the guest of honour, Gladys Young OBE, presented a prize in memory of her sister, E H Young.

Emily Hilda Young had been a prolific and popular novelist in the earlier part of this century, though few today still read her work. Born in the north of England, she married a solicitor, J A H Daniell, and went to live in Bristol which became the setting for many of her novels. Daniell was killed at Ypres in 1917; thereafter, his widow set up a *ménage à trois* with Ralph Henderson, the Head Master of Alleyn's School in Dulwich, and his wife – an extraordinary arrangement affording at that time every possibility for scandal and a wrecked career had it come to public notice. The relationship survived undetected, however, and Mrs Daniell, under the name of E H Young, continued her writing of novels that in some of their aspects reflected the double life that she herself led. After Henderson's retirement, she and he moved to Bradford on Avon. More books followed, and, as Mrs E H Daniell, she became a Governor of the Fitzmaurice Grammar School. She died of lung cancer in 1949, the E H Young Prize for a subject on a classical theme being awarded annually from 1951 to commemorate her close involvement with the school. The first recipients were Wendy Wadsworth and Graham Matthews.

In the 1947-1955 period, the annual Speech Day continued in its well tried and conventional format, with a little formal music, an address from the Chairman, the Head Master's report on the school's progress, a few well chosen words from the guest of honour, the distribution of prizes, and votes of thanks. As has already been said, the venue was now the Alexander Cinema and the first distributor of prizes at this new venue was Sir Philip Morris of Bristol University. He was followed successively by Rear Admiral Rodney Scott, Miss D Reader Harris, former Deputy General Secretary of the National Association of Girls' and Mixed Clubs and newly appointed Head of Sherborne Girls' School, the Venerable E A Cook, Archdeacon of Bath, Gladys Young, Major Jack Cooper BSc, AMIEE, of the BBC, the Bishop of Salisbury, Miss Burgoine, and the Lord Herbert, Lord Lieutenant of Wiltshire. He took the place of Henry Rosen, a Headmaster of some 30 years earlier, who declined the invitation for the Speech Day of 1955. (Jack Cooper was the first former pupil to be invited back in this role. One of John Crompton's young scholars from 1906 to 1913, he gained the school's first distinction in the School Certificate examination, remembered Mr

Baker as the best teacher ever, and recalled with pleasure his trips "to the top of Trowbridge Road" to play football.)

Many boys and girls were honoured on these occasions for their successes and contributions to school life, none more so than Claude Say who received the Sixth Form prize from Rear Admiral Scott in 1948. He had been School Captain that year, gained his HSC and won a County Scholarship, joined the RAF and went to Bristol University for 3 years. After that he was posted as an engineer to Woomera, retiring in 1985 after living and working for 30 years in Australia, and it was from there that he recently penned a few notes:

> "Johnny Otter: sports master and maths teacher *extraordinaire* – he gave me the calculus, God bless him! – short, stocky, ex aircrew – can you believe we actually used Euclid's geometry.
> Mr Brosnan: if he was displeased with you, he called you a 'chump' – always had a stinking, bubbling pot of glue on the boil. I fancy he even kept it going during the hols.
> Miss Burgoine: a lovely lady; to her the world was full of colour. She had a crippled leg, but she never complained. We all loved her, so warm was she and gentle.
> Minnie Rhodes: I must include Minnie. A north-country lass, young and 'with it' – minuscule, but a ball of fun and energy.
> Mr Percival: old fella – very strict history teacher – one of the olde school – firm but sarcastic; a very interesting character.
> In biology, next to the Wimshurst machine our most prized possession was a dinkum human skull called George. He spent most of the time safely hidden away in a box. What amazed and delighted us was that the top of the skull was removeable."

In August 1951, Charles Edward Stewart Flemming, well respected family doctor and eminent Bradfordian as well as a man closely connected with the development of the school over almost half a century, died. His widow presented the school with an Encyclopaedia Britannica in memory of her husband, and arrangements were put in hand for his photograph to be hung in the school's entrance hall alongside those of his former colleagues and friends, Lord Fitzmaurice and Canon Clarke.

Other matters to receive attention during the early years of the new Head's tenure were school hours, tennis courts, Bibles, blazers, and potato-peelers. From September 1948, the afternoon session was extended until 4.00 pm, with full parental approval; the tennis courts were also extended – spatially rather than temporally – so that at last they were of full size; the Head suggested that each pupil, on the occasion of his leaving the school, should be given a Bible, a suggestion turned down by the Governors; and purchase was authorised both of a stock of blazers that were on offer at a bargain price and of a power-operated potato-peeler for use in the kitchen.

None of these is an item of high educational significance, but the blazers and potato-peeler are interesting in that they were bought from the Endowment Fund which under Geoffrey Avery was put to greater use than at any time previously. It produced an income of about £410 a year, which, together with the rent of £40 from Clifford House, gave the Governors about £450 a year to be used at their discretion. Broadly, the heads under which this money was spent were:

a) maintenance grants for pupils whilst at school and at university;
b) £50 annually for the Head to spend on concerts, school visits etc;
c) £100-£120 on each occasion to subsidise exchange visits to France;
d) expenses for Speech Day, Sports Day etc;
e) expenses in connection with the school's participation in rowing;
f) stage electrical work and dramatic productions;
g) maintenance of the Headmaster's house.

The Endowment Fund enabled the Governors and the Head to obtain items that were desirable rather than necessary, and to enrich school life in countless small ways that added up to a significant and recognisable benefit. In 1950, for example, as well as spending small sums on the Mistresses' Common Room and on furniture for the Head, though they do not fit neatly into any of the above categories, purchases were made of violins and a cello prior to the starting of a class in stringed instruments, and of a wireless set for school use. And the Fund came into its own again in 1953, Coronation year, when it paid for bunting and flood lighting, the re-painting of the flag-pole, commemorative trees that were planted in the playing field, and a subsidy for a school trip to London to see the Coronation decorations and the Trooping of the Colour.

Money was made available by the Education Committee for the commemorative trees mentioned above, but additional cash from the Endowment Fund allowed 25 trees in all to be bought – poplars, beech, lime, flowering cherries, and copper beech – to augment the chestnuts planted by Lord Fitzmaurice in Victory Field some 28 years earlier. And in Coronation year, Geoffrey Avery was able to write:

"It was by a strange turn of circumstance that Miss Burgoine took leave of us at this time, for her gift to the school in memory of her 34 years with us was also of trees. Miss Burgoine gave a magnolia, a tulip tree, and a copper beech. The magnolia was given pride of place in the corner to the left of the gate and already it has bloomed. Please do not call it a tulip tree, as passers-by have already miscalled it; the tulip tree is to the right of the gate. In some 15 years time it will bear flowers shaped like a tulip, beautiful in themselves yet coy, not easily distinguishable save by those who seek them, for their petals will be greenish. In 20 or 30 years time the tree should reach more than 80' in height – a companion to the elm, whose place it may one day usurp as the greatest tree within sight."

The elm, alas, was deemed to be dangerous in 1954 and was felled the following year, and today the magnolia, the tulip tree, the copper beech, and many of the rest are gone. Lord Fitzmaurice's chestnuts, however, remain.

If there was one single issue and one preoccupation that dominated the whole period of Geoffrey Avery's headship, however, it was the disgraceful inadequacy of the buildings and the threat that this inadequacy posed to the school's very existence. As has already been said, the possibility of reconstruction which was vaguely there when he took up his post receded as the weeks and months went by. The Governors declared in 1947 that a much better staff room was needed; in 1948 they decided that additional hutments were required in default of more permanent structures, and a working party, consisting of Governors, HMI, the Head, and officers of the Authority, was set up to examine the problem; science classrooms and laboratories were identified as being a most urgent need; but in the following years, there was a clear statement from the Authority that new, or extra, buildings of any kind were just not affordable.

Some headway seemed to have been made when, in 1952, the Wiltshire Development Plan was submitted to, and accepted by, the Minister of Education, but even here there was unhappiness in that the Fitzmaurice Grammar School was found not to have been scheduled as a boarding establishment. So often had plans for rebuilding been frustrated, and so constant had been the rejection by the Authority of suggestions for the admitting of a regular two-form entry, that slights were all too easily found and threats to the school's continuance suspected where they really did not exist. In this instance, the Director of Education explained that this was not an indirect hint that the school might close. It was simply an indication that the grammar school at Bradford on Avon did not need a boarding element, the very furthest pupil coming from no more than 8 miles away. Failure to achieve an adequacy of accommodation for its pupils, then, continued as a running sore throughout these years.

An HMI report of 1954 says:

"The last published report on this school in 1937 enumerated nine major defects in the buildings which were described as 'unsuitable for the school's needs'. Since then a kitchen-dining room has been added, and a classroom of the old-fashioned gallery type has been converted for teaching biology. For this purpose it is too small, and, in other ways, is most unsatisfactory. Most of the defects recorded in 1937 still persist, and the conclusion reached seventeen years ago that 'the school is heavily handicapped by inadequate buildings' is still true. It would be tedious to describe all the deficiencies already on record. It is sufficient to state that only by extensive building can most of the present adverse conditions be removed and the full needs of the school met....For many years, the inadequate and out-of-date premises have greatly hampered and made burdensome the life and work of the school. There can be no real relief from most of these restrictions until additional building gives the school the facilities it so sorely needs."

These were the depressing conclusions of the inspectors in October 1954, and they contrast vividly with their up-beat and optimistic findings about the organisation and morale and quality of teaching at Fitzmaurice Grammar School. Their report in these sections must have gladdened the hearts of both Governors and Head.

Of Geoffrey Avery himself they say: "He orders the affairs of the school with admirable smoothness and efficiency, and his government is resolute and far-sighted. Under his direction, which is humane and dignified, the life and work of the school have been strengthened and enriched." They acknowledge the debt owed to Arthur Percival, and of the rest of the staff – 12 in all, 7 being in their first posts and 9 appointed in the last 2 years – they observe: "Despite their lack of experience, the staff show teaching skill well above the average. They are vigorous and hard-working, generous in their attitude towards the school, and very ready to meet the varied demands made upon them by a school of this size." The positive feel to these general comments was repeated when the inspectors looked at individual subject areas. "All the teaching is inspired by sincerity and conviction" (scripture); "[Mr Percival] is a skilful and persuasive teacher"; "there is....no weakness in the teaching of this subject, and much of it is very good indeed" (French); "[Miss Lawson] has made a promising beginning and infected the pupils with her own enthusiasm"; "there is considerable vitality in the teaching and a stimulating range of materials is used" (art). Admittedly, these are selective quotations, but they accurately indicate the tenor of the report and they give an impression of a unified, competent and effective team that was working under strong leadership.

Above: Mr G W Avery, Headmaster 1947-1955.

Below: Cast of 'Pygmalion', with Messrs Smith, Freeth and Revill, centre, 1957.

A First-class School
The Fitzmaurice Grammar School:
1954-1968

THE INSPECTORS' REPORT OF OCTOBER 1954 was a good one and in most ways it must have been encouraging for everyone connected with the school; but, of course, not everything ran smoothly all the time.

In 1954 there had recently been a fire in the laboratory; examination results (as ever) sometimes caused disappointment; there was a disturbing theft of money from the Head's cupboard (followed by the County's refusal to provide him with a safe); and the relevant authorities had reason to complain of some of the boys (but not girls, seemingly) throwing stones from the playing field wall that bounded the canal into the canal itself. Dire warnings were issued about the consequences should this offence be repeated and the culprits apprehended. Nevertheless, building problems apart, it was a happy school which Geoffrey Avery led and from which he resigned in April 1955 in order to take up the headship of a new grammar school at Crawley in Sussex. He, like most of his predecessors, left Bradford to seek new and greater challenges elsewhere.

In the advertisement for a new Head, Fitzmaurice was described as a co-educational grammar school of 200 pupils, and in the brief interregnum between Avery and his successor, Norman Bradshaw, presided over again by Arthur Percival, a few loose ends had to be tied up. For example, Geoffrey Avery was asked back to plant trees in commemoration of his leadership of the school, and he accepted the honour. The ownership of Clifford House, residence of all six of the school's previous Heads, came under scrutiny because there was the anomaly of the Head Master's being an employee of the County Council but a tenant of the Endowment Trust. Should the position be regularised by the sale of the house to the Council? And from the County Council came the suggestion, unwelcome to the Governing Bodies of both Fitzmaurice and the Secondary Modern School, that Bradford on Avon should be the scene for the setting up of that uncomfortable hybrid, a bilateral school. It was unanimously declared locally that within the County there were places far more suitable for such an experiment. So there was no shortage of matters of controversy to greet Mr Bradshaw when he left King Edward VII Grammar School, Melton Mowbray, for the Fitzmaurice Grammar School at Bradford on Avon.

David Rees was a pupil from 1952 to 1960. Son of Anne Rees, mentioned earlier as having taught at the school for many years, he knew some of the staff socially and informally, and he is an interesting commentator on the change of leadership of Fitzmaurice at this time. "Sam" Farrar and Geoffrey Rowntree he saw as essentially "patrician" and all that that implies – men who were liberal, generous, natural leaders, and with a certain social distinction. Crompton, too, would probably have merited the same description. Geoffrey Avery, however, had an army background, having held a high rank in the Military Police, and he did not enjoy quite the same relationship with his Governors or his senior colleagues as had his predecessors. With Norman Bradshaw there was another shift, this time to that of wholehearted professional, and it is from roughly the time of his appointment that a significant rise in Fitzmaurice's fortunes can be traced.

During the first 60 years of its history, the Fitzmaurice Grammar School (and the County School before it) had never achieved greatness. On occasion, indeed, it had sunk to significant depths of mediocrity and from time to time its future had been seriously in doubt. From the mid or late 50s, however, it won a growing reputation and achieved an enviable degree of excellence, the beginning of its entry to the first division of Wiltshire schools coinciding roughly with Norman Bradshaw's assumption of the headship.

Bradshaw is remembered as a tough, energetic, dynamic sort of man who did a lot for the school in the short time he stayed in Bradford. This was for three years only, and then he left in July 1958 for the headship of the grammar school at Tiverton in Devon. (Both in character and the brevity of his stay he had something in common with Henry Rosen 30 years earlier.) But in one important respect at least he had better luck than almost all those who had gone before him. During the period of his leadership of the school, it acquired its first new permanent buildings for more than half a century, and it is both the physical expansion of the grammar school and the quality of its academic results that are the dominant themes of its history from 1958.

In view of its widespread unpopularity, the suggestion that Bradford on Avon should be provided with a bilateral school was quickly dropped by the Local Authority. Also dropped was the idea of selling Clifford House. £3,000 had been thought a reasonable asking price, with £2,250 eventually agreed as being acceptable. What had been overlooked was the fact that Norman Bradshaw's rent for the property had been negotiated when he had been appointed, and any raising of that rent (which would have been an inevitable consequence of the property's being sold) would have contravened the terms of his appointment. So that idea was dropped – or, at least, held in abeyance until the headship should change again. The same fate befell the new Head's wish to reform the

House system that had operated, largely successfully, since Henry Rosen had introduced it so many years ago. He proposed that the four Houses should be mixed rather than being for boys and girls separately. The novelty of this suggestion shocked the Governors and met with hostility in other quarters, so they first insisted that, should the change take place, the name Fitzmaurice must be retained for one of the new Houses, and then, having gauged the strength of the opposition, they were emboldened to ditch the idea altogether.

If these were all negative results, positive things were also being achieved. Dramatic productions – modestly – had long been meaningful school activities, principally as inter-House competitions and as presentations of short plays or excerpts from longer works. In 1957, however, Ken Revill and John Smith produced *Pygmalion* which was pronounced a resounding success. The tennis court was resurfaced. Mr Fellowes, a former captain of Lancashire, coached the boys in cricket. In 1956, first year pupils got an unexpected holiday when it was decided that, because of the numbers wishing to be present, they would be excused attendance at the annual Speech Day. In 1957, a rowing team was entered in the Nottingham Regatta. And Goodalls became the sole suppliers of school uniform. Previously, the school itself had bought and sold certain items from the Endowment Fund, but any remaining items were now handed over to the official suppliers at cost price less 20%. (The clothing account was found to have been accurately kept, Miss M'Quhae was thanked for her careful accounting, and "it was agreed that the two ties which appear to be short should be 'written off' and that the supply of panties which seemed to be unsaleable be given to the Head Mistress of the Junior School for use as she thinks fit"! What did she do with them?)

A far more important matter, however, was the extension of the accommodation that had been sought for so many years. This was a development that had two limbs, one being the phased provision of completely new buildings and the other the acquisition of the residence known as Summerfield House, 2 Trowbridge Road.

Towards the end of Geoffrey Avery's regime one of the Governors had suggested that, as there was clearly no money available for new buildings, the purchase of a suitable house in the neighbourhood should be investigated. She had had a specific property in mind, but unfortunately it proved not to be available. Now, a year later, the large house on the corner of Junction Road and Trowbridge Road came on the market and the Local Authority was urged to buy it at the asking price of £4,750. (The rider was added that they should not see this as an alternative to, or as a way of delaying the provision of, the block of new classrooms that was scheduled for 1956.) Completion was achieved on 30 October 1956, and thereafter there was a rolling programme of adaptation with a view to its being used for Sixth Form teaching, music, pottery, and as a book store. A room was also to be provided for the girl prefects, the boys taking over the old book store. There were several staff flats on the first floor of the property, one of which was offered to Miss Pickworth in 1957 when it was vacated by Kathleen Hyde, and L F Parsons was taken on as part-time gardener at the house as the additional work that this entailed was too much for Groundsman Kranz to undertake. Summerfield, then, though its conversion was not completed until 1959, was a real bonus and a significant addition to the school's facilities.

The permanent building that had been promised – the first new permanent building on the site since 1905 – was to be a block of three classrooms at the back of the original building and down towards the Junior School. It was to have been up and ready for the start of term in September 1956. But, not unusually, there was a delay, and this delay was compounded by a change in plans. Instead of three classrooms, it was decided that a chemistry lab, a prep room, and a single classroom should be built. A tender for £7,551 was accepted, building started, building was halted, September 1957 was hoped for, Christmas came and went, and finally, early in 1958, all was done. In parallel with this provision went pressure for a new physics lab and, as a further development, a new biology lab, but by the time of Norman Bradshaw's leaving the improvements remained as a chemistry lab and prep room, a new classroom, and the facilities provided by Summerfield House.

It was perceived that the boiler house in the Junior School which was close to the new building could be used to heat the lab, particularly as the Head Mistress had no objection to this plan; Bill Rawlings was appointed Lab Assistant from September 1957; and Groundsman Kranz was given an allowance for the extra work that he had to do around the new chemistry lab.

Though Bradshaw was an Oxford English graduate, he was early in his recognition of the importance that science would come to hold in the second half of the twentieth century. The old lab of 1897, with its gold lettered *Laboratory* on the door, its high stools, and its casually scattered collection of assorted chemicals and acids, was a Victorian relic and both inappropriate and inadequate for the teaching of science in the 1950s. The provision of new labs at this time owed much to the vigour with which he urged the necessity of better facilities for the teaching of science.

As accommodation became somewhat easier, so the number of pupils on roll increased. By 1955 the school was two-form entry throughout, the old, incredibly clumsy system of alternating a one-form with a two-form entry having been abandoned. (Not only had it been difficult to administer; it had been subject to manipulation, for parents had tended to choose the school for their children in the two-form entry years, looking elsewhere when they knew that only one form was to be admitted.) And this change was another factor in Fitzmaurice's move from second (or third) class status to something much better. A total of 200 on roll was reached for the first time in the early 1950s, with 215 in 1955, 224 in 1957, 297 in 1959, and 337 in 1961. But the really significant figure was the virtual doubling of the number of pupils in the school between the early 50s and the mid 60s, with the creation by Norman Bradshaw of a real Sixth Form. This was something that he set about with determination, working deliberately to create a more dynamic institution with a Sixth Form of substance as its crown.

Some of the pupils, as had always been the case, caused problems – the train boys from Melksham, for example, who could have been better controlled (it was thought) had corridor-type coaches been available on their trains. Others brought the school nothing but credit – the public examinees of 1956 who, at the highest level, produced three County Scholarships. And so it was to a school that was confident and expanding that Philip Edmonds was appointed in January 1959. John Smith had been officially appointed Deputy Head and Nora Lawson Senior Mistress in September 1956, and now, between the going of Bradshaw and the arrival of Edmonds from the headship of Yorebridge Grammar School at Leyburn in Yorkshire, they, for a term, were in charge of Fitzmaurice Grammar School.

The teaching staff for the Bradshaw years was:

Head Master:	Norman Bradshaw (1955-1958);
Deputy Head:	Arthur Percival (1950-1956), John Smith (1956-);
Senior Mistress:	Nora Lawson (1956-);
English:	Kenneth Revill (1953-), Eunice Cadogan (Mrs Moore) (1957-), Roy Day (1954-1958), Frances Potter (1958);
Maths:	Sidney Johnson (1952-);
Science:	Albert Jelfs (1948-1956), Thomas Ratcliffe (1956-), Peter Schrecker (1956-), Nora Lawson (1952-);
Mod Langs:	John Smith (1945-);
History:	Arthur Percival (1921-1956), Marjorie Pickworth (1956-);
Geography:	Kathleen Hyde (Mrs Brown) (1953-1957), Ronald Price (1957-);
RE:	Margaret McNeill (1955-);
Art:	Cicely Cox (Mrs Lishman) (1953-1955), Mrs Sheila Wright (1956-);
Woodwork:	Arthur Freeth (1955-);
Dom Sci:	Sylvia M'Quhae (1953-);
Boys' PE:	Harry Haddon (part-time) (1954-58);
Girls' PE:	Mrs Day (1955), Helen Mellor (1955-1958).

Percival, of course, was one of those who had given a lifetime of service to the school, and he retired in 1956 after acting as Head and then overseeing the arrival of the new Head Master. Ilse Stein recalled his skill as a raconteur; others remember him differently. For Jo Uncles he was a good historian and an interesting teacher, but strict and not very approachable. Graham Hayter remembers "a white haired, unsmiling man, whose lessons were uninspiring lectures, and sadly the subject never came alive for me". The memories of former colleagues are rather different. They recall, for example, that the length of staff meetings was often determined by the time of departure of Mr Percival's train to Bath, and for many years there was a tacit acknowledgement of his right to ownership of the most comfortable armchair in the men's staffroom. Whatever the flavour of individual memories of Arthur Percival, he, like a handful of other men and women, was one of the great formative influences at Bradford's grammar school.

Ted Jelfs's acceptance of promotion at Ilfracombe Grammar School led to the appointment of Tom Ratcliffe as Head of Science. Peter Schrecker, Eunice Cadogan, and Margaret McNeill were additions to the staff to help cope with the increased numbers. (Ratcliffe and Schrecker were both appointed to strengthen the science teaching, and both were from a recent service background, Ratcliffe having had wartime experience in naval intelligence in Turkey whilst Schrecker was a German refugee who had served in the RAF.) Harry Haddon, who was a part-time teacher, left in order to go to college to become professionally qualified. And this was the staff that Philip Edmonds inherited. Appointed to the positions in 1951, Arthur Baker and S C Tucker continued throughout as Chairman and Vice Chairman respectively of the Board of Governors.

After graduating from Oxford, Philip Edmonds had taught at Shaftesbury and Lydney Grammar Schools before serving in India with the Royal Artillery during the War. He returned to Lydney as Senior English Master after his stint in the army, and just prior to his appointment to Bradford on Avon had served as Head for five years at Yorebridge. He and Norman Bradshaw were temperamentally chalk and cheese. Where the latter had been a combative, busy, thrusting individual, Edmonds was gentle, even tempered, and willing to listen to points of view that were different from his own. John Smith, his Deputy, was later to describe him as "patient, good humoured, slow to anger, magnanimous, and immensely tolerant"; Lilian Oakman (who taught at Fitzmaurice in 1953 and who was taught by Edmonds at Lydney) remembers him as "a gentleman and a fine teacher". And it was a school that was clearly in the ascendant as far as academic achievement was concerned that he joined in January 1959.

For the period of his headship, there were, of course, changes, and the number of teachers at the school grew considerably. The following list, however, has two caveats attach to it. The first is that staff are listed under their principal subject specialisms, but many taught across two or more areas. (Examples would be Miss Diamond who taught both games and French, as did Mr McColl, and Miss Doubtfire was involved in science as well as RE.) A second caveat is that there were a great number of visiting and part-time teachers who taught at the school for as little as one half day a week or for as much as four or four and a half days so that few would realise that they were not, in fact, full-time staff. In science there were Dr Maxwell, Beatrice Johnston, Dr Steven, and Mrs Harries; Mrs Ratcliffe began by teaching occasionally and part-time, as did Margaret Hore; and there were others – Mrs Wright, Mrs Wilson, Mrs Corcoran, Mrs Lowe....

Headmaster:	Philip Edmonds (1959-1968);
Deputy Head:	John Smith (1956-);
Senior Mistress:	Nora Lawson (1956-1963),
	Sylvia M'Quhae (Mrs Adams) (1964),
	Mrs Kathleen Ratcliffe (1964-);
English:	Kenneth Revill (1953-), Colin Steele (1959-),
	Eunice Cadogan (Mrs Moore) (1957-1959),
	Christopher Brown (1965-1966),
	Mrs Virginia Evans (1965-);
Maths:	Sidney Johnson (1952-), Geoffrey Swift (1959-),
	Lynne Powell (1965-);
Science:	Thomas Ratcliffe (1956-), Peter Schrecker (1956-1959),
	Mrs Heather Field (1960), Joan Timbrell (1960-1962),
	Islwyn Thomas (1962-), Nora Lawson (1952-1963),
	John Hicks (1964-), Barbara Doubtfire (1963-1964);
Mod Langs:	John Smith (1945-),
	Donald McColl (1958-1967), Mrs Vaughan (1967),
	Katrina Paroussi (Mrs Howell) (1967-),
	Ruth Diamond (1959-1964), Joan Davies (1964-);
History:	Marjorie Pickworth (Mrs Wilson) (1956-1963),
	Douglas Anderson (1963-), Mrs Margaret Lowe (1968-);
Geography:	Ronald Price (1957-1959), Mrs Kathleen Ratcliffe (1960-);
RE:	Margaret McNeill (1955-1966), Duncan Smith (1966);
Music and Art:	Mrs Sheila Wright (1956-1959), Robert Davis (1962-1965),
	Maureen McGregor (1965), Mrs Enid Corcoran (1968-);
Woodwork:	Arthur Freeth (1955-1967), John Blake (1967-);
Dom Sci:	Sylvia M'Quhae (Mrs Adams) (1953-1964);

Boys' PE:	Harry Haddon (1960-);
Girls' PE:	Diana Wiffen (1958-1959), Mrs Margaret Hore (1959);
General:	Janet Collier (1964-1965).

Again, some footnotes may be in order.

Philip Edmonds was taken seriously ill in October 1962 and was away from school for three or four months. During that time, John Smith took over the reins, and Mrs Page, Mrs Sheldon, and Miss Macdonald lent a hand to cover the Head's absence. Another substitution was that of Sheelagh Daunt for Donald McColl. He was seconded for the 1965/66 school year to receive instruction in the teaching of Russian, so she temporarily took his place in modern languages before going off to teach at the Girls' High School in Trowbridge.

John Smith was Edmonds' Deputy for the whole period, but Nora Lawson's post of Senior Mistress passed briefly to Sylvia M'Quhae in January 1964 before she left a couple of terms later to become Mrs Adams (returning later part-time), and then Kitty Ratcliffe assumed the office.

By this time, the two senior teachers on the staff (Head and Deputy Heads excepted) were Sidney Johnson and Ken Revill, and Mr Johnson recalls with a degree of amusement how his colleague had blotted his copybook immediately he was appointed. He failed to turn up at school on that first morning and had to be summoned to work by a telephone call from the Head. He also recalls that it was Revill who played the piano (very loudly) at assembly every morning and the school invariably marched from the Hall to its first lesson to the strains of *In a Country Garden*.

In a more serious vein, he tells how he reached a stage in his career when he had to teach more maths and cut down what had been a quite considerable commitment to games. At this point he was introduced to Harry Haddon, player-manager of Trowbridge Town. A former Royal Navy PE Instructor, Haddon put on an impromptu gymnastics display that was sufficiently impressive for Sidney Johnson to ask for his recruitment to the staff as a way out of the games difficulty. This explains his part-time employment at the school from 1954 to 1958. In that year, he was released by the school to go to College to obtain a teaching certificate, and after a crash course with Roy Day to enable him to qualify for entry to St Paul's at Cheltenham, he spent two years there, obtained professional recognition (with a distinction in PE) and returned to Fitzmaurice in 1960 where a full-time post had been kept open for him.

It is noteworthy that, with the increase in size of the school, the better opportunities for advancement, and the greater professional satisfaction to be derived from belonging to a successful organisation, the teaching staff tended to stay longer. No more was there a frantic annual turnover; indeed, a significant number of those who served under Edmonds stayed on into Gerald Reid's time and were still there when the grammar school finally closed in 1980.

Pupil numbers had reached what at that time was an all-time high of 245 in 1958. By 1968 they were 387 – a 58% increase in ten years – and they remained in the high 300s for the whole of the mid and late 1960s. So this decade saw Fitzmaurice transformed from a small, struggling selective school to a fair-sized grammar school with a considerable and highly academic Sixth Form, staffed by a well qualified and ambitious teaching force who viewed the school as desirable in its own right rather than a stepping-stone to somewhere better. Much of the credit for this must go to Norman Bradshaw, with his constant emphasis on the importance of a flourishing Sixth Form, and Sidney Johnson thinks that its reputation was sealed by the Open Oxbridge Scholarships gained by David Rees and Geoffrey Copland (sons of former teachers at the school) in 1960. Both went on to gain 1st class degrees, Rees at Downing College, Cambridge, and Copland at Merton, Oxford.

The 1961 results were better, and in 1962 they were better still, particularly at A level. 1963 saw the best examination results for some years, and they were improved upon the following year, at least at O level, in which an average of 5.8 passes per pupil was achieved. In 1967 the O level results were poor, the A level the best ever, whilst in 1968 there was an improvement at O level and a 76% pass rate at A level.... And so the roll call of successes continued. It had not always been so. Neither the Fitzmaurice Grammar School nor the County School before it had always been able to take pride in consistently good results and enjoy the genuine academic achievement of their pupils both at school and at college and university thereafter.

And for all these boys and girls more buildings were needed. The extent of these, by the time of Norman Bradshaw's departure was, as has been said, Summerfield on the corner of Trowbridge Road and the new chemistry lab and classroom down by the primary school. These were added to in Philip Edmonds' time by the tacking on of a physics lab to the recently built science block, the acquisition of two classrooms that were vacated when the new secondary modern school was opened, and the obtaining of some Prattens. A new biology lab failed to materialise, and there were two considerable complications to the whole business of improving the school's accommodation. The first was the proximity of the Trowbridge Road Primary School to Fitzmaurice; the combining of the buildings of these two institutions for the benefit of one or the other was mooted from time to time and always eventually rejected as being impractical The second was the publication of DES Circular 10/65 and all that it implied.

A positive development, then, was the building of a physics lab in 1960 at a cost of £6,494 as an addition to the chemistry lab of 1958. It was not originally

Above: 1st team tennis, 1958. Back, left to right, Jocelyn Rabbitts, Heather Gerrish, Miss Mellor, Lesley Masters, Yvonne Brown; front, Sylvia Prosser, Jane Brown, Judith Webster, Suzanne Knott.

Below: 1st team cricket, 1960. Back, left to right, Clifford Rule, Maurice Isley, Colin Howell, Robin Hanny, Leon Hall, David Way, Geoffrey Copland; front, Raymond Davis, David Culverhouse, Grant Noble, Geoffrey Payne, Ronald Holdway.

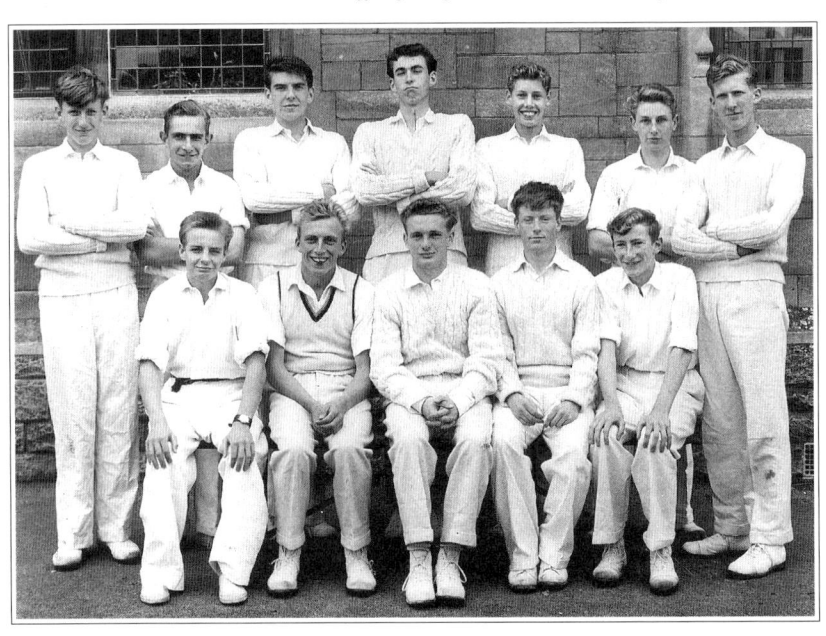

Above: 1st team hockey, 1962. Back, left to right, Janet Lally, Judith Edwards, Eileen Barry, Pamela Green, Margaret Mitchell, Lindsay Noble, Jean Dawe; front, Marie Evans, Heather Spear, Pat Wilkins, Pamela Howlett (capt), Celia Hynes.

Below: 1st team football, 1962. Back, left to right, Mr H Haddon, Stuart Carrier, Stephen Hills, Richard Saxty, Simon Hanny, Leon Hall, Clifford Rule, Brian Pearce; front, Robert Morgan, David Stillman, Richard Clarke (capt), Anthony Whitfield, Jonathan Brown.

fitted with blackout, but this was a deficiency that was soon put right. Another positive gain a couple of years later was the taking over of the two rooms that had up to then been used for practical subjects by pupils from Trinity but that were rendered surplus to their requirements by the opening of the new school in Ashley Road in 1962. (Both the science rooms and the older practical rooms were taken over by the primary school when the grammar school closed, and both are still there, still in use, the practical block having had a large door let into it so that it can be used to garage a minibus.)

More changing accommodation for boys was also provided. The girls' cloakrooms had been improved by a substantial addition in 1928; the boys' facilities, however, were still much as they had been for more than 60 years. "Present amenities are completely primitive. It is suggested that....the pavilion should be extended to offer showering facilities for games players. Provision is also most urgently needed for PE staff who have no amenities whatever for showering and changing," wrote Edmonds to his Governors. So, after prolonged expressions of concern that developed into really rather frantic representations to the CEO, a minor project was approved whereby the boys' changing rooms in the pavilion could be extended. These had been terribly cramped, and the extension effected a marginal improvement on the quite dreadful conditions under which the boys had previously washed and changed.

In the early 1960s there was also pressure for the provision of a new biology lab. It proved unavailing, so this branch of science continued to be taught in the old laboratory on the first floor of the old building of 1897.

These were all piecemeal developments of the years 1959 to 1962, but behind them, a grander, more cohesive design for the rebuilding of Bradford's grammar school was being developed – but its realisation was a distant prospect indeed. In February 1961, the Head reported to the Governors:

> "It is a matter of very grave concern that the school's building development is dependent on the removal of the Bradford on Avon County Junior School to new premises, the building of which has not yet even been sanctioned for inclusion in a programme. It would, therefore, appear highly optimistic to suppose that rebuilding here can be completed in less than five to seven years, perhaps more....Additional accommodation at Summerfield House and in the new laboratory block has really done no more than keep pace with the larger numbers in the Sixth Form and improve the facilities for the teaching of certain subjects. Meanwhile, in many respects the school has completely outgrown its original premises. It would clearly be wrong to wait on a distant prospect of improvement while at least a complete school generation suffers from inadequate accommodation."

Philip Edmonds then goes on to detail small improvements that could be made in the interim. One was an extension to the pavilion changing facilities which, as we have seen, actually happened. Another was an abortive attempt to get a biology lab built, and a third was the building of a new hall on the high ground between the science block and the canteen as an earnest of bigger and better things to come. This plan, too, came to nothing. All that happened on the ground was the provision in 1965 and 1966 of a couple of mobile classrooms between the science block and the main building that provided three more, quite pleasant, teaching spaces.

To return to the grand, albeit distant, plan – the nub of it was the displacement of the junior school from its site a couple of hundred yards or so behind the Fitzmaurice Grammar School, and the taking over of its buildings, suitably extended, by the secondary school. This plan sank in 1963 when, at a meeting between the Head, the Chairman of Governors, and officers of the LEA, it was decided that it was simply not viable because of the many dispersed teaching blocks that were implied by the idea and because of the practical difficulty of remodelling the old grammar school building. It would have created a very bitty and disadvantageously scattered school. So the formula was reversed. Perhaps the junior school should be extended to take in the grammar school's site and buildings, and Fitzmaurice could look forward to a sort of rebirth in entirely new premises. No objection in principle was raised against this by the Governors. (Subsequently, Arthur Baker – by this time Vice Chairman, having relinquished the Chair in favour of Mervyn Uncles – made known his strong objections to moving out of the 1897 building. After all, it was the school around which his life had revolved for 60 years.) J H Bradley, the Chief Education Officer, saw merit in the proposal. The primary school could be left where it was, and the new labs and classroom could be added to it and used by it when the grammar school was rehoused. "But Circular 10/65 seems to preclude the Government's agreeing to this," he added ruefully.

Circular 10/65, therefore, needs a word or two of explanation, and what I wrote in my earlier book, *The Trowbridge Schools Revisited*, can be repeated here:

> "The Education Act of 1944 introduced the new and radical principle of secondary education for all, and it saw the vehicle for this change as being a tripartite system of grammar, secondary modern, and technical schools, though, in the event, few gestures towards the establishment of the latter were made. The so-called 11+ exam determined to which type of school a pupil should be allocated. There were sheep and there were goats; one was accepted or rejected. From the very beginning, however, there were Local Authorities that were uneasy about this early and, in the main, irrevocable casting of the dye. The West Riding, for

example, wanted no truck with selection, and so, sometimes for ideological reasons and sometimes because they fitted in well with the local situation, a number of all-through, or comprehensive, schools were established that educated pupils of a range of abilities under one roof, albeit, perhaps, in differently titled and organised divisions. At first they were few – 13 by the end of the 1940s, 27 by the mid 1950s, and 126 by 1959. Leicestershire followed the West Riding and London as an advocate of comprehensive education, but this was a journey into the unknown; both the general public and teachers themselves viewed it with caution and sometimes with downright hostility. Selection had its acknowledged weaknesses, but it was a system which everyone knew and understood.

Robin Pedley, in *The Comprehensive School*, details these reservations:

'Grammar school teachers were often a little fearful of being called on to teach difficult and backward boys and girls. They had had dull pupils before the war, it is true, but they were usually the docile dull from respectable fee-paying families. They disliked the possibility of losing their hitherto superior status in the town. They thought that school standards in scholarship and behaviour would suffer if the doors were flung open to all. Many had little or no understanding of the interests and needs of the non-academic pupils, and felt honestly that such pupils would be better taught by teachers who did understand them. Conversely, the non-graduate heads and staff of the former elementary schools were apprehensive about being passed over for graduates in competition for the top jobs in the comprehensive system. Some graduates too, realising that their prospects of a headship in a grammar or comprehensive school were nil, chose to carve a niche for themselves in the secondary moderns: better to reign in hell than serve in heaven.'

So, although the abolition of selection at the age of 11 came to form a part of socialist political philosophy, the advantages and disadvantages of comprehensive schools were discussed by all sections of the community during the 1950s and early 1960s. Wiltshire set up a Special Sub-Committee in 1963 to consider secondary reorganisation in the County, and it was not unmindful of the fact that its discussions would be much more than merely an academic exercise if a Labour government came to power. And this, of course, is what happened. In October 1964 Labour won the general election, and in July of the following year DES Circular 10/65 signalled a change in the organisation of secondary education in this country; selection was to disappear and all-ability schools were to be set up by Local Authorities. Its provisions did not come as a bombshell to administrators, but in schools like the [Fitzmaurice Grammar School] worst fears were realised and feelings of despondency, anxiety about the future, and of impending loss were powerfully felt. The proposals for secondary reorganisation were threatening and destructive of an order with which those who taught in selective schools were comfortable and to which they had become accustomed; and it was probably an imperfect appreciation of these feelings held by ordinary classroom teachers and the parents of their pupils that was at the root of much of the unhappiness that accompanied educational reorganisation over the next 10 or 15 years."

Mr Bradley was right. Circular 10/65 had put any idea of building a new grammar school out of court, but 15 years were to elapse before the changes it advocated actually came into being in Bradford on Avon.

The 1960s, then, was generally a time of frustration, unfulfilled hopes, and fears about the future, so much so that a long, well balanced, and moderate letter went from all the members of the teaching staff to the CEO, with a copy to Sir Robert Grimston MP, expressing their exasperation at what was not happening. The Minister himself, Sir Robert Boyle, was drawn into the correspondence, but nothing was done and the kerfuffle eventually died down. That was in 1962. In 1965 the Governors arranged to see Dennis Walters MP with a view to his arranging a meeting with the Minister, a confrontation that was first postponed and then cancelled. Nevertheless, these were serious moves and indicative of the mood of deep discontent that prevailed.

A few positive steps forward were taken. In addition to those already mentioned, the prefects – by self-help and a little assistance from the Endowment Fund – created a room for themselves, and the LEA bought some rather unpromising land at the back of the junior school which it thought Fitzmaurice might be able to develop and use at a later date.

Whilst all this was going on, from 1963 onwards Wiltshire was looking at different models of reorganisation. 1965 saw Melksham nominated as the first area to undergo this operation, with pupils from that town ceasing to be eligible for Fitzmaurice once the process was completed. Trowbridge and Bradford on Avon were next in line. Betty Edwards, Clerk to the Governors, in a letter of 1966 to her old Head Master, Sidney Farrar says: "The word 'comprehensive' is beginning to rear its ugly head. The legal department at County Hall is trying hard to trick us into getting their hands on the Endowment. The Governors are fighting for all they are worth to keep the Endowment under their control." And, of course, from 1965 or 1966, as she said, the word "comprehensive" dominated all discussions about buildings and reorganisations and the future of individual secondary schools.

In 1947 there had been confusion about the respective functions of the Governors of the Fitzmaurice Grammar School and the Governors of the Foundation, with the consequence that the latter were not even constituted and, by 1966, had effectively not existed for almost 20 years. This oversight was rectified at a meeting of 19 May 1966 when the Foundation was once again properly set up, with 6 members appointed by the UDC, 3 by the County Council, 2 by the RDC, with 4 coopted. Almost the first act of this reconstituted Board was to appoint 3 members to serve on the Joint Working Party that had been established by the County Council to consider the matter of comprehensive education in Bradford on Avon.

The negotiations and public consultations of 1966, 1967, and 1968 were tortuous and lengthy. There was little room for manoeuvre on the basic issue which was the combination of the Fitzmaurice Grammar School and the Holy Trinity Secondary Modern School to form a single comprehensive school on the Trinity School site, its name to be the St Laurence Voluntary Controlled Comprehensive School with six forms of entry, but in the detail there was ample opportunity for controversy and dissent. This detail involved the wording of the Trust Deed, the precise definition of the new school's religious basis, the catchment area to be served, the buildings that would be required, and a host of organisational and legal considerations, all of which had to be thrashed out in an atmosphere that was often reluctant and resentful.

If the impending closure of Fitzmaurice and the establishing of a comprehensive school in the town were the background to everything else that happened in, and to, the school in the late 1950s and the 1960s, life for its pupils and staff continued on the surface much as usual. Arthur Baker continued as Chairman of Governors with Mervyn Uncles as Vice Chairman when Tucker stood down in 1959. Two years later, the positions of Chairman and Vice Chairman were reversed at Baker's request when he began to feel the need to take a less active roll in public affairs. He died, still as Vice Chairman, in 1964, aged 82. Arthur Baker had joined the school as science teacher in 1905. Narrowly missing out on being appointed Head in 1929, he eventually retired in 1945. He became a Governor in 1947, Vice Chairman in 1949, and Chairman in 1951, reverting, as has been seen, to the position of Vice Chairman in 1961. The school had been his life; he, in turn, had had a huge influence on the way that it had developed. A big fish in a small pond, he had thriven on the provincial politics of Bradford on Avon and the restricted stage of its grammar school. One has the feeling that this was the milieu with which he was comfortable, and that in his later years, because of the narrowness of its boundaries, he had perhaps become overly proprietorial in his management of the school's affairs. Nevertheless, its history was his history.

Other people, too, caused ripples and had their moments and excitements during these years. To mark his headship, Norman Bradshaw had presented a cup for girls' tennis when he left; Miss Pickworth went for a year to the John

Above: Entrance Hall showing, left to right, Honours Board, portrait of Canon Clarke (see page 136), portrait of Arthur Baker (see page 95), and portrait of Lord Fitzmaurice (see frontispiece) above the plaque commemorating his Chairmanship of the Governing Body. The portrait of Dr Flemming is out of shot to the right.

Left: Mr P H Edmonds, Headmaster 1959-1968

Bartram High School in Philadelphia for an exchange that involved a Mr La Paglia's coming to Bradford; Geoffrey Swift also went on an exchange – less excitingly, to Trinity School for two months; and John Smith did a course in preparation for teaching A level German, with Joan Davies promoted to take charge of that subject in 1965. In 1958 Miss Eastman resigned as School Secretary, Noreen Brady being appointed in her place and beginning what was to prove to be a long period of service in that position. Caretakers came and went – Collins, Davis, Selby, Stokes, Whittle, and, finally, Perce Millard – and in January 1969 Groundsman Kranz retired after tending the school's fields and gardens for just short of 22 years. (Sidney Johnson remembers F A Kranz as an excellent gardener and an easy man to get on with provided one didn't attempt to tread on his carefully manicured grass.) Bainton replaced him.

Grant Baker joined the Governing Body in 1959, and after the death of Arthur Baker Mrs Brown became Vice Chairman of Governors. John Stillman brought great credit to himself and to the school by his national success in tennis; a cup, therefore, was purchased and, from 1966, was presented annually for the boys' tennis championship. And Bill Rawlings, the Lab Assistant, found himself overworked with the opening of the new science block, so an additional Assistant was needed. Rawlings continued with chemistry and physics, but Enid Wicheard (formerly Enid Dobson, a pupil at the school from 1942 to 1947) was appointed by Philip Edmonds a few days before his death to service biology in the old laboratory that looked out on to Junction Road.

Year by year, however, Fitzmaurice provided in the 1960s (and on into the 1970s) a rich cultural environment for the young people of Bradford, crowned in most cases with academic success, and in many by distinction. The full-length school play became an accepted feature of the calendar – *The Admirable Crichton, You Never Can Tell, The Lark, Antigone, The Crucible, The Importance of Being Earnest, The Merchant of Venice, Major Barbara, The Boy Friend*.... Ken Revill was the inspiration behind these productions, all of which, apart from *The Admirable Crichton* which was put on in St Margaret's Hall, were produced with maximum difficulty and inconvenience in the school gymnasium. Virginia Evans, John Smith, Sylvia M'Quhae, and Marjorie Pickworth were also heavily involved, and a very promising young actress who took the lead in a number of these productions was Pamela Weston. From the long list of plays that he produced from 1957 onwards, however, for the sheer fun that it generated, *The Boy Friend* in 1974 still stands out in Revill's memory as his favourite.

After a few early years at Hemsworth Grammar School in Yorkshire, he spent the rest of his teaching career at Bradford and was the instigator of much of what the school offered extra-curricularly in drama, music, and the spoken word. He had initiated and then developed a choir. With the arrival of Robert Davis, brass and woodwind instruction was made possible, and soon a fledgling orchestra was formed. It, and the choir, made a concert debut in May 1964 in Trinity Church. It was soon to perform successfully at the County Festival, and, under Maureen McGregor, the St Margaret's Hall concert by choir and orchestra of 1967 was pronounced outstanding. Both music and drama, therefore, were important to the school.

A little more unusual was the emphasis laid on formal debate. It had long held a place in inter-House competitions, but 1958 saw the first venture into inter-school debating, the Fitzmaurice team in both that and the following year being Lesley Masters and David Rees. From this beginning, debating became a major activity, and by the mid 1960s the team was winning through on a fairly regular basis to the final rounds of the County competition that were held in Bath.

These successes were celebrated at Speech Day in late November, an occasion that differed little from the Prizegivings of the early years of the century. They were important in that they were the forum for a reporting on the year's events and the public face of the satisfaction taken in the school's achievements. And there were, of course, occasional excitements – as Sidney Johnson recalls: the eminent academic, for example, who dried up in mid speech and was totally incapable of continuing, and the guest who was apparently so wearied by the length of the Chairman's introduction that she uttered one tart sentence to the effect that everyone had had quite enough, and then sat down. These must have been splendid moments. More usually, the format was entirely predictable; Chairman's address, Headmaster's report, speech from the guest of honour, distribution of certificates and awards, and votes of thanks – with the leavening of a little music and song. The highlight, of course, was the guest's totally unanticipated request that the school should be granted a holiday to mark the occasion, and the unrestrained pleasure with which the granting of his petition was greeted. Year in and year out this ritual was enacted at the Alexander Cinema in November, 1958 being the one exception. In that year the cinema closed. Speech Day, therefore, was temporarily moved to the deconsecrated methodist church, with a reversion to the old venue – now, rather more grandly, St Margaret's Hall – in 1959.

The burden of both the Chairman's and the Headmaster's addresses came increasingly to be dominated by the two crucial issues of the 1960s – the appalling situation created by the school's inadequate buildings, and the growing threat of enforced change posed by the need to introduce comprehensive education. These were gloomy themes, and a succession of distinguished visitors did their best to dispel the pessimism with more uplifting thoughts. The roll-call of these guests in the 1960s is an interesting one: Alan Bullock (Censor of St Catherine's Society, Oxford and well known television personality), Miss A F McDonald (former Headmistress of Monmouth School for Girls), Father Slade (a former pupil of the 1920s), Sidney Farrar (a former Head of the school who had just retired from his headship at Chippenham after 22 years), Prof A D C Peterson (Director of the Department of Education at Oxford), D R Wigram (Head of Monkton Combe School) – and so on. It was customary for the guest to be entertained to lunch at The Swan by some of the Governors, but from 1963 onwards the Headmaster arrogated this responsibility to himself more domestically at Clifford House.

Jennifer Fox, formerly Jennifer Baker, remembers one of these notabilities very well.

> "At some time between the wars, Bill Slade walked round the building on the ledge below the top windows – or so the story goes. I met him once in the 60s but didn't think to ask about the escapade. He later joined some teaching monastic order. The Slades were a big family but I doubt if any are left in BoA now."

And she goes on:

> "During my time as a pupil (1952-1959) a window fell out of the science room above the front door. Luckily it was during lesson time so no one was hurt, but the dent remained in the tarmac by the door for many years. Less fortunate was the original occupant of the huge stone coffin – probably Saxon or Roman – found at Budbury or Ashley, I think. It spent many years in the entrance hall and must have been the oldest waste paper basket in any of the schools in the County."

1968 was to be a year of significance, but a number of other matters that occurred in the early and middle years of the decade should be recorded. Bradshaw had failed in his attempt to reform the House system at Fitzmaurice; Edmonds was more successful. In 1960, Sidney Johnson prodded the staff into recommending that there should be 4 mixed Houses rather than the time-honoured 2 for boys and 2 for girls, and, under greater pressure than they had been a few years earlier, this time the Governors agreed. The name "Fitzmaurice" disappeared (the justification being that the founder was permanently remembered in the name of the school anyway), "Flemming" taking its place. This resulted in the reallocation of some of the old Cups, the Blake Cup, for example, being awarded for hockey under the new system, the Cowlishaw Cup for football, the Frankell Cup for school work, and the Pinckney Cup for champion House. Donald McColl prodded, too. He complained to the Governors that interest in football among the boys was flagging. Many of the grammar schools in Wiltshire only played rugby, and so Fitzmaurice's footballers had to be content with a very limited fixture list, principally involving local secondary modern schools. The Governors saw his point and granted extra money to allow the team to travel further afield to more exciting locations.

Where prodding did not pay off was in staff agitation for representation on the Governing Body. They tried it in 1964 and the answer was "No". They tried again in 1968, but with no more success. It was an exercise in democracy too dangerous to appeal to an innately conservative management.

Gifts were now received on a more than occasional basis from parents who were grateful for the quality of education, and the examination success, that their boys and girls had received – sometimes cash, sometimes something more tangible like a garden seat; when he stepped down from the position of Chairman, Arthur Baker established a science prize to be awarded annually from the interest on £100-worth of Defence Bonds that he donated to the school; and a year later, extensions to the school telephone were daringly installed in the men's staff room, the new laboratory block, and the recently acquired practical rooms.

The years of Philip Edmonds' headship, then, were a time of expansion, high academic achievement, and a burgeoning of clubs and activities of all sorts. But hand in hand with this positive, optimistic ethos went a deep dissatisfaction with what was felt to be the Authority's indifference to the school's plight over accommodation. At the 1963 Speech Day, he was moved to say:

> "I sometimes ponder gloomily on the fact that virtually no progress appears to have been made towards our final development during the five years I have been here....Our hall/gymnasium is now, frankly, ridiculous for either purpose for which it was intended. With our dining room and kitchen we have been forced to admit defeat and to arrange for some 70 pupils to make use of the central kitchen [in the town]."

(The lunch "hour" had earlier been extended to last an hour and a half to accommodate three sittings, pupils from the last sitting often being late for afternoon school. This was modified in 1963 in the way that Edmonds describes above.) The second negative factor was the possible demise of the Fitzmaurice Grammar School implied by the increasingly insistent pressure for reorganisation.

Philip Edmonds bore the brunt of all this conflict. He was a heavy smoker, but it is easy to believe that the stress and worry which must have been constant during these discussions were a factor in the fatal heart attack that he suffered in 1968. He died on 25 October, at the end of the half-term holiday. A fine teacher and widely respected as a most caring and gentle man, his loss was widely and deeply felt. Mrs Edmonds sent £100 to be used for a prize to be presented annually in her husband's memory, and from November 1968 to April 1969 John Smith was appointed Acting Head.

Form 2P, 1968-1969.
Back row, left to right, David Kirkpatrick, Rupert Davis, Simon Taylor, Peter Dawson; boys standing, Michael Franklin, Philip Retter, Cameron Melrose, Ian Hedges, Alan Viles, Nicholas Stronach;
girls standing, Jayne Strong, Bridget Gover, Claire Chedzoy, Susan Price, Jean Harper, Sarah Newman, Joanne Pollard, Jane Walters;
girls seated, Anthea Mead, Susan Schofield, Christine Harvey, Miss Lynne Powell, Angela Ebdon, Clare Smith, Susan Scott; front row, Mavis Webb, Jane Watts, Hilary Moore, Melinda Finn.

Endgame
The Fitzmaurice Grammar School:
1968-1980

JOHN SMITH'S ACTING STEWARDSHIP ran for six months or so until the new Head was able to take up his post in April 1969. From Northern Ireland and with a degree from Belfast, Gerald Reid was a modern linguist who came to Bradford on Avon from the deputy headship of Helsby Grammar School for Boys in Cheshire, and he it was who had the daunting task of maintaining the school's morale and upholding what by now was its fine academic record whilst, at the same time, preparing for a reorganisation to which not all his colleagues felt committed. So if the problem of Fitzmaurice's buildings dropped away for the first time in many years simply because it was obvious that little would be done with an entirely new comprehensive school on the horizon, the achieving of academic excellence year by year was one preoccupation, as were the preparations, both administrative and practical, for a differently organised sort of school.

The huge rise in pupil numbers – from 245 in 1958 to 387 in 1968 – has already been mentioned, and this trend continued steadily until, by 1976 and 1977, there were almost 440 on roll. It is accounted for by the progress through the school into the Sixth Form of several small three-form entries. At this time, too, each year group tended to get bigger as it progressed through the school, and there were substantial numbers who transferred to Fitzmaurice's Sixth Form from Trinity and some of the independent schools.

Summerfield had been a useful addition in the late 1950s, but the rooms were small and, as compared with purpose-built accommodation, it was of limited value. Clifford House, too, had been pressed into service when Gerald Reid and his family left it in 1970, with the ground floor devoted to school use (teaching space and the Deputy Head's office) and the top floor set out as a flat. This was first let to Peter Argyle, and when Rod Stewart moved out of it in 1976 there were hopes that the upper floor could be used for teaching purposes, but, as this was deemed not to be possible on grounds of safety, Clifford House, like Summerfield, turned out to be of only marginal benefit. A mobile classroom was obtained in 1969. This was used for the teaching of music, the art room thus being freed completely for that activity. Even more excitingly, a mobile lab arrived in 1974. These two structures, which were more attractive and acceptable than might be thought, were set up in the field at the back of the main school, the lab having been transported from Amesbury. They provided some alleviation to the problem of teaching space, but essentially the permanent school buildings remained unaltered, desperately crowded and inadequate in every way, despite the seemingly inexorable rise in the number of pupils.

The Sixth Form by the 1970s was substantial, and in the Upper Sixth there was always a solid cohort going on from school to university and other forms of higher education. In 1976, for example, the Upper Sixth numbered 34. Of these, 15 went to university, 4 to polytechnics, 3 to colleges of education, 4 into banking, 3 to the MOD, 1 joined the sports centre at Bath University, 1 went into hotel reception, 1 into farming, and, at the time of the review, 2 were unemployed. This was not untypical of the picture year by year. The A level results were generally, at worst, satisfactory, and often distinguished, with a steady stream of young men and women achieving two or three grade A passes. From this list of successes during the 1970s, individual names spring out. Quite outstanding results were obtained by such as Tony Walker, Alan Barker, Sally Masters, Patricia Diprose, David Ponting, Martin Eales, Chris Taylor, Andrew and Nicholas Stronach, Oliver King, Neil Carden, Honey Schrecker, Frazer Winterbottom, Christine Sorensen, Stephen Bartram, Jacqueline Copeman, Mark Taylor, Michael Pankiewicz, Philip Watts, Mark Gray.... the last three gaining Oxbridge entrance in the same year when one or two such successes annually was the more usual score. And the list could be extended considerably. At O level, the picture was similar, with the average pass rate often being more than 6. A low of 5.1 was recorded in 1974 and a high of 6.6 the following year, but a reduction required on economic grounds by the Local Authority in 1977 to 8 from 9 as the maximum number of subject entries per pupil militated against this figure's being bettered in the future. The all-round consistency and excellence of these successes was the cumulative result of encouragement, expectation, aspiration, and the quality of the instruction provided by a teaching staff that was unusually stable and experienced.

As has previously been noted, plays and concerts continued to mark the school year, as did visits at home and abroad, and the annual sports and winter and summer games produced outstanding team and individual performances. In 1975, Debbie Miles won the Under 15 Wiltshire Cross Country race, came 3rd in the South West Area competition, and 20th nationally out of some 400 competitors. The rowers, too, distinguished themselves. At the Gloucester Junior Head of the River races in 1975, the Fitzmaurice entrants won the Schools Fours, the Junior Fours, and the Under 16 Fours, and were selected to represent the Western Counties in the Regional Championships. A little later, they took first place at the Reading Regatta and first place and the gold medal at the National

Schools Championships. In his annual Report, therefore, Gerald Reid was regularly able to speak of the wealth of extra-curricular activities available to his pupils – extracts from that of 1975 giving a flavour of the school's vitality in its final years.

> "The Charity Committee has been active; the biggest event of the year was the fete in September, but there were also several fund-raising discos. A cheque for £200 has been sent to Cancer Research, and our sponsorship of a student through Aid to Children has been continued. [This was Manoharan, an Indian boy, whom the school sponsored through his secondary education.]
>
> Although there were no tennis matches and a slightly reduced list of cricket fixtures, hockey and football teams continued to contest a full range of events. The hockey results were excellent and the 1st XI again won the Devizes Rally. Sandra Watts, Joanna Alsop and Kay Wicheard have represented the County 1st and 2nd XIs. Last year's 1st XI football team was young, but the experience gained has meant that a virtually unchanged side has had a very successful start to this season. Richard Thomas, Kevin Haynes and Michael Carden have represented the County. Our unreorganised state has meant that on almost every occasion we have played schools two or three times bigger than ourselves. Pride of place among sporting achievements must, however, go to the rowing four coached by Mr Barrie Burke, captain of the Bradford on Avon Rowing Club. They have made an almost clean sweep of regattas from Chester to Boston to Bristol....
>
> Non-sporting activities followed very much their usual pattern, but the normal range of educational visits was supplemented by what will, I hope, be an annual event and a small step towards better international understanding. In October 1974 I spent some time in Sully-sur-Loire in the French Department of the Loiret, which is twinned with Wiltshire. As a result of this, we had in June and July an exchange of 29 pupils and two staff with the school in Sully.... Other Continental excursions were to the Rhine in October and Austria for winter sports at Easter; in this country there was the Lake District trip, whilst after O levels there was a sailing camp at Cerney Wick for Fifth Formers, some of whom also worked, for the first time, at National Trust Camps.
>
>   Musical activities continued the year round, and the hours spent in lunch-time and after-school rehearsals were brought to fruition in concerts, of which we had two – one in St Margaret's Hall and one in our own building. The latter featured Captain Noah and his Floating Zoo, a performance which was so popular that a repeat was staged the next morning for the whole school."

This is a record of real educational achievement and opportunity. There were times in the past when the situation was not quite so happy; that the 70s was a period of success was due to a number of coinciding factors, one being the school's retention of an experienced and committed teaching force. Stability and stagnation are different. The former imperceptibly becomes the latter when teachers outlive their effective shelf-life, initiative and innovation and excitement giving way to complacency and performance based simply on habit. In this scenario, a routine that has proved satisfactory in the past requires little thought or effort in its being repeated, but what was successful first time round has lost its inspiration and freshness. In this decade, Fitzmaurice Grammar School enjoyed the benefits of stability whilst avoiding the evils of stagnation, and the Head was able to boast in 1975 that there had been only 10 resignations of full-time members of the teaching staff in the past 7 years. In particular, English, maths, physics, chemistry, modern languages, history, geography, and some of the minority subjects retained their senior teachers, to the academic benefit of their pupils. For the period of Gerald Reid's headship, then, the staff changes at the school were as follows:

Headmaster:	Gerald Reid (1969-1980);
Deputy Head:	John Smith (1956-1978), Sidney Johnson (1978-);
Senior Mistress:	Mrs Kathleen Ratcliffe (1964-1977), Margaret Tottle-Smith (1978-);
English:	Kenneth Revill (1953-1980), Colin Steele (1959-), Mrs Virginia Evans (1965-1980);
Maths:	Sidney Johnson (1952-), Geoffrey Swift (1959-), Lynne Powell (1965-);
Physics:	Tom Ratcliffe (1956-1977), Mrs J M Creese (1976-1977), John Warburton (1977-);
Chemistry:	Islwyn Thomas (1962-1972), Anthony Hull (1972-), Stuart Ferguson (1979-);
Biology:	John Hicks (1964-1969), Rita Andrews (1969), Anne Baker (1970-1972), Colin Sumner (1972-1975), John Blowers (1975-), Jill Bayley (Mrs Lynch) (1973-1976), Janet Williams (Mrs Dawe) (1976-1979), Diane Satterthwaite (1979-);
Mod Langs:	John Smith (1945-1978), Peter Knight (1978-), Joan Davies (1964-), Mrs Katrina Howell (1967-1969), Colin Whittle (1969-1970), Mrs Ruth Rees (1969-1971), Robert Hawkes (1971-);
History:	Douglas Anderson (1963-), Mrs Margaret Lowe (1968-1971), Adrian Thomas (1971-1976), Clive Main (1976-1979), Timothy Wilbur (1979-);

Geography:	Mrs Kathleen Ratcliffe (1960-1977), Margaret Tottle-Smith (1978-), Raymond Wilkinson (1974-1977), Alistair Thomson (1977-);
RE:	Duncan Smith (1966-1969), Peter Argyle (1969-1972), Roderick Stewart (1972-1976), Brian Heavisides (1976-1979), Mrs Margaret Gadd (1979-);
Music and Art:	Maureen McGregor (Mrs Boys) (1965-1974);
Music:	Elizabeth Buchanan (1973-);
Art:	Mrs Sallie Burden (1974-);
Woodwork:	John Blake (1967-);
Boys' PE:	Harry Haddon (1960-);
Girls' PE:	Mrs Margaret Hore (1959-);
Housecraft:	Mrs Joan van Ryssen (1977-).

Only the Head himself, Ken Revill, and Virginia Evans retired when Fitzmaurice closed, all the other 23 full-time members of staff in 1980 going on to teach at the new comprehensive school. And, as ever, the permanent staff was augmented from time to time by a cohort of part-time teachers: Mrs Enid Corcoran (music, 1968-1969), Mrs Jennifer Harries (science, 1968-1969), Mrs Jean Brown (science, 1969-1970), Mrs Jean Catchpool (geography and biology, 1971-1973), George Ayres (maths and physics, 1971-1974), Mrs Ann Williams (modern languages, 1972-1973), Mrs D Sumner (geography, 1973-), Mrs E K Symes (German language instructress, 1974-1978), Mrs E S Adams, who was formerly Miss M'Quhae (1964-1977 after her full-time service), Mrs Margaret Gadd (1976-1978), Mrs Beatrice Johnson (1977-1979), Timothy Hammond (chemistry, 1978-1979), and others.

The Deputy Head, John Smith, retired in 1978 after serving the school for 33 years, and he was replaced by Sidney Johnson. Smith was one of that small band of men and women who gave a lifetime of dedicated service to Fitzmaurice; he left £100 to the school, the interest on which was to go for an award in French studies, to be known as the Jasper Prize, and which was to take the form of French books, copies of French paintings, French wine, or some other gift with a French flavour. Very tragically he was killed a few years later in a car accident in North Wales. Tom Ratcliffe, Head of Science, was taken seriously ill in 1976 and in the emergency thus created Mrs Creese helped out, as did Len Newell of the John of Gaunt School in Trowbridge with advanced level work. Ratcliffe resigned in 1977 and died shortly afterwards. His wife, who was Senior Mistress, also left at this time. A happier story was that of Lynne Powell who for the school year 1970-1971 enjoyed an exchange with an American teacher, Karen Spriegel. Miss Spriegel came to Bradford and took over not only Miss Powell's

Above: Lower Sixth Form, 1968-1969, with Mr Steele

The staff at the time of the closure of the Grammar School in 1980.
Back, left to right, Alistair Thomson, Tony Hull, Geoff Swift, Peter Knight, John Warburton, John Blowers, Stuart Ferguson, Tim Wilbur, Bob Hawkes, Harry Haddon, John Blake.
Centre, Joan Davis, Lynne Powell, Doug Anderson, Colin Steele, Virginia Evans, Joan Van Ryssen, Margaret Osbourne, Mireille (French Assistante), Sally Burden, Margaret Gadd.
Front, Ken Revill, Marilyn Maundrell, Noreen Brady, Sid Johnson, Gerald Reid (Headmaster), Meg Tottle-Smith, Enid Wicheard, Diane Satterthwaite, Liz Buchanan, Margaret Hore.

Opposite below: A gathering of heads at the Fitzmaurice Grammar School's first reunion in June 1980.
Left to right: Norman Bradshaw, Sydney Farrar, Mrs Dora Edmonds (widow of Philip Edmonds), Geoffrey Avery, Geoffrey Rowntree and Gerald Reid.

maths classes but also her flat in Summerfield House, while Miss Powell went off to experience the rather different climate of American education at a secondary school in Colorado Springs. And Douglas Anderson, 35 years after his appointment to Fitzmaurice Grammar School, retired only this term (summer, 1998) from his history post at its successor, the St Laurence Comprehensive School in Bradford.

By this time, foreign language assistants were a regular feature of school life, young men and women coming for a year from Europe (and occasionally North Africa) to supplement the work of the modern languages staff, and from rather closer to home help was forthcoming from the lecturers at Trowbridge College in subjects like sociology, economics, and business studies.

Long-serving members of the non-teaching staff also retired during this period. As was said earlier, groundsman Kranz left in 1969 after 22 years, Bill Rawlings, the Lab Assistant, went in 1973 after 15 years (though his service really began as a pupil in the 1920s), Mrs Sunderland who had served hundreds of thousands of school meals over very many years went in 1974, and Perce Millard retired in 1976 after 16 years as Caretaker. All were replaced, but some of the new men and women remained for a comparatively short time, the position of Groundsman in particular being difficult to fill satisfactorily. However, Andy Gerrish in School Meals, and David Alsop, the Caretaker, stayed and eventually went on to work at St Laurence.

Enid Wicheard had been appointed by Philip Edmonds as an additional Lab Assistant only days before his death. Her territory was the old laboratory – by this time, the biology lab – in the main building. Like Bill Rawlings she was a former pupil and is today one of the two Governors appointed by the Trustees of the Lord Fitzmaurice Educational Trust. And one other departure needs mention. After 23 years as Secretary to the Governors, Mrs Edwards retired in 1972, to be replaced by John Shehan. Mervyn Uncles and Mrs Brown, however, were returned year after year as Chairman and Vice Chairman respectively of that Governing Body, and Mrs Brady (by now with an assistant, Mrs Maundrell) passed her twentieth anniversary in the post of School Secretary.

Of course, from time to time little scandals and difficulties blew up, modest innovations were attempted, and variations to well established routines were introduced. For example, such was the press of numbers in St Margaret's Hall that from 1968 only pupils in the fourth year and upwards were able to attend the annual Speech Day celebrations. And because of the number of pupils, morning assembly could no longer accommodate everyone, so on four days of the week (Monday was different) three only of the four Houses by rotation were got together, the odd one out having its own assembly elsewhere. Two flowering cherries were bought and planted to enliven the school's front lawns, and the

Foundation funded other small but worthwhile ventures – the purchase of a greenhouse, a present to Len Newell for the help he had given during the difficulties posed by Tom Ratcliffe's illness, the subsidising of swimming lessons rather than music tuition from 1978, and backing for the school magazine. So a further word now needs to be said about *The Gudgeon*.

From its inception in 1930 it continued year in and year out, through thick and thin, through Peace and War, in the same modest, self-effacing format that has been described earlier. And then, in 1954, without explanation or excuse, it suddenly blossomed into a larger, gaudier, more strident publication. In that year it grew to be 25cms x 19cms, greenish, and with a larger type-face, though the contents were much the same as before. The following year it was blue, and in 1956 bright yellow; and bright yellow it continued until 1968. These were very readable magazines that maintained a record of what was happening in the school as well as providing a platform for the creative energies of prospective poets and story tellers. In the 70s, however, as costs increased, the quality of production fell away, and *The Gudgeon* in its later days became a pale shadow of its former self, both contents and visual presentation, despite financial help from the Foundation, falling from the high standard set by the earlier publications.

In 1976 there was yet another abortive attempt by the teaching staff to secure a place for one of their number as an observer at Governors' meetings; the reason for the request's being refused this time was that the Taylor Report was expected shortly and it would be unwise to preempt that Report's recommendations on the subject of staff observers or, indeed, staff Governors. A year earlier the Governing Body itself had been reorganised. In its new form it consisted of 4 Foundation Governors (Messrs Uncles, Bowyer, Benjamin, and Mrs Brown), 2 from the West Wilts District Council (Mrs Blease and Mrs Maulton), 2 from the Bradford on Avon Town Council (Baker and Mrs Rodway), and 4 from the County Council (Messrs Couzens and Webb, Col Dudley Smith, and Mr Ramsey, the parent representative).

Gerald Reid presided over these various changes, sometimes happily, occasionally less so. In tune with the times, 1971 saw some of the pupils of the school attempting to organise themselves as a small but militant group seeking "reform" in certain directions. This caused him concern. It held a meeting, but its stridency and calls for action were soon dissipated. More constructively, his plans for the forming of a School Council came to fruition in 1971. This was not the school's first venture into this area of democratic management, but this time round the Council was rather more successful than it had been in the past, its Charity Committee in particular being active and achieving positive results. The following year Mr Reid's plans for a Parents' Association were also implemented, and soon that body was functioning to the benefit of the school in a number of directions. And Mr Tugwell replaced Mr Moore as the resident farmer.

Some roughish land beyond the junior school had been acquired speculatively in the early 1960s with the idea of its eventually being made into a proper playing field. A part of it was soon marked out for football and hockey, thus "saving the grass on the main school field", but in 1965 Mr Moore of Leigh Green Farm was allowed to rent 5 acres of it, and in 1972 a grazing licence was granted to a Mr Tugwell for the same patch of grass, so, though it belonged to the school, the use being made of it as a playing field was only half-hearted.

When Gerald Reid was appointed to the headship of Fitzmaurice in April 1969 he was obviously aware of moves nationally to reorganise grammar and secondary modern schools on comprehensive lines, and he was also quite clear about the plans that had been made locally to amalgamate Fitzmaurice Grammar School with the Trinity Secondary Modern School. On the other hand, he was told that his appointment was not short-term and that he could look forward to a substantial period in the post to which he had been appointed. And so it turned out. The discussions in very general terms about the principle of ending selection which had been buzzing about in the 1950s and 1960s had become more pointed in Wiltshire in 1963 with the setting up of the Special Sub-Committee to consider reorganisation. Labour came to power in 1964, and in 1965 Circular 10/65 brought the issue into even sharper focus. After that, in 1966, 1967 and 1968, the decision was taken to combine the two schools on the Trinity School site as the new St Laurence Comprehensive School – and then everything went quiet! This was mainly, but not solely, for financial reasons. Lack of money repeatedly prevented the provision of the necessary accommodation, and no one was prepared for the scheme to go off at half-cock on a temporary, split-site basis or in inadequate buildings. Another reason for delay was the argument that developed over the wording of the Trust Deed. The consequence was a period of some 6 or 7 years in which virtually nothing happened and a whole entry of boys and girls entered, progressed, and left the school to go into employment and further and higher education with the threat of closure always present, but unrealised.

Gerald Reid is insistent that impending reorganisation did not cast a cloud over these years. The school went about its business and concentrated on achieving results of which it could be proud in any company. Eventually, however, things moved on, and in 1975 the Local Authority wrote to the two schools in these terms:

> "During consultations in the winter of 1967/68 on the comprehensive reorganisation proposals for the Bradford on Avon area....the intention was then

expressed to delay reorganisation until sufficient buildings were available on the one site. Since then the economic state of the nation has deteriorated, whilst parental demands for the abolition of the 11+ and the establishment of comprehensive schools have grown. You may know that as a result of this the County Council in considering its objectives has instructed the Education Committee to look again at those areas which do not yet have comprehensive schools to see if it is possible to reorganise them more quickly but with fewer new buildings."

Things were beginning to move again. They had to, because the town's near neighbours, Trowbridge and Melksham, both now had comprehensive schools and Bradford's retention of selection was causing administrative difficulty. First, however, the idea of a quick fix solution such as a split-site school had to be knocked on the head. And this knocking on the head was done in an admirably practical way. The two Heads organised a walk for themselves, representatives from the DES, Local Authority officials and HMI, from one school to the other, to illustrate the difficulty that would face staff and pupils if this solution were considered. It took place in November 1975 from the station car park to Trinity – a pretty good uphill slog – and thereafter no more was heard of a split-site school.

The Working Party on reorganisation reported in March 1976 on the original scheme and possible alternatives to that scheme. Originally, the plan had been for an all-through comprehensive school on the Trinity site. "The premises for the school would be those of the present Trinity School, with the extensions in the 1970/71 building programme and with further extensions to replace the inadequate and largely temporary accommodation of Fitzmaurice Grammar School"; and the provision would be for 6, or possibly 7, forms of entry. After early disagreement, the wording of the Trust Deed had finally been agreed by the joint promoters, the Salisbury Diocesan Council (for Trinity) and the Fitzmaurice Foundation (for the Grammar School) in this form:

> "The Governors shall have regard to the fact that the school [the new St Laurence School] derives from a Church of England and a Christian Faith foundation and therefore, except in so far as religious instruction may be required by law to be given in accordance with an agreed syllabus, the religious instruction to be given in the said school shall reflect this fact."

It was the hammering out of this wording that had proved to be so difficult. The marriage of an Anglican foundation to a Non-Denominational establishment was unusual rather than unique, but with each tenaciously fighting its corner a formula satisfactory to both was not easily, or quickly, achieved. (Interestingly, the actual name *St Laurence* had been an early concession to the established church by the other side.)

Possible alternatives to a single, all-through school were the split-site solution, an 11-16 school on the Trinity site with a transfer at 16+ to the Fitzmaurice building, and an 11-16 school on the Trinity site with a transfer at 16+ to Trowbridge. As has been seen, the first was easily disposed of, and, after several spirited, high-level meetings, the other two were seen to present unacceptable difficulties. The Working Party's report, therefore, reaffirmed the original decision.

In the summer of the following year, 1977, there was a joint meeting of the Governing Bodies of the two schools, chaired by the Rev David Ritchie, Chairman of the Trinity Governors, with officers and the two Heads in attendance. This meeting accepted the recommendations of the Working Party, but one or two new details emerged: the proposed date for the establishment of the St Laurence Voluntary Controlled Comprehensive School would be September 1980; it would be for 1,155 pupils; there would be 4 Foundation Governors, 2 nominated by the Salisbury Diocesan Council and 2 by the Fitzmaurice Foundation; an Instrument of Government would be drawn up specifying, among other things, the composition of the school's Governing Body; and 3 members of this Body and 3 officers would appoint the new Head. There was one matter on which the meeting had a firm view, and it proved to be a matter about which they had their way. The normal composition of the Governing Body would have been for it to have 4 Foundation Governors, 4 nominated by the District Council, and 4 by the LEA (one of whom would be a parent). However, it was felt that, rather than have 4 nominated by the District Council, 2 only should come from that body and that the other 2 should be the nominees of the Town Council because of the high proportion of pupils in the school who would live in the town.

The timetable for these various moves was outlined, but in the event, of course, it slipped somewhat, so that in January 1979 the Fitzmaurice Governors were expressing concern "at the delay in forming the new St Laurence Board and the fact that no step appeared to have been taken in appointing a new Headmaster". (There was no mention of a possible Headmistress!) A month or two later these matters had been dealt with, but the delay, whilst not particularly damaging from an administrative point of view, was distressing personally to a number of people. Gerald Reid, in particular, was left in limbo for many months. It was an unhappy situation about which his Governors had things to say.

The new Governing Body was: Squire and the Rev Ritchie (nominated by the Salisbury Diocesan Council), Uncles and Mrs Brown (nominated by the Foundation), Viles and Mrs Newman (from the District Council), Col Dudley

Smith and Mrs Rodway (Bradford Town Council), and Capt Bradley, Mrs Kain, Bridgwater, and Lamble, the parent representative (from the County Council). It met for the first time on 29 March 1979 in the Westbury House Annexe, and among its first tasks was the appointment of the Head of the comprehensive school. This was F H (Bill) Wheeler from Cumbria, Gerald Reid being offered, and accepting early retirement, to the publicly expressed regret of the Fitzmaurice Governors. And from this point on the three Governing Bodies worked in parallel.

The other matters that had to be dealt with were administrative formalities and, increasingly, a physical drawing together of the two staffs to ensure as smooth a change-over as possible in September 1980. To this end, staff training days were utilised for the sharing of information about curricula, syllabuses, and teaching materials; visits were made by each staff to the school of the other; and experience was sought from other comprehensive schools in the County. The pupils, too, managed to get together through the organising of joint trips and by such stratagems as the entering of a combined hockey team at the Devizes Festival. A few further valedictory rituals remained to be performed. There was the final Reunion of former pupils on 21 June 1980, an occasion of which all who were present (and there were close on a thousand) still have vivid memories, and there was the rather subdued, domestic prizegiving at the end of the summer term when Mr Reid said his goodbyes to the pupils, his colleagues, and the school which he had led with distinction for over 11 years.

And so, on 15 July 1980, the Fitzmaurice Grammar School sent its pupils home for their summer holidays for the last time.

Just before its closure, Gerald Reid wrote:

> "When the new school is completed, it alone will provide the secondary education for the children of Bradford, assuming the traditions and responsibilities of the two present schools. Few can doubt that Lord Fitzmaurice, with his foresight and confidence in Bradford, would have supported the new venture as fully as he did the school which today proudly bears his name."

The Fitzmaurice Grammar School has now disappeared from the educational scene, and sadly a number of items in which the town could have taken pleasure disappeared with it – the plaque commemorating the founding of the school by Edmond Fitzmaurice, for example, which was displayed in the entrance hall for almost 50 years, and the school's honours boards of which no trace can be found. The building in Junction Road, too, was a sad sight for a number of years as dereliction set in, though few would have mourned unduly the demolition of the gym, the woodwork room, or the Gallipoli hut. The school's ghost was not finally laid for some time, however, because there ensued a protracted argument about the fate of the Trust. Lord Shelburne fought to have it returned to the family; Mervyn Uncles, on the other hand, felt that it should be retained for educational purposes. And he it was who won. The money is administered today by Trustees who use it for the benefit of the boys and girls of the St Laurence School.

Bradford on Avon's grammar school had had a thoroughly successful final twenty years or so, but its name had not always been synonymous with success. For most of its 83 years it was an ill-equipped little institution with buildings totally inadequate for its purpose, and, curiously, it never had a pupil who went on to become a household name. Nevertheless, throughout its life it had the ability to inspire great affection among those who taught and learnt there, and despite its manifest shortcomings, both material and academic, there will be few who do not agree with Ilse Stein's sentiment, quoted earlier: "It is my time at Fitzmaurice that I look back on as being the halcyon days."

A Postscript by Gerald Reid
My first sight of Bradford on Avon was on a Friday morning in January, 1969. I left my car in the Swan car park and was heading for Fitzmaurice Grammar School to have the meeting with John Smith, who was Acting Head, and the other four candidates to be interviewed that afternoon, see over the School and be briefed about the post. The town looked its best on a sunny morning and, fascinated by its charm, I failed to realise that my watch had stopped, and consequently arrived late!

Our tour of the School left me with different impressions: the facade of the original building was splendid; once inside there was a sense of tradition but material conditions were far from ideal. We joined the staff for coffee and talked of general educational matters. John Smith spoke of the School and, as I told him later, his pride in the achievements and the general atmosphere of purposeful calm made me realise that this would be a post worth having. I was delighted to be offered the Headship and looked forward to 17th April, my first day.

I quickly learned that my first impressions were accurate. The LEA had sent a television reporter to the School the previous year to investigate staff reaction to inadequate conditions. He had left, disappointed, because the staff's reluctance to complain left him without a story. They were much more interested in getting on with the job in spite of the inadequacies of the surroundings. It was very obvious that there was a great sense of pride, professionalism (in the best sense) and togetherness among the staff, enthusiasm and desire to do well from the pupils, and interest and cooperation from the parents. Keith has rightly written of the School's "ability to inspire great affection among those who taught and learnt there". Once established, I never felt a desire to move on.

The stability of senior members of staff was most important; newcomers quickly saw what standards were expected, old-fashioned virtues of punctuality, courtesy and dependability were the norm and my job was the easier for it. The Governors were interested and helpful without interfering. It helped, of course, that many were former pupils. I was reminded of a phrase in the details sent to applicants from the LEA. "The School is small but its standing is high both in the county and in the town." Eighteen years after the closure I look back and ponder the reasons for the sense of happiness which old pupils feel. (Even now, a reunion is being planned by pupils who are in their mid-forties.) The conclusion I have reached is that the small size meant that everyone knew and so remembers most of one's fellow-pupils. Only yesterday I heard two, both well into their seventies, talking in the golf club locker room about what had become of some of their contemporaries.

Schools, being man-created, are necessarily imperfect and to judge yesterday's achievements by today's standards is a trap into which it is easy to fall. Equally, nostalgia is a great aid in forgetting faults and errors. Bearing these qualifications in mind, I like to think that Fitzmaurice, pupils, staff, parents and governors, added something to this town for which so many feel so much affection. I am happy to have been a part of it.

The demolition of the Gallipoli hut in 1985.

Above: St Laurence School staff in 1998.

Below: St Laurence Jazz Band rehearsing in the Music Centre, opened 1997.

Towards 2000

THE STORY OF BRADFORD ON AVON'S SCHOOLS now needs, very briefly, to be told to the present day – that is, for the primary schools, from 1928 to 1998, and, for St Laurence, for its less than 20 years of life from 1980 to 1998.

As we have seen, the town's elementary schools were reorganised in 1928. Young Jack Gingell was at Christ Church when this happened and he remembers nothing of this major educational upheaval. He had more important things to think about. He had already learnt his letters under Miss Butcher.

> "The way she did it was to write a capital A on the blackboard, and then a B, and so on. We had to copy these letters exactly by tracing them with a finger in sand-trays that we were all given. And after that we did the small letters. It was a very effective method because, when we had finished, all we had to do was shake the sand-tray and the letters disappeared. As clear as if it was yesterday I can still see Miss Butcher leaning over my shoulder to check if I had done it right. She was a very good teacher. She had ginger hair and lived in Church Street opposite where Lloyds Bank is now."

Christ Church School had one dozen of these sand-trays on its inventory at this time, their total value being six shillings.

By 1928 he had been taught by Miss Butcher, Miss Lapham, and Miss Hayes (all uncertificated), and he had made the acquaintance of another teacher whom he came to respect and admire – Frank Musselwhite. Henry Chappell who taught him woodwork in the workshop at the secondary school, however, was feared rather than liked.

Mrs Elizabeth Wilkinson was appointed Head of Christ Church at the 1928 reorganisation, the only newcomer to the staff as a result of that reshuffle being Mrs Dunning, a certificated teacher who lived in Sladesbrook and who is also still remembered by Jack Gingell. Mrs Wilkinson stayed until 1932. In that year, Miss Margaret Padmore began her 23 year period of office, which, of course, spanned the difficult wartime years, and it was as a result of her work at that time – not least, in her accommodating between 800 and 900 evacuees – that she was awarded the MBE. The first evacuees arrived as early as September 1939. There were over 100 of them, mainly from Dagenham, and with them came two of their teachers. The immediate crisis over, however, they soon started to drift home, and four months later fewer than half remained. Later in 1940, a fresh wave arrived from Ilford and West Ham, and this swelling of numbers caused extra classroom space to be sought – at the British Legion Hall in Masons Hill, the Lambert Room, the Wesleyan Chapel in Coppice Hill, the Huntingdon Chapel, and the Crusader Hall in New Road. This remained the pattern, and it was the sort of difficulty – an ever-shifting school population that compelled a juggling of inadequate resources – that schools typically had to cope with in those wartime years. An innovation rather than an improvisation was the supplying of school dinners. These were first brought in from a central kitchen in Holt in September 1942 and after that date, of course, they became an institution.

From 1955 to 1973 Leslie Carr was Head, and it was during his time that the old premises on Mount Pleasant were vacated and a move made to new buildings with access from Sladesbrook and Berryfield Road. The new junior school opened first, leaving the infants marooned in Mount Pleasant. Land had been acquired from Mr Feltham of Leigh House Farm in 1955 and the new school was built in 1957. Christ Church (C of E Controlled) Junior School thereafter was an entity distinct from its infant counterpart. However, the infants' school moved into adjacent premises ten years later, opening in April 1968 and being known as the Berryfields Park County Infants School. Its first (and only) Head was Mrs K M Baxter. She stayed until 1981 when her retirement coincided with an alarming fall in the number of children on roll (a drop from over 200 to little more than 100 in 13 years), so the opportunity was taken of amalgamating infants and juniors into the Christ Church (C of E Controlled) Primary School.

John Messer was Head from 1973 to 1994, and Peter Mountstephen from that date.

The old buildings given by Captain Palairet and Miss Poynder still stand in Mount Pleasant, looking somewhat forlorn and uncared for, but they have recently been listed and there is hope that restoration and preservation will soon be undertaken. They form a striking contrast to the cheerful, open and grassy accommodation afforded by the modern Christchurch Primary School. (Or is it Christ Church Primary School? The latter is affirmed by history; the contraction, however, seems gradually to have been adopted in the late 1980s and has now the respectability of official recognition.)

South of the river in 1928, and planned to accommodate the town's expansion in that direction, there was a parallel situation to that at the top of the hill. The brave new world of Bradford on Avon's reorganised schools was taking shape and an integral part of it was the opening of a new junior school on a site between the Trowbridge and Frome Roads. It had no church affiliation at all, but, although not strictly speaking the successor to the British Girls' School, the closing of the one and the opening of the other were sufficiently closely linked for it to be seen as such in some ways.

Under the headship of Alice Davis from Trinity Infants, the new Trowbridge Road School – the "council" school – was a solid, rectangular, five-roomed building with its in-line office and four classrooms backing on to an open wooden verandah; it provided classrooms that were much more spacious and convenient than those of the old Mason's Lane building. At its opening it took children up to the age of 9 – class III ("the babies") under Mrs Brown, classes I and II (the infants) under Mrs Pratt, standard Ia and Ib with Mrs Davis, and standard IIa and IIb with Miss Rudman – all four teachers having come from the former Trinity Infants'School. There were 55 boys and 50 girls on the opening day.

Inspection revealed that it was "a very pleasing and satisfactory school". It was felt that "this is a very pleasant and well ordered school in which teachers and pupils seem to be on the happiest terms". "And," say the inspectors, "it has been a pleasure to visit this ideally situated school." So it met with official approval. Sadly, Mrs Davis had to retire for reasons of ill-health in 1932, her successor being Miss Fanny Lawrence, and she it was who saw the school through to the outbreak of war and just beyond. During her headship it was visited by Lord Edmond Fitzmaurice. Educated at Eton and Cambridge, and in his time a statesman of international repute, he nevertheless maintained a keen interest in education in Wiltshire and, in a very practical way, in the welfare of boys and girls of all conditions in Bradford on Avon. So he went to look at the Council School one afternoon in 1933. By this time he was a very old man, but he visited every group in turn and afterwards "addressed the children, telling them he would arrange to give them a tea very shortly". Like the visit itself, this treat, which took place a week later, was no empty gesture towards paternalism; it was evidence of Edmond Fitzmaurice's lifelong belief in the importance of people and of education.

In 1935 two further classrooms were added to the original four, enabling the school to expand to six classes because by this time numbers were closer to 200 than the 105 of 1928.

Wartime brought evacuees – 111 from Barking, together with 2 of their teachers, Misses Bland and Lewis, in September 1939. They were soon emboldened to go home, but a second wave arrived from Ilford the following March, and with them came Misses Bateman and Parry. Extra accommodation had to be sought in Church House, but the greatest disruption of all came from the pupils having to vacate the school every time the sirens sounded to take shelter in the Mushroom Quarry. This constant and total dislocation of school routine could not be allowed to continue, and soon a modified sort of shelter was found within the school itself under the desks in the various classrooms.

In November 1940 Fanny Lawrence gave way to Miss Grace Greiner. It was she who introduced a form of junior Speech Day that was held in the Town Hall in December 1942 and again in 1943. On this latter occasion the prizes were to have been distributed by the Captain of the Norwegian submarine *Ula* (a vessel that had been adopted by the school) but at the last minute and, one assumes, to the huge disappointment of the children, he was called away at short notice to do submarinely things. No more thereafter was heard of a formal Speech Day for the Trowbridge Road Junior School.

Victoria Brice-Tribe became Head in 1944, beginning a 24 year tenure in that post, and in 1968 Hugh Solomon succeeded her. It was in his term of office that further expansion took place. The accommodation of 1928, added to in 1935, was now further extended by the acquisition of two mobiles – a single hut and a double classroom. A kitchen/hall/practical area was provided in 1973, and when the Grammar School closed in 1980, its science block, that was closer to the junior school than it was to the main Fitzmaurice building, was converted for use as four infants' classrooms. And Mr Solomon employed self-help and entrepreneurial ingenuity in converting the former home economics HORSA (the building just off the Frome Road that had been used by Trinity School until 1962 and then by the Grammar School) into a garage for his minibus. Both these buildings remain today.

Jo Uncles had an early, and continuing, connection with the school.

> "From 1925 to 1928 I went to Trinity Infants' and went up through Mrs Brown's, Miss Pratt's, and Mrs Cowlishaw's classes. Then from 1928 to 1929 I went to the new school where Mrs Davis was Headmistress before going back up to Trinity Senior School for the three years. Then I went to the Grammar School. In Trinity Senior School there were Gaffer Harris, who was slightly deaf, and Mr Musselwhite. Mr Musselwhite was a great caner, and I can see him now with his cane kept down his trousers' leg and hooked over his belt.
>
> I went back to the Trowbridge Road School as a Student Teacher. Fanny Lawrence was then the Headmistress and I disliked her intensely. I thought she was unpleasant to her staff, particularly to poor Miss Young, and she made me say a formal Good Afternoon to her before I left school every day. Sometimes she deliberately kept me waiting. She was often to be seen driving her little Austin up the middle of Trowbridge Road.
>
> During the War I did firewatching at the school. Three of us would be on duty, two teachers and me, and if the siren went we had to report to the warden who was on duty at the Trowbridge Road entrance. By this time Miss Greiner was Head. She, of course, was suspected of being a German spy and it was common knowledge that she used to signal to enemy aircraft at night from her

window!

I actually taught at the school from 1959 to 1981, under Miss Brice-Tribe and Hugh Solomon. Victoria Brice-Tribe always called herself Queenie. She had a twin sister who was called Alberta and who lived in Bournemouth, I think."

So Miss Uncles' memories of the Council School span more than half a century – from its opening in 1928 to 1981.

Perhaps the most memorable event of the 1980s was the renaming of the school. The staff suggested that Lord Fitzmaurice's name should be perpetuated by its being adopted by the junior school; so, after negotiation with Governors and the LEA, in July 1985 the former Trowbridge Road Council School officially became the Bradford on Avon Fitzmaurice County Primary School.

Led today by David Hester who followed Hugh Solomon in 1992, its expansive and exciting curriculum is a striking contrast to that of the tight but narrow little ship commanded by Alice Davis seventy years ago.

And, finally, Bradford on Avon's secondary school, now nearly 20 years old – the St Laurence School (Voluntary Controlled: Church of England and Fitzmaurice Foundation) – takes boys and girls from the Christchurch and Fitzmaurice primary schools and from those of the villages that neighbour the town. Its recently appointed Head is Nicholas Sorensen and its Chairman of Governors Patrick Squire. As has been seen above, Mr Squire was a member of the "shadow" Governing Body appointed in 1979 and from his vantage point of having been a Governor for the whole of the school's life he has a unique oversight of its development since its inception.

A conscious effort was made to free the new school of the burden of carrying undesirable historical baggage from its predecessors, and today the old schools are remembered principally in the names of two of St Laurence's components, the Fitzmaurice Library and the Trinity Hall. There are other reminders (like the carrying forward of the Fitzmaurice badge, but with an increase in the number of gudgeon from one to two, symbolising St Laurence's creation from the union of the two former schools), but one feels that the present day comprehensive is essentially forward-looking rather than given to glancing over its shoulder at ghosts from the past.

Nevertheless, Nicholas Sorensen stresses his awareness of St Laurence's dual inheritance. He is conscious of the liberal, secular tradition that stems from the work and vision of Edmond Fitzmaurice, and he values the respect for spiritual values that springs from the school's roots in the established church through the Trinity Foundation. For him, this melding of philosophies results in a striving to provide the best possible education for the young people of Bradford on Avon at a time when many of the old certainties upon which the former pupils of

Fitzmaurice and Trinity could rely are no longer there. He and his staff are educating for an uncertain future; the pupils, therefore, need to be adaptable and, above all, to understand the learning process. So a mastery of *how* to learn is today just as important as (or more important than?) *what* is learnt.

St Laurence, of course, has many natural advantages. Its catchment area is not exactly ring-fenced but the school has no local rivals, and in that sense it is truly comprehensive. Bradford on Avon is an attractive little town that acts as a magnet for aspiring professional families, and the proximity of the University of Bath with all its extra-mural and on-site facilities tends to draw the academically ambitious to the area. It has, therefore, a great deal going for it, but it has worked hard at developing an earned identity and reputation rather than relying simply upon its geographical good fortune. Its pupils represent a range of abilities and come from a broad spectrum of social and economic backgrounds. Any desire to sit back and believe that success will come as of right, therefore, would be doomed to failure.

If there is one thing that it retains from its two predecessors it is, according to Patrick Squire, a strong sense of community and a feeling shared by pupils and staff that they belong to a family whose members have a mutuality of interest. Bill Wheeler and James Wetz were its first two Heads. Now, under Nicholas Sorensen, it is aware of the enormous possibilities opening up for its pupils in the field of technology. At the same time and as something of a counterbalance it is pressing ahead with its application for Specialist School Status in the Performing Arts to reinforce its reputation in that area and to maintain the impetus given by the recent building on its site of the Wiltshire Music Centre. It seeks to provide a rounded education; its ambitions are multi-faceted.

This history has told the story of Bradford's schools over almost three centuries, and low as well as high points have been clearly discernible as the story unfolded. St Laurence secondary and Christchurch and Fitzmaurice primary schools are today in the ascendant and all three look set fair to serve the young people of the town handsomely as the twenty-first century dawns.

The badge of St. Laurence School. It is an adaptation of the Fitzmaurice badge, the two gudgeon sybolising the union of the two former schools.

Appendix A

Headteachers of the County School and the Fitzmaurice Grammar School:

Charles Watkins	1897-1900
John Crompton	1900-1926
Henry Rosen	1926-1929
Sydney Farrar	1929-1939
Geoffrey Rowntree	1939-1947
Geoffrey Avery	1947-1955
Norman Bradshaw	1955-1958
Philip Edmonds	1959-1968
Gerald Reid	1969-1980

Chairmen of the Bradford on Avon Technical Education Committee and, thereafter, of the Governing Body of the Grammar School:

Erlysman Pinckney	1891-1904 (Technical Education Committee)
Lord Edmond Fitzmaurice	1904-1905 (Technical Education Committee)
Lord Edmond Fitzmaurice	1905-1935
Rev W H M Clarke	1935-1936
Dr C E S Flemming	1936-1947
Rev W D Galsworthy	1947-1951
A H Baker	1951-1961
M Uncles	1961-1980

Appendix B

List of Awards Made to Pupils of the Fitzmaurice Grammar School

1. **Public Service Awards**
These were two awards that were often, though not always, made to the Head Boy and Head Girl. They were instituted by Lord Fitzmaurice in 1927.

2. **The A H Baker Prize**
This was for "outstanding achievement in science subjects". It was awarded annually and regularly in memory of the teaching service of A H Baker, science master from 1905 to 1945 and Chairman of Governors from 1951 to 1961.

3. **The E H Young Prize**
First awarded in 1951, the E H Young Prize, given by her sister, Gladys Young, commemorated the years that the novelist served, under her married name of Mrs E H Daniell, as a Governor of the Fitzmaurice Grammar School. Initially awarded for an essay on a classical theme, it was later given for "outstanding achievement in Arts subjects".

4. **The P H Edmonds Prize**
Mrs Edmonds gave £100 in March 1969 to mark her husband's headship of the Fitzmaurice Grammar School. It was presented annually thereafter, the interest the capital provided going towards an award "for Literary and Dramatic achievement".

5. **The F J Smith Prize**
£100 provided for an annual prize to be given in memory of F J Smith who taught at the school from 1945 to 1978, for many years as Deputy Head. It was awarded from 1978 to 1980. He wished it to be for good work in French, and had asked for it to be known as the Jasper Prize, Jasper having been his nickname.

6. **The Flemming Prize**
This shield for Public Speaking was awarded in 1947, 1948, and 1949. Thereafter no record of it has been found.

7. **The Cannings Seals Prize**
Awarded in 1975 and 1976, this was for "outstanding achievement in maths/science subjects at O level". Its origins are unclear, as is what happened to it in the last years of the school's existence.

List of Cups Awarded for House and Individual Distinction in Sport
Many of the cups that were originally presented for one purpose were assigned for a different purpose in 1960 when the House system was overhauled.

1. **Blake Cup**
Presented by Miss Helen Blake in memory of Miss J E Blake in 1927 for girls' work, and later for junior winter games.

2. **Cowlishaw Cup**
Presented by F J F Cowlishaw in 1927 for boys' games, later for senior winter games.

3. **Frankell Cup**
Presented in 1927 by Alfred Frankell for boys' work, then for school work, later for netball, and latterly for netball and basketball.

4. **Pinckney Cup**
Originally given by Captain E C Pinckney of Wraxall Lodge in 1927 for girls' games, it was eventually awarded to the champion House.

5. **Slade Cup**
A cup for cross-country running, the Slade Cup was given in 1929 by H E W Slade who had been School Captain from 1927 to 1929.

6. **Old Main Cup**
On being wound up in 1931, the Bradford on Avon Swimming Club presented this cup for boys' swimming. It was later awarded for senior swimming.

7. **Selfe Cup**
Mrs E Selfe gave this cup for girls' athletics (later senior athletics) in 1941.

8. **Watkins Cup**
Mr and Mrs W H Watkins gave this cup for boys' athletics and it was later awarded for success in senior athletics.

9. **Scarisbrick Cup**
Presented by Mrs J L Scarisbrick for girls' swimming, it was later re-allocated to junior swimming.

10. **Bradshaw Cup**
This cup was given in 1958 by Norman Bradshaw for girls' tennis. It was later awarded for senior summer games.

11. **Harris Cup**
The cup given by C Harris was for junior summer games.

In addition there were the Gilbert, Stillman, and Copland Cups for athletics, the Matthews Cup for swimming, the Jonathan Head Barrow Cup, a road-safety award, a gymnastics shield, and a Parent's Association Jubilee Cup for a third year project.
A Drama Shield also appeared for a short time in the late 1960s and early 1970s, and one wonders if it was a belated reappearance of the Flemming Prize. Most of these trophies are no longer presented but are today in secure storage in Bradford on Avon.
Most of these trophies are no longer presented but are today in secure storage in Bradford on Avon.

Appendix C

This short article by Ellis Darby appeared in the *Holy Trinity Parish Magazine* in August 1962 (See the illustration on page 63).

TRINITY SCHOOL

At the time of writing, the combined ceremony of Dedication and Opening of the New School is imminent, and the School Emblem as printed here appears on the programme.

As the School never appears to have possessed anything in the form of a crest, it was decided to make use of an engraving on a brass plate inlaid in the tombstone of Thomas Horton, which latter stands in a very dark corner at the east end of the north aisle. In this portrayal of the Holy Trinity, the robed figure of God the Father is enthroned. He supports the Crucified Christ between His knees, while the Dove of the Holy Spirit rests on one arm of the Cross.

A drawing was made from a rubbing of the engraving, and a commercial artist friend added the ribbon and lettering. The whole was then reduced to one-sixth of its original size by the printing blockmakers.

Thomas Horton was a " merchant of the staple," or a " clothier." Doubtless he was a rich clothier since, as well as founding a Chantry, he was responsible for building not only his own house on the site of the present Abbey House, but also Church House (now known as Church Hall), the original " Chantry " for his Chantry Priest, and nearly all of the north aisle of Holy Trinity Church itself.

He must have prepared his own tombstone before his death, since the inscription on brass, beginning, " Of your charity pray for the soul of Thomas Horton and Mary his wife . . . ," omitted the dates of their respective deaths.

The family tree shows that Thomas Horton died at Westwood on 14th August, 1530, and other records suggest that his wife, Mary, was living in 1538, but died in or before 1545.

Why were these dates never inscribed on the brass? Was he not so rich a clothier when he died? Were his heirs parsimonious or indifferent, or more likely, did the tombstone fall a victim to the turbulence of the Dissolution, bearing in mind that about 1532, one Traywell (or Tropnell) was burnt at the corner of the Shambles and Woolley Street as an early Protestant, and that in 1540, William Byrd, ~~Baptist~~ [Papist], and Vicar of Bradford on Avon at that time, lost his living for his criticism of the Protestant ways of Henry VIII, while his patron, Lord Hungerford, lost his head?

With due deference to Canon Jones,

—H. E. DARBY.

INDEX OF NAMES
(Page numbers in italic refer to illustrations)

Abbott, Miss J 174
Abrahamson, Mary 87
Adams, E A 122, 139
Adams, Mrs E S (see M'Quhae, Edna Sylvia)
Adye, Dr 105
Alexander, Minnie 49
Alexander, Roma 150, 155, *159, 160*, 178
Allen, Miss (music) 71
Allen, Miss (PE) 87
Allwright, Agnes 119-121, 132
Alsop, D 214
Alsop, Joanna 209
Anderson, D 191, 210, *213*, 214
Andrews, Rita 210
Angell, A E 164
Angell, J L 156
Arbuckle, Mary 42-43
Archard, Kathleen 50
Archard, K M 104
Argyle, P 207, 211
Arnold, M 137
Arnold, Mrs 55
Arthur, Kate 47
Asquith, H H 134
Atkins, V F 64-65
Aust, A C 68
Aust, W 68
Austin, Patricia *159*
Avery, G W 163, 169-171, 173, 176-177, 181-183, *184*, 185-187, *212*, 229
Ayres, G 211

Baber, Miss 107
Bailey, Miss A *34*
Bainton, Mr 202
Baker, A H 57, 85, 87, 90, 94, *95*, 97, 99-100, 103, 105, 107, 115, 118-122, 131-132, 138, 147-148, 150, 154-155, *158*, 161-164, 172-173, 180, 190, 197, 200, *201*, 202, 205, 229, 230
Baker, Anne 210
Baker, H Grant 202, 215
Baker, Jennifer 161, 204
Baker, M *159*
Baker, Mrs 161
Barker, A 208
Barnes, Ethel T 98, 100, 104, 106-108, 114
Barrett, Mrs Sarah 31
Barry, Eileen *195*
Barry, Rev P 60
Bartram, S 208
Baster, Miss 110

Bateman, Miss 225
Bath, Marquess of 137
Battiscombe (HMI) 110
Baxter, Mrs K M 224
Bayley, Jill 210
Beath, Mabel 49, 53
Beavan, J F 164
Beddoes, Mrs 45
Beechey, W H J *34*
Bell, Rev Dr A 13
Benjamin, C 50
Benjamin, J 21, *152*, *153*, 215
Bethell, Miss J H 173
Bigwood, C 122
Bird, Hannah 106-107, 118-119
Blake, E 93
Blake, Helen 93, 117, 230
Blake, J 191, 211, *213*
Blake, Julia 49, 77, 80, 87, 92-93, 95, 97, 99-100, 104-107, 114, 118-119, 121-122, 131, 170, 230
Blake, Lilian 77, 80, 95
Blakeney, Mrs Evelyn 171
Bland, Miss 225
Blease, Mrs J 215
Blease, T Y S 164
Blowers, J 210, *213*
Boaden, Agnes *34*, 38-39, 41-44
Boden, Mona 170
Bonnet, Mlle Simone 118
Booker (pupil) 132
Booker, F J 99
Borrett, Nellie 50
Borrett, V 50
Bowyer C H S (Governor) 215
Bowyer, H 102
Bowyer, Mary 42
Bowyer, W 50
Boyd-Maunsell, N 171
Boyle, Sir R 199
Boys, Mrs Maureen (see McGregor, Maureen)
Bradley, Capt 219
Bradley, J H 197, 199
Bradshaw, N 171, 185-186, 188-190, 193, 200, 204, *212*, 229, 231
Brady, Mrs Noreen 60, 201, *213*, 214
Bray, R C 156
Brayley, Miss 47-48
Breen, G T 86, 92, 94-95, 98-99, 107
Brice-Tribe, Alberta 227
Brice-Tribe, Victoria W 226-227
Bridge, Mr (HMI) 126
Briggs, Mrs 171
Bridgwater, Mr 219

Broad, Minnie 43
Brosnan, Pat *141*
Brosnan, W H 99-100, 102, 106-108, 118-120, 148-149, 154-155, *158*, 160-161, 180
Brown, C 191
Brown, E J 156
Brown (ironmonger) 118
Brown, Jane *194*
Brown, Mrs (caretaker) 100, 110
Brown, Mrs (primary teacher) 225-226
Brown, Mrs B A 202, 214, 215, 218
Brown, J R M *195*
Brown, Mrs Kathleen (see Hyde, Kathleen)
Brown, Mrs Lilian (see Oakman, Lilian)
Brown, Yvonne *194*
Bruce, W N 21
Bryant, C W B 32, *34*
Bryant, Mrs Mercy 32, *34*
Bubb, J 20
Buchanan, Elizabeth 211, *213*
Bull, Clara 46-47
Bull, Monica *159*
Bullock, A 203
Burbidge (caretaker) *156*
Burbidge (farmer) 102
Burbidge, Mrs 157
Burchell, Ada 54
Burden, Mrs Sallie 211, *213*
Burgess, Kate 47, 51
Burgoine, Dorothy 98, 100, 106-107, 114, 117, 118-120, 148-149, 154, *158*, 162, *164*, 169-171, *175*, 179-181
Burke, B 209
Burton, Miss 156
Butcher, Miss 223
Butler, R A 17
Butt, J T 20
Byfield, C 30

Cadogan, Eunice 189, 190-191
Cairns, Lady 138
Campbell-Bannerman, H 134
Cannon, J A 171
Capon, Margaret C 138, 148
Carden, M 209
Carden, N 208
Carey, G 57
Cargill, Marion 119, 121, 126-127
Carpenter (pupil) 106
Carr, L 224

233

INDEX

Carrier, S *195*
Carter, Messrs 160
Catchpool, Mrs Jean 211
Challis, Mrs Roma (see Alexander, Roma)
Chancellor, Messrs 69
Chapel, Sgt J 98
Chappell, H 99, 106, 223
Chard, E *50*
Chard (farmer) 102
Chard, H 29
Chard, Hilary (see Lywood, Mrs Hilary)
Chard, Hilda *50*
Chedzoy, Claire *206*
Christopher, Mr 114, 118
Chrystal, J M 151
Clark, Miss 121
Clarke, Canon W H M 57, *130*, 133, *136*, 138, 180, *201*, 229
Clarke, R M *195*
Claxton, Miss Evelyn 118
Clegg, Mary 49, 52-54
Cleveland, B *50*
Cockrom, Mabel 49, *50*
Cole, Mrs Mona (see Boden, Mona)
Collier, Janet 192
Collins, Mr 176, 2020
Collins (benefactor) 105
Collins, Dora (see Neathey, Mrs Dora)
Colquhoun, C J 80, 83, 85, 95
Comley, Alma *141*
Comley, R *130*
Compton, Mr (solicitor) 135
Comrie, M 171
Coombs, Fanny 47-48
Cook, Ven E A 179
Cook, Rose 43
Cooper, Iris *159*
Cooper, J A 90, 179
Copeman, Jacqueline 208
Copland, C C 148, 161, 170-171, 179
Copland, G M 193, *194*
Corby, S 170
Corcoran, Mrs Enid 191, 211
Cottle, P 98
Coudray, Irene 156
Coupland, H 132
Courtney, G 149
Courtney, Mrs Winifred 138, *141*, 148-149, *158*, *159*, 161
Cousins, M 132
Cousins, W *50*
Couzens A H 215
Cowlishaw, A 20
Cowlishaw, F J 20, 117, 231

Cowlishaw, F W 20, *22*, 24, *34*, 49, 90-91
Cowlishaw, P 20
Cowlishaw, Mrs Ruth 57, 226
Cowlishaw, S J 20
Cox, Cicely 170-171, 189
Creese, Mrs J M 210-211
Crisp, Mr 101
Crompton, Mrs Isabel 115, *120*
Crompton, J 70-73, 79, 83, 86-87, 92, 94-95, *96*, 97, 99-100, 105, 107, 110, 114-116, 118-120, *120*, 121, 131, 171, 179, 186, 229
Crompton, J R 104
Culley, R 98
Culverhouse, D J *194*
Cummins, Betty 170-171

Dainton, Enid *141*
Dallimore, Constance 139, 156
Daniell, Mrs E H 164, 179, 230
Daniell, J A H 179
Darby, H E 60, 62, 64, 148, 162, 169-170
Darch, N B 156
Daunt, Sheelagh 192
Davies, Joan 210
Davis, Mrs Alice 31-33, 225-227
Davis, Enid 171
Davis, Jean 149, 161-162
Davis, Joan 191, *201*, *213*
Davis, Mr (caretaker) 202
Davis, R 191, 202
Davis, Raymond L *194*
Davis, Rupert *206*
Davison, C 65
Dawe, Jean *195*
Dawe, Mrs Janet (see Williams, Janet)
Dawson, P *206*
Day, E 170-171, 189, 192
Day, Mrs 170, 189
Dean, Edwina 140
Diamond, Ruth 191
Dilke, Sir C 133
Diprose, Patricia 208
Dobson, Enid (see Wicheard, Mrs Enid)
Dotesio, Mrs 156
Doubtfire, Barbara 191
Dubois, Mlle Mireille 118
Dunning, Mrs 223
Dyer, Gertrude 46-47

Eales, M 208
Eastman, Miss 201
Eastwood, W 138, 148, 154, 161, 162
Ebdon, Angela *206*
Edmonds, Miss 37

Edmonds, Mrs Dora 205, *212*, 230
Edmonds, P H 189-193, 197, *201*, 202, 204-205, 214, 229, 230
Edwards (butcher) 118
Edwards, G *50*
Edwards, Judith *195*
Edwards, Mr *130*
Edwards, Mrs Betty 172, 199, 214
Edwards, R *130*
Ellery, Mr 176
Elliott, B
Elliott, Evelyn 98, 100, 106-107, 119, 121
Elton, Sir A 108
England, Lucy 30
Evans, Marie *195*
Evans, Mrs Virginia 191, 202, 210-211, *213*

Falkner, Marion *141*
Farr, Mrs K 87, 100
Farrar, Mrs *130*
Farrar, S 118-121, 123, 127, 129, 132-133, 136, 138-139, 147-148, 154, 171, 186, 199, 203, *212*, 229
Farrell, Aileen 119, 121
Fassnidge, H 35
Fatt, Ellen 36
Fellowes, Mr 187
Feltham, Mr 224
Ferguson, S 210, *213*
Field, Mrs Heather 191
Finn, Melinda *206*
Finney, J H 117, 132
Fitzmaurice, Lord Edmond George-Petty 2, 24, 54, *66*, 67-68, 70, 73, *75*, 76, 83-86, 90, 100-102, 105, 117, 122, 131, 133-135, 137-138, 170, 172, 180-182, *201*, 219, 225, 227, 229, 230
Flemming, Dr C E S 100, *130*, 133, 135, *136*, 138, 143, *159*, 164-165, 169, 172, 178-180, *201*, 229, 230
Ford, Bessie 46
Ford, Mrs (caretaker) 100
Ford, Mrs Jessie (see McCulloch, Jessie)
Forster, Sir M 86
Forster, W E 15, 16
Foulds, Barbara Elizabeth 149, 162, 170-171
Fowle, Maud 43
Fox, Miss 156, 169
Fox, Mrs Jennifer (see Baker, Jennifer)
Frankell, A 117, 132, 231
Franklin, M *206*

234

INDEX

Freeth, A *184*, 189, 191
Fricker, R *130*
Fry, Sarah 30
Fuller, G P 68, 134
Fuller, Sir G 147
Furbner, W 19

Gadd, Mrs Margaret 211, *213*
Galsworthy, Rev W D 169, 172-173, 229
Gare, Doris Irene 138, 149, 155, *158*, 161
Gatacre, Lady 138
Gay, Miss J *174*
Genders, Mrs Blanch 30
Genders, J 30
Gerrish, A 214
Gerrish, E *159*
Gerrish, Heather *194*
Gerrish, I *130*
Gerrish, J *130*
Gerrish, Mrs A
Gibson, Dr 149
Gill, L F 156
Gilpin, Dr J 149
Gingell, J 223
Gittings, Miss 47
Gladstone, W E 134
Glasspool, Mrs Molly 119
Goodall (outfitter) 118, 187
Goodwin, Doreen 119
Gornall, R *130*
Gorst, Sir J 79
Gorvett, A 98-99, 106
Goschen, Mrs C H 64
Gough (solicitor) 122-123
Gover, Bridget *206*
Gray, M 208
Green (caretaker) 157, 176
Green, Pamela *195*
Green, Rev Claude 60
Greenland (pupil) 125
Gregory, Evelyn *141*
Greiner, Miss Grace 216, 226
Griffiths, Dr 157, 173
Griffith, Miss 121
Grimston, Sir R 60, 199
Grist, J 20
Guillamore, Lady 138
Gunstone, Miss 51
Gurney, Lady 164
Gutman, Fritz 161

Haddon, H 170-171, 189-190, 192, *195*, 211, *213*
Hall, L G *194*, *195*
Hallett, T L 70-72, 87, 97, 98-99, 107 114
Hammond, T 211
Hanny, R R *194*

Hanny, S C *195*
Harding, Emily 43, 45-46
Hardy, Mrs 157
Harman, Misses *34*
Harper, Jean *206*
Harries, Mrs Jennifer 191, 211
Harris, A 31-33, 57, 226
Harris, C 231
Harris, Diane Reader 179
Harris, Rose 52
Harrison, Mr 176
Harvey, Christine *206*
Harvey, Sarah 36
Harvey, Susan 36
Hawker, Annie 43
Hawkes, R 210, *213*
Hawkins, Miss M *174*
Hawkins, Sarah 30
Hawkins, T 30
Hayes, Miss 223
Haynes, K 209
Hayter, G 155, *159*, 190
Hayter (caretaker) 139, 156
Hazell, Mrs 139, 156
Heamon, A 170
Heavisides, B 211
Heavyside, J 55, 72
Heavyside, Mrs 55
Heavyside, Private 134-135
Henderson, R 179
Henson, J W 72
Herbert, the Lord 179
Herring, M *130*
Hester, D 227
Hewett, G E 104
Hewett, Gladys 90
Hicks, J 191, 210
Hill, S G 156
Hillier, Miss A *174*
Hills, L 99, 101, 116, 118
Hills, S *195*
Hitchcock, Joan *141*
Hobbs, Margery *141*
Hobhouse, Sir J 31, 102
Hobhouse, Mrs 138
Holbrow, G C V *130*, 138, 164, 169
Holder, Phyllis 138, *148-149*, *158*, 162
Holdoway, Messrs 62
Holdway, R P *194*
Holt, H *34*
Hope, R 170
Hopkins, Ellen 46
Hopkins, F *130*
Hopkins, Molllie 51, 54
Hopkins, Mr 51
Hopkins, Mrs (cook) 156
Hore, Mrs Margaret 191-192, 211, *213*

Horton, T 19, 35
Howard, Rev H 41
Howell, C G *194*
Howell, Gertrude 38
Howell, Mrs Katrina (see Paroussi, Katrina)
Howlett, Pamela *195*
Howse, Dorothy 121
Hull, A 210, *213*
Humphrey, Mrs 49
Humphries, H 31
Humphries, Mrs Mary 31
Hunt, P J 157
Huntley, D *159*
Hurry, Hope 99, 107, 118-119
Hyde, Kathleen 170, 188-189
Hynes, Celia *195*

Iles, Mrs Doris 121
Inker, J 31
Innes, K (see Struckmeyer, K)
Isley, M K *194*

J, Mr 59
Jackson (agricultural engineer) 160
Jackson, Vera 57
James, L 122
Jelfs, A E 169-171, 189-190
Jenkins, J 119
Jenkins, Mr 176
Jennings, Dorothy *50*
John, Mrs Catherine (see Proudlock, Catherine)
Johnson, Miss 71, 95
Johnson, S W 170-171, 177, 189, 191-193, 203-204, 210-211, *213*
Johnston, Mrs Beatrice 191, 211
Jones, Bessie 119, 121-122, 126-127
Jones, Emily 49
Jones, Frances 43, 45
Jones, G C 59-60
Jones, Harriet 42-43
Jones, Rev W H 40
Jordan, Kathleen 171
Jowett, Kathleen 99, 107

Kain, Mrs Jean 219
Kay-Shuttleworth, Sir J 14
Keen, Maria 36-38, 49
Kelly, Brigadier 151
Kemp, G 30
Kennard, Mrs 138
Kernutt, L W 57-58, 119-120, 138, 148
King, A 121
King, C M 179
King, K H 156
King, O 208

235

Index

King, W 30
Kirkpatrick, D *206*
Knight, Ada 43, 45
Knight (inspector) 73
Knight, Jane 42-43
Knight, P 210, *213*
Knott, Suzanne *194*
Knowles, Betty 151
Kosyleski, Mrs Annie 102
Kranz, F A 169, 176, 188, 202, 214

Lally, Janet *195*
Lambert, Mr 137
Lamble, J H 219
Lancaster, J 13
Lane, S S 24, 49
Lansdowne, Lord 133
La Paglia 201
Lapham, Miss 223
Lawrence, Fanny 225, 226
Lawson, Nora 170-171, 183, 189, 191-192
Leatham, Mr 117
Lees, W 100
Leslie, Mrs 156
Lewis, J 29
Lewis, Miss 225
Likeman, Mary 38-39, 42-43
Linsell, Lady 62
Linsell, Lt Gen Sir W 62
Lishman, Mrs Cecily (see Cox, Cecily)
Little, Georgina 44, 45-49
Livermore, Emma 37-38
Long, Emily 42-43
Long, J 73
Long, L *50*
Long, Miss 36
Loram, T 120
Lowden, Miss 71, 73, 76, 78, 80, 95
Lowe, Mrs Margaret 191, 210
Lowe, R 15
Lucas, J 151
Lynch, Mrs Jill (see Bayley, Jill)
Lynn, Mona 119, 121
Lywood, Joan *159*
Lywood, Mrs Hilary 127, 147, 154-155, 162

McColl, D 191-192, 204
McCulloch, Jessie 49
McDonald, Sgt 98
McDonald, Miss (Governor) 64
McDonald, Miss A F 203
Macdonald, Miss (teacher) 192
McGregor, Maureen 191, 202, 211
Maclean, Dot *50*
Maclean, Muriel *50*

McLean, Sgt 71

McNeill, Margaret 189-191
M'Quhae, Edna Sylvia 170-172, 187, 189, 191-192, 202, 211
Maddison, Gwendoline 54
Maggs, Miss M *174*
Maier, L D 148
Main, C 210
Maizey, Fanny 36-37
Mallinson, Miss 51
Malpas, Mrs Margaret (see Prince, Margaret)
Manoharan 209
Marchant, J 29
Martin, J L 98
Martin, T 110
Masters, Lesley *194*, 203
Masters, Sally 208
Matthews, Dr E R 173
Matthews, G 179
Matthews, J *159*
Mattock, Meta 132
Maulton, Mrs D 215
Maundrell, Mrs Margaret *213*, 214
Maxwell, Dr G 191
Mayell, B *50*
Mead, Anthea *206*
Mellor, Helen 189, *194*
Melrose, C *206*
Merrett, J 25
Merrick, Ellen *34*, 36
Merrick, Sophie *34*, 36
Messer, J 224
Methuen, Lady 138
Methuen, W 19
Miles, Debbie 208
Millard, P 202, 214
Miller, R 156
Mireille, Mlle *213*
Mitchell, Margaret *195*
Mizen, Dolly *50*
Mizen, Ivy *50*
Mizen, Nellie *50*
Moore (farmer) 216
Moore, H 135
Moore, Hilary *206*
Moore, Mary 132
Moore, Mrs Eunice (see Cadogan, Eunice)
Moore, 2nd Lt S A 135
Morgan, R J L *195*
Moroney, Nora 119
Morris (asst caretaker) 122
Morris, Miss E 30
Morris, S *130*
Morris, Sir P 179
Mortimer, L B 156
Moulton, J 25

Moulton, Mrs 138
Mountstephen, P 224
Mullings, Mrs 100
Mumford, June *159*
Munford, Winifred (see Courtney, Mrs Winifred)
Murphy (pupil) 106
Musselwhite, F 57-60, 223, 226

Napoleon 133
Neathey, Mrs Dora 148-149, *158*, 162
Neathey, H 149
Newell, L 211, 215
Newman, Mrs 218
Newman, Sarah *206*
Niblett, Miss G *174*
Nichols & Bushell (grocer) 118
Noble, G *194*
Noble, Lindsay *195*
Norris, Keziah 36-38, 49
Norris, Mary *50*
Nott, Mrs Mona (see Lynn, Mona)
Nourry, Mons 71

Oakman, Lilian 170, 190
Osborne, Rev A F 62, 64
Osbourne, Margaret *213*
Ostler, Phyllis 103
Otter, R 60, 120, 129, *130*, 132, 140, 148, 150, 154, 156, 161, 165, 169-170, 180
Ovens, Dorothy 31
Ovens, Winifred 30
Overy, F G 157, 169

Padmore, Margaret 223
Page, Mrs 192
Palairet, Capt S H 31, 224
Palmer, Col 117
Palmer, Lady Alexandra, 138
Palmer, Marion 122, 139
Pankiewicz, M 208
Panzetta, F 60, 119
Panzetta, Mrs Evelyn (see Elliott, Evelyn)
Parkinson, Miss 54-55
Paroussi, Katrina 191, 210
Parker, Capt 110
Parkes, Mrs 143, 150
Parry, J 92
Parry, Miss 225
Parsons, L F 188
Patch, J 35
Patrick, Mr 68
Payne, G *194*
Payne, Norah *50*
Pearce, B *195*
Pearson, Miss (HMI) 126

236

INDEX

Pedley, R 198
Pepler, R *159*
Percival, A B 106-107, 117-120, 132, 148, 150, 154-155, *158*, 162, 169-171, 180, 183, 185, 189-190
Percival, Betty (see Wayling, Mrs Betty)
Percival, Nell *50*
Perkins, R P D 156
Perry, J 31
Perry, Mrs Jane 31
Peterson, Prof A D C 203
Pfeiffer, Miss 80, 95
Phillps, Anne (see Rees, Mrs Anne)
Phillips, E J 161
Pickworth, Marjorie 188, 189, 191, 200, 202
Pinckney, Capt E C 117, *130*, 231
Pinckney, E 67-68, 70, 78, 84-85, 95, 229
Plowman, A 99
Pocock, Miss 86
Pollard, Joanne *206*
Ponting, D 208
Poore, Admiral Sir R 92
Potter, Frances 189
Powell, Lynne 191, *206*, 210-211, *213*, 214
Poynder, Isabella 31, 224
Pratt, Mrs 225-226
Price, R 189, 191
Price, Susan *206*
Priestley, May 119-120, 132, 138, 148
Prince, Margaret 148, 162, 170
Prosser, Sylvia *194*
Proudlock, Catherine 148, 162, 170
Pugsley, Messrs 118
Pullinger, W 32, 58, 78, 109, 119, 129

Rabbitts, Jocelyn *194*
Raikes, R 13,
Ralph, Margaret *141*
Ramsey, Mr 215
Ransom, Jennie 51
Ratcliffe, Mrs Kathleen 191-192, 210-211
Ratcliffe, T 189-191, 210-211, 215
Rawlings, B 188, 202, 214
Rawlings, Priscilla *141*
Rawlings, W S 87
Read, C 156
Read, Lydia Jane 37-38

Rees, D 186, 193, 203
Rees, Miss D *174*
Rees, Mrs Anne 119-120, 148, 162, 170-171, *175*, 186
Rees, Mrs Ruth 210
Reid, R G H 193, 207, 209, 210, *212*, *213*, 215-216, 218-220, 229
Retter, P *206*
Revill, K 170, *184*, 187, 189, 191-192, 202, 210-211, *213*
Rhodes, Minnie 99, 148, 162, 170-171, 180
Rice, G E 170-171
Richardson, Rev A T 57, 99
Ridley, A 31
Ritchie, Rev D C 65, 218
Robinson, Esther 119
Robinson, H G 119-120
Robinson, Mrs 31-33
Roblin, Mrs Yvette 170-171
Rocke, Col 155
Rodway, Mrs J 215, 219
Rogers, E *159*
Rogers, Rev J 19, 63
Rose, Ida *50*
Rose, Muriel *50*
Rose, P *50*
Rosen, H S *75*, 115-121, 123, 129, 131, 133, 171, 179, 187, 229
Rossiter (radio) 118
Rowley, B *130*
Rowntree, G C 147-148, 154, 165-167, 169, 171, 186, *212*, 229
Rowntree, Sarah 165
Rowntree, Simon 165
Rowntree, Susan 165
Rudman, Miss 156, 225
Rule, C F *194*, *195*
Russell, Lt Col H T 157, 169, 172
Russell, Miss P 169
Ryder, Mrs Ilse (see Stein, Ilse) 165

Salisbury, Bishop of *136*, 138, 179
Sartain, N *159*
Satterthwaite, Diane 210, *213*
Saunders, D 106-107
Saxty, R *195*
Say, C 180

Scarisbrick, Mrs 126, *130*, 231
Schofield, Susan *206*
Schooley, Miss 110
Schrecker, Honey 208
Schrecker, P 189-191
Scott, Ada 49
Scott, Rear Adm R 179-180
Scott, Susan *206*
Scratton, Mrs 117
Sealy, Enid *141*
Selby, Mr 202
Selfe, Mr 102, 128
Selfe, Mrs E 231
Sharp, Mrs Annie 47-48
Shehan, J 214
Shelburne, Earl of 133-135, 220
Sheldon, Mrs 192
Silcock, T B *66*, 69
Simmonds, Mrs Alfreda 54
Sims, W E 110, 122, 157, 178
Skinner, Ereline 118-119, 121
Slade, Fthr H E W 117, 203-204, 232
Slade, H W 164-165, 169, 172
Sleightholme, T *159*
Slocombe, I 31
Smith, Clare *206*
Smith, Col D 215, 218
Smith, D 191, 211
Smith, F 20
Smith, F J 148, 161, 169-171, *184*, 187, 189-192, 201-202, 205, 207, 210-211, 220, 230
Smith, G 179
Smith, Mrs (cook) 122
Smith, Mrs (teacher) 37-38
Snelling, Miss 80, 95
Solomon, H 226-227
Sorensen, Christine 208
Sorensen, N 227-228
Sparks, J 41, 46, 48
Spear, Heather *195*
Spriegel, Karen 211
Squire, P 218, 227-228
Stapleton, J 29
Steele, C 191, 210, *212*, *213*
Stein, Ilse 149-150, 154, 157, *159*, 161, 165-167, 190, 220
Stein, Mrs Elise 148, *158*, 161, 166-167
Steven, Dr Muriel 191
Stevens, Ald W E 60
Stewart, R 207, 211
Stillman D J *195*
Stillman, J 202, 231
Stills, C C 30
Stinchcombe, Miss 47
Stokes, Mr 202

237

Index

Storrier, Matilda 43
Strangeways, Rev D 64
Street, A G 138, 150
Street, Miss 86
Stronach, A 208
Stronach, N *206*, 208
Strong, Jane *206*
Struckmeyer, K 129, 143-144, 147
Sturgis, Miss 121
Summerell, O *130*
Summers, W 86
Sumner, C 210
Sumner, D 211
Sunderland, Mrs 214
Sutton, Miss 86
Swanborough, Mrs A 164
Swift, G 191, 201, 210, *213*
Swift (parent) 20
Swinfield, Jane 37-38
Symes, Mrs E K 211

Talbot, Miss 138
Tayler, A J 65
Taylor, C 208
Taylor, J 68
Taylor, M 208
Taylor, Marjorie 119
Taylor, S *206*
Thomas, A 210
Thomas, I 191, 210
Thomas, R 209
Thomson, A 210, *213*
Thorne, Miss P *174*
Thornton, J 133
Tiley, Caroline 38-39, 42
Tiley, Miss T *174*
Tiley, R *159*
Timbrell, Joan 191
Tottle-Smith, Margaret 210-211, *213*
Tracey, Hon Mrs Hanbury 114, 138
Trapwell, Miss 49
Tucker, Emily 39
Tucker, S C 164, 173, 190, 200
Tugwell (farmer) 216
Turner, Annie 47
Turner, J 20
Turner, Mary *159*
Turner, Miss (teacher) 171
Tutton, A E 21

Uncles, Dolly *50*

Uncles, Jean *159*
Uncles, Jo 138, 140, 190, 226-227
Uncles, M 197, 200, 214-215, 218, 220, 229
Uncles, Nellie *50*

Vallis, Jean *159*
Van Ryssen, Mrs Joan 211, *213*
Vaughan, Mrs 191
Vennel, Phyllis *50*
Venton, Ella *34*, 49
Venton, Mrs *34*
Viles, A *206*
Viles, W C 218
Vincent, Mrs 118
Vine, Dorothy 98, 100, 107

Wadsworth, Wendy *174*, 179
Walker, A J 208
Walker, Mrs 49, 52
Walsh, P 99
Walters, D 199
Walters, Jane *206*
Walton, Mrs 100
Warburton, J 210, *213*
Wase, C 19
Washford, Miss J *174*
Watkins, C G 70-72, *74*, *75*, 86, 95, 229
Watkins, Miss 49
Watkins, Mrs W H 231
Watkins, W E 68, 70
Watkins, W H 143-145, 163, 231
Watts, Jane *206*
Watts, Jean *159*
Watts, Miss (secretary) 156
Watts, P 208
Watts, Ruth 119-120, 122, 138, 148
Watts, Sandra 209
Way, D H *194*
Waygood, Mrs Agnes (see Boaden, Agnes)
Wayling, Mrs Betty 116, 120
Weaver, C *50*
Webb, M 215
Webb, Mavis *206*
Webb, N H 156
Webber, Joan *141*
Webber, Mrs Littleton 138
Webster, Judith *194*
Weeks, J 165
Wells, P 179

Weston, Pamela 202
Wetz, J 228
Wheeler, F H 219, 228
Wheeler (pupil) *50*
White, G N 31, 71-72, 87, 97-98
White, Miss D 31
White, Mrs Ada 31
White, R 100
Whitehouse, Miss 150
Whitfield, G A *195*
Whittle, C 210
Whittle (caretaker) 202
Wicheard, Kay 209
Wicheard, Mrs Enid 202, *213*, 214
Wicks, J *159*
Wiffen, Diana 192
Wigram, D R 203
Wilbur, T 210, *213*
Wilkins, A 87, 105, 122-123, 154, 157, 176
Wilkins, Pat *195*
Wilkins, W 41
Wilkinson, H 32-33, 57-58
Wilkinson, Mrs Elizabeth 32-33, 223
Wilkinson, R 211
Williams, I 71, 73, 76, 80, 95
Williams, Janet 210
Williams, Mary 119-120
Williams, Megan (see Yelland, Mrs Megan)
Williams, Mrs Ann 211
Willmer, B K G 156
Willson, Mrs Katharine 86
Wilson, Mrs Marjorie (see Pickworth, Marjorie)
Wiltshire, Archdeacon of 62
Winterbottom, F 208
Wood, Margaret *159*
Wray, Marjorie 118-119, 121
Wright, Mrs Sheila 189, 191

Yates, Joan 120, 138, 149
Yelland, Mrs Megan 148-149, 154, *158*, 161-162
Young, Gladys 179, 230
Young, Miss 226
Young, Mrs E H (see Daniell, Mrs E H)
Young, Sir H 164

About the Author:

Keith Berry was born at Wakefield in Yorkshire and educated, first, at Queen Elizabeth Grammar School, Wakefield, and then at the University of Liverpool. After graduating, he spent three years in the RAF in Germany, during which time he worked on defence against atomic, biological, and chemical warfare, and played rugby. In 1956, he began his teaching career at Ripon Grammar School. At Ripon, and then at Broxbourne, Hertfordshire, and Tavistock in Devon, he taught English before moving to the Deputy Headship of a large London comprehensive school. From 1971 he was Head of the Tom Hood Senior High School in Waltham Forest, and from 1979 of the John of Gaunt School in Trowbridge.

After retirement in 1991, he produced two books of local interest – *The John of Gaunt School and the Trowbridge High Schools: the First One Hundred Years* (1994), and *The Trowbridge Schools Revisited* (1996).

He has lived in Bradford on Avon for almost twenty years and, when not writing, he spends time in neglecting his garden, following the diminishing success of Bath Rugby Club, and dispensing justice as Deputy Chairman of the West Wilts Bench of Magistrates. Work with a national charity and the activities of the Bradford on Avon Preservation Trust, of which he is Deputy Chairman, also occupy his time.

With the completion of his third book – *Bradford on Avon's Schools* – he hopes to be able to spend more time on some of these activities, as well as on travel and cruising, a recently acquired enthusiasm.

Keith Berry is married with two sons.

More books of local interest from Ex Libris Press:

BRADFORD VOICES: *A Study of Bradford on Avon in the Twentieth Century*
by Margaret Dobson
This book is a remarkable achievement and a fitting tribute to a century of life in Bradford on Avon.
256 pages; Illustrated; ISBN 0 948578 89 0; Price £9.95

BRADFORD ON AVON: PAST AND PRESENT
by Harold Fassnidge
This updated edition remains the standard history of the town.
192 pages; Illustrated; ISBN 0 948578 62 9; Price £7.95

WHERE WILTSHIRE MEETS SOMERSET
20 Best Walks in the Country around Bath, Bradford on Avon, Trowbridge, Westbury, Warminster and Frome
by Roger Jones
A completely revised and redesigned edition of a book which has been going strong since 1982.
128 pages; Illustrated; ISBN 0 948578 94 7; Price £5.95

A SENSE OF BELONGING: *History, Community, and the New Wiltshire*
by John Chandler
120 pages; Illustrated; ISBN 0 948578 93 9; Price £5.95

THE PROSPECT OF WILTSHIRE
Words by John Chandler; pictures by Jim Lowe
The first and only full-colour book dedicated to the beauties of this special county.
112 pages; full colour photographs and maps throughout; hardback; ISBN 0 948578 74 2; Price £14.95

THE DAY RETURNS: *Excursions in Wiltshire History*
by John Chandler
This is the perfect dipping into book for all lovers of Wiltshire.
256 pages; Illustrated; ISBN 0 948578 95 5; Price £9.95

EXPLORING HISTORIC WILTSHIRE Volume 1: North
EXPLORING HISTORIC WILTSHIRE Volume 2: South
by Ken Watts
Each volume comprises 176 pages and includes a comprehensive index.
Vol. 1 ISBN 0 948578 85 8; Vol. 2 ISBN 0 948578 92 0; Each Volume £7.95